Let's Dance a Waltz

2

Natsumi Ando

Characters & Story

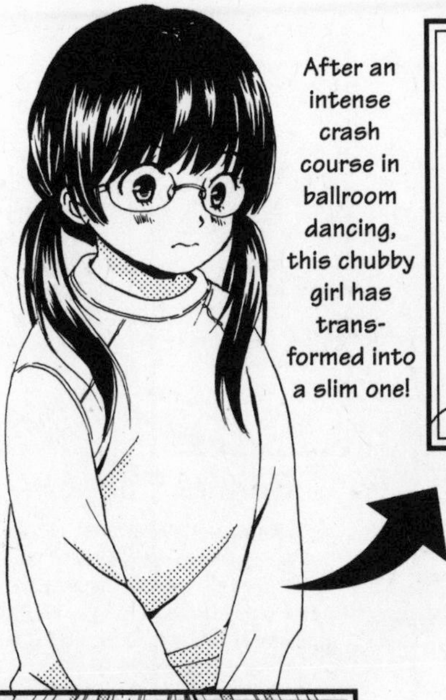

After an intense crash course in ballroom dancing, this chubby girl has transformed into a slim one!

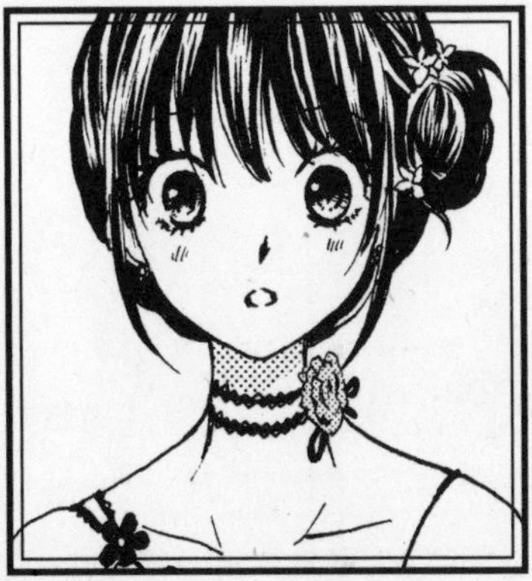

Himé Makimura

A plain, ordinary middle school girl and beginning ballroom dance student. She's doing her very best to live up to her name and be a princess so that she can be Tango's partner!

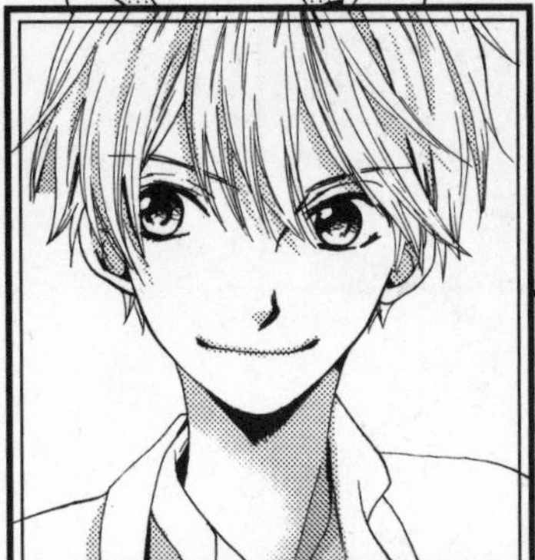

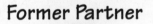

Tango Minami

Himé's classmate whose family runs a dance school. He unexpectedly ended up introducing Himé to ballroom dancing! He insists that he has no plans of ever returning to the world of competitive dance.

Former Partner

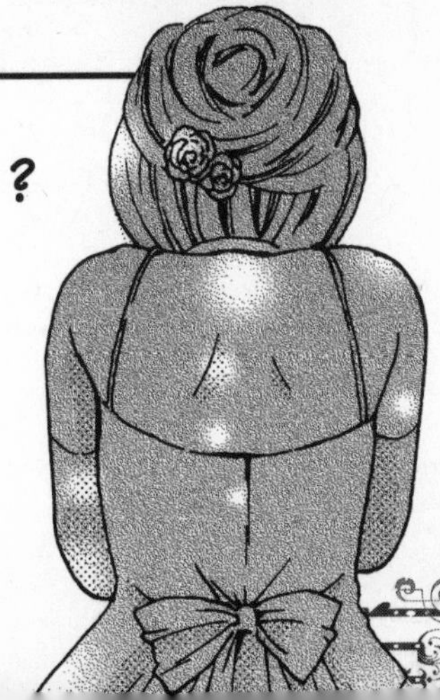
?

Let's Dance a Waltz

Lured by a poster she happened to see in town, the plain, almost invisible girl Himé Makimura goes to a trial class at a dance school. Who should she run into but her super athletic and popular classmate Tango Minami!

Himé is determined to be his partner, but Tango tells her, "I will never take a partner again."

Meanwhile, Yūsei invites her to dance with him in a competition. Is this part of his plan to bring Tango back into ballroom dancing...?! After an intense crash course that results in her losing 20kg (44lbs.), Himé's first dance competition is about to begin!

Sumiré Shiraishi

A longtime friend of Tango's. She and Yūsei are currently the star couple of the Minami Dance School. She's a young beauty whose sophisticated charm makes it hard to believe she is only in middle school.

Partners

Yūsei Sudo

A longtime friend of Tango's. He and Sumiré are currently the star couple of the Minami Dance School. He wants to bring Tango back to the world of dance.

Contents

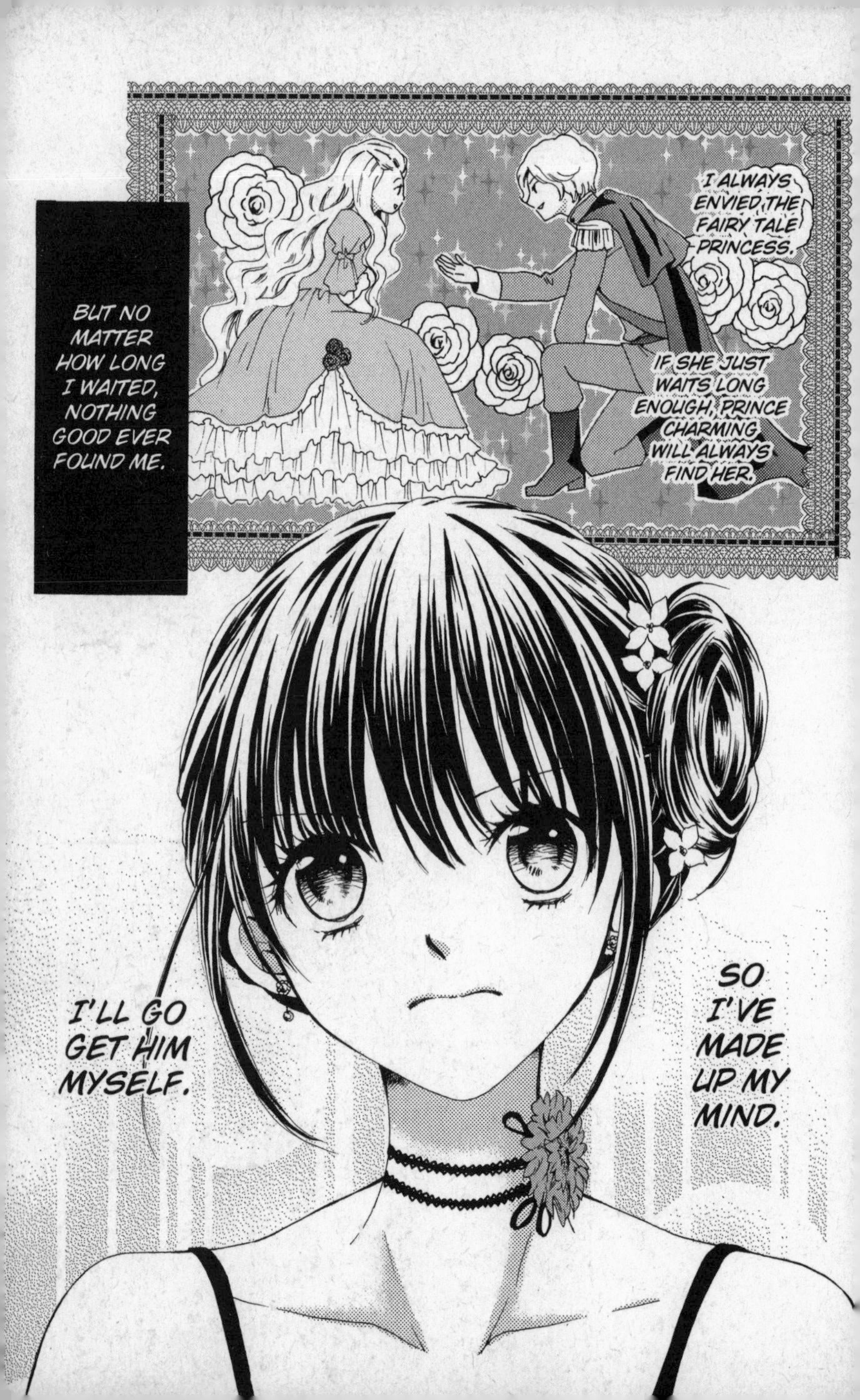
I ALWAYS ENVIED THE FAIRY TALE PRINCESS.
IF SHE JUST WAITS LONG ENOUGH, PRINCE CHARMING WILL ALWAYS FIND HER.
BUT NO MATTER HOW LONG I WAITED, NOTHING GOOD EVER FOUND ME.
SO I'VE MADE UP MY MIND.
I'LL GO GET HIM MYSELF.

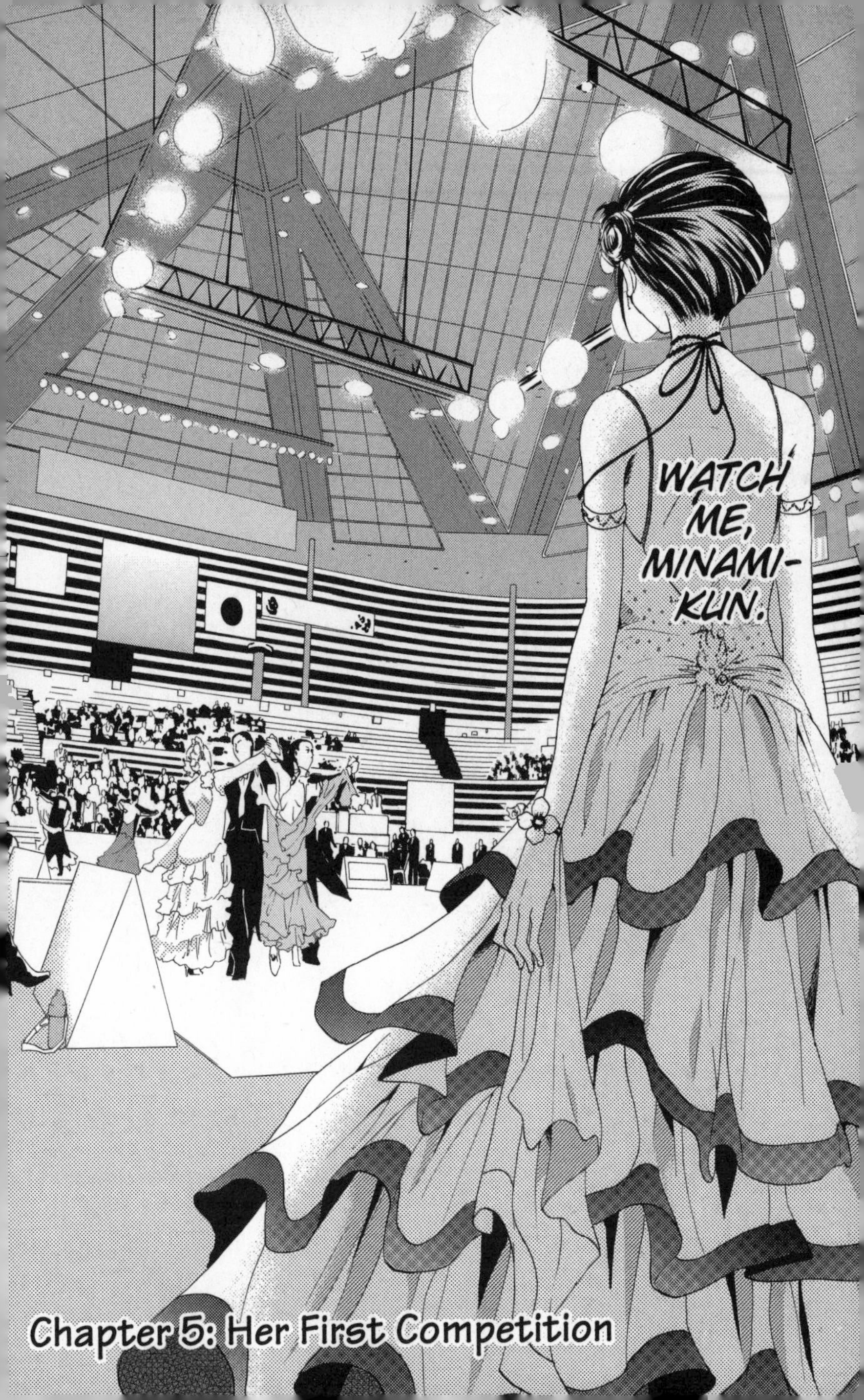
WATCH ME, MINAMI-KUN.
Chapter 5: Her First Competition

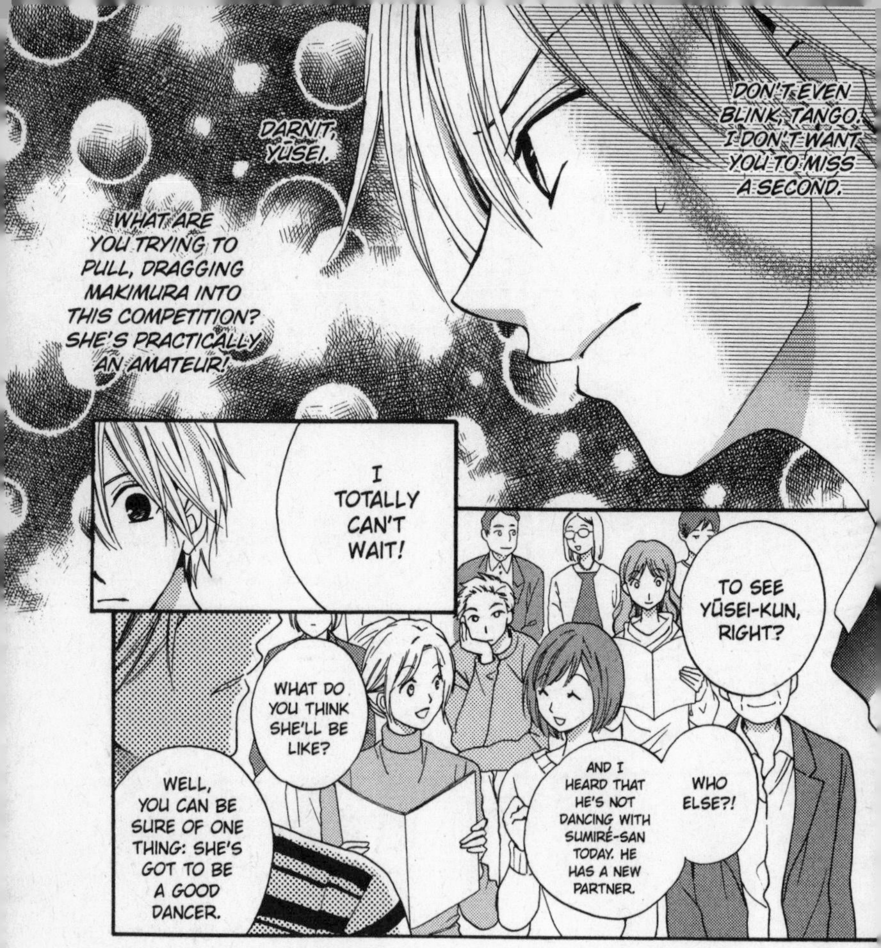
DON'T EVEN BLINK, TANGO. I DON'T WANT YOU TO MISS A SECOND.
DARNIT, YŪSEI.
WHAT ARE YOU TRYING TO PULL, DRAGGING MAKIMURA INTO THIS COMPETITION? SHE'S PRACTICALLY AN AMATEUR!
I TOTALLY CAN'T WAIT!
TO SEE YŪSEI-KUN, RIGHT?
WHO ELSE?!
AND I HEARD THAT HE'S NOT DANCING WITH SUMIRÉ-SAN TODAY. HE HAS A NEW PARTNER.
WHAT DO YOU THINK SHE'LL BE LIKE?
WELL, YOU CAN BE SURE OF ONE THING: SHE'S GOT TO BE A GOOD DANCER.

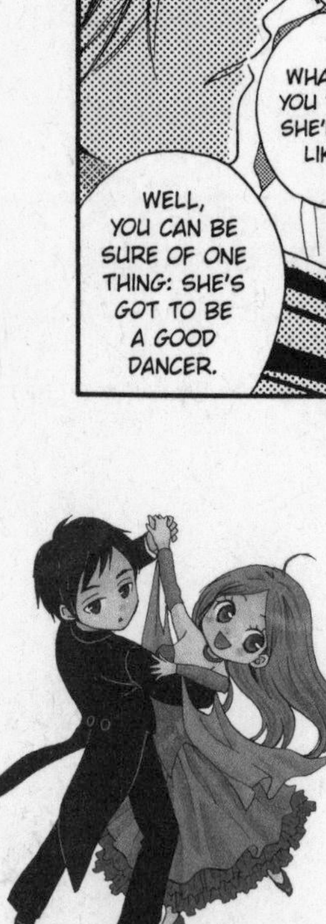

The Waltz

An elegant dance in 3/4 time. It is characterized by the upward and downward movements of the body, with the rise on the first beat, and the fall on the third. As they waltz, the dancers draw a circle around the dance floor. It's such a popular style of dance that it's almost synonymous with the term "ballroom dance."♪

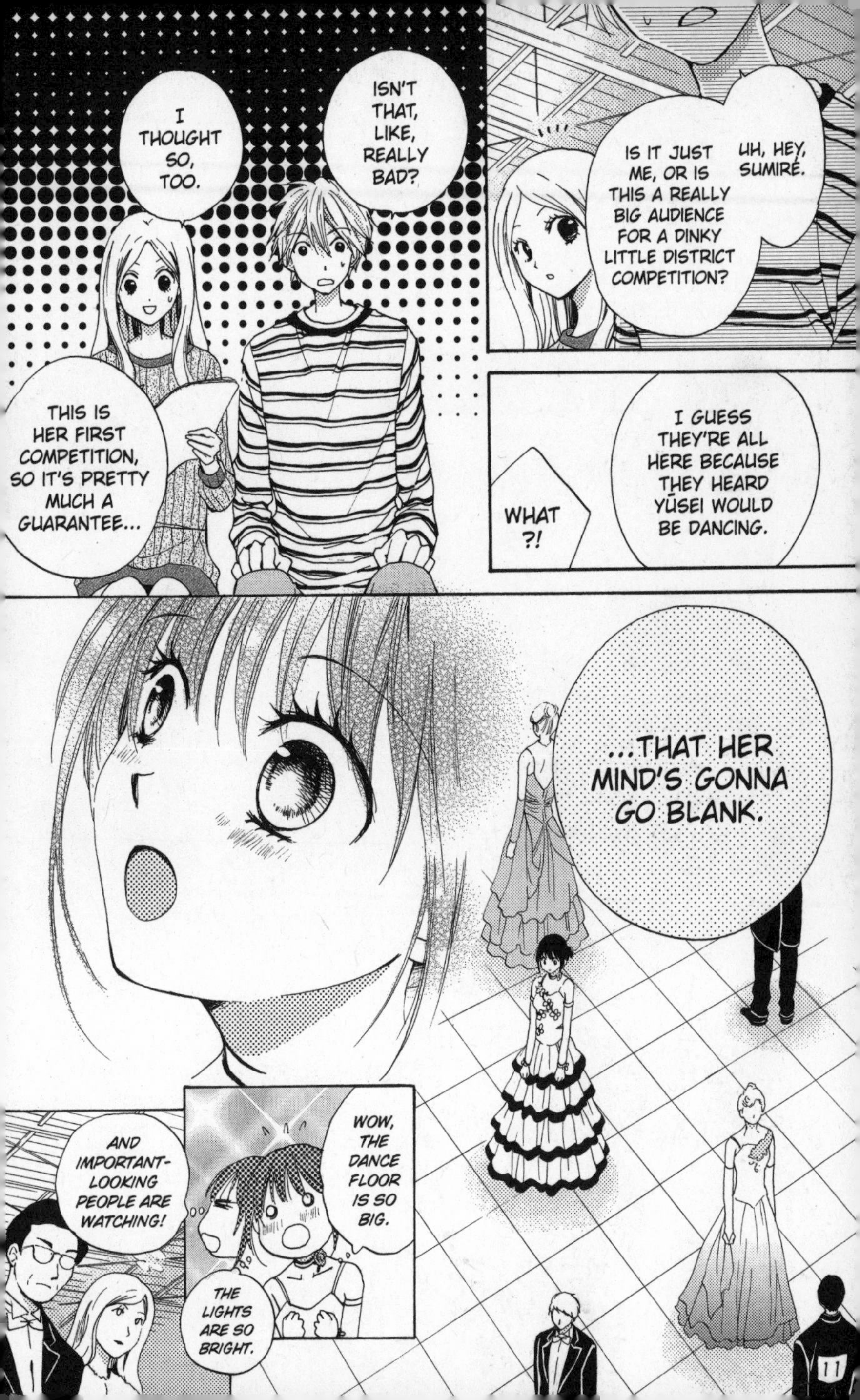
UH, HEY, SUMIRE.
IS IT JUST ME, OR IS THIS A REALLY BIG AUDIENCE FOR A DINKY LITTLE DISTRICT COMPETITION?
I GUESS THEY'RE ALL HERE BECAUSE THEY HEARD YŪSEI WOULD BE DANCING.
WHAT ?!
ISN'T THAT, LIKE, REALLY BAD?
I THOUGHT SO, TOO.
THIS IS HER FIRST COMPETITION, SO IT'S PRETTY MUCH A GUARANTEE...
...THAT HER MIND'S GONNA GO BLANK.
WOW, THE DANCE FLOOR IS SO BIG.
THE LIGHTS ARE SO BRIGHT.
AND IMPORTANT-LOOKING PEOPLE ARE WATCHING!

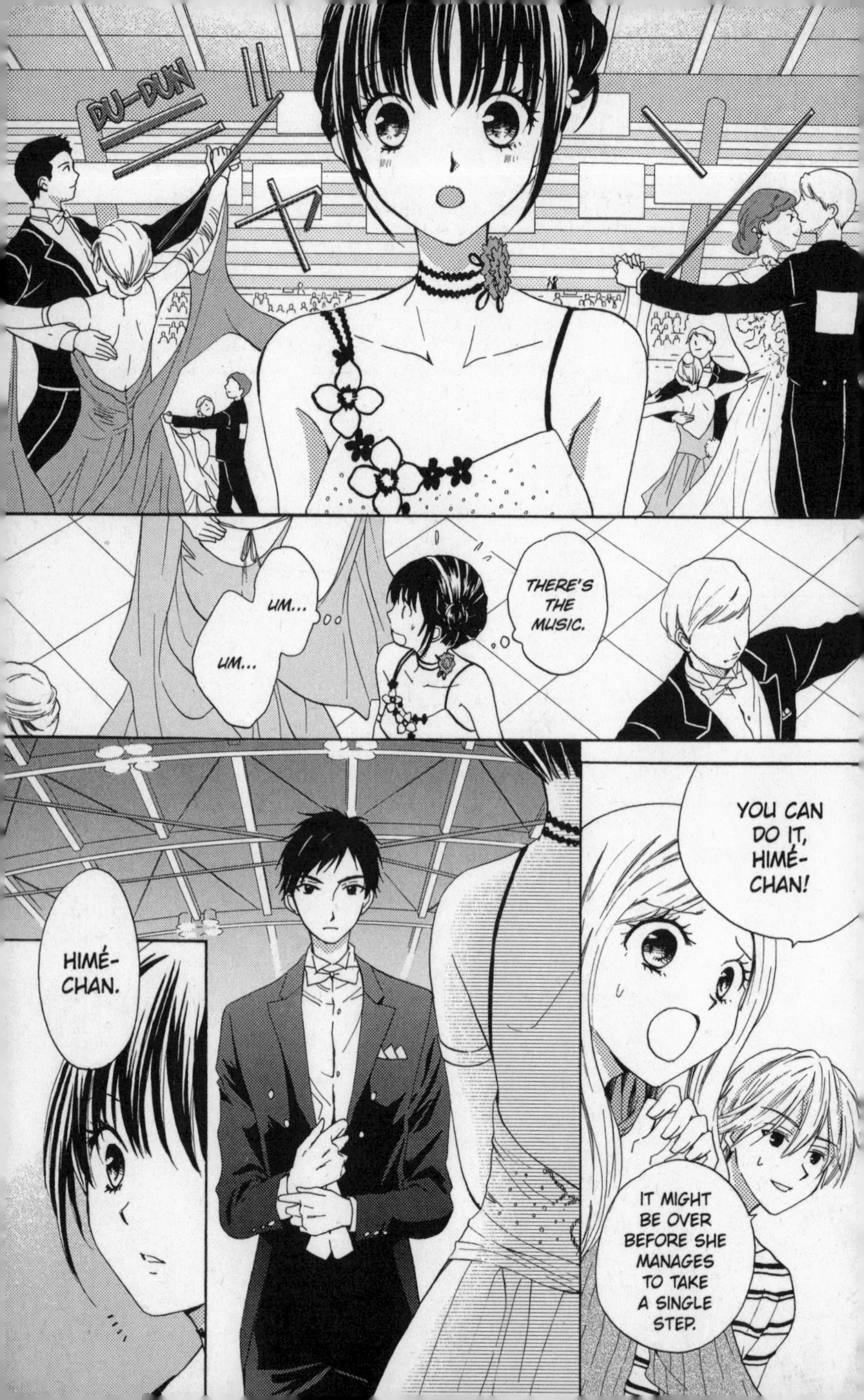
DU-DUN
THERE'S THE MUSIC.
UM...
UM...
YOU CAN DO IT, HIMÉ-CHAN!
IT MIGHT BE OVER BEFORE SHE MANAGES TO TAKE A SINGLE STEP.
HIMÉ-CHAN.

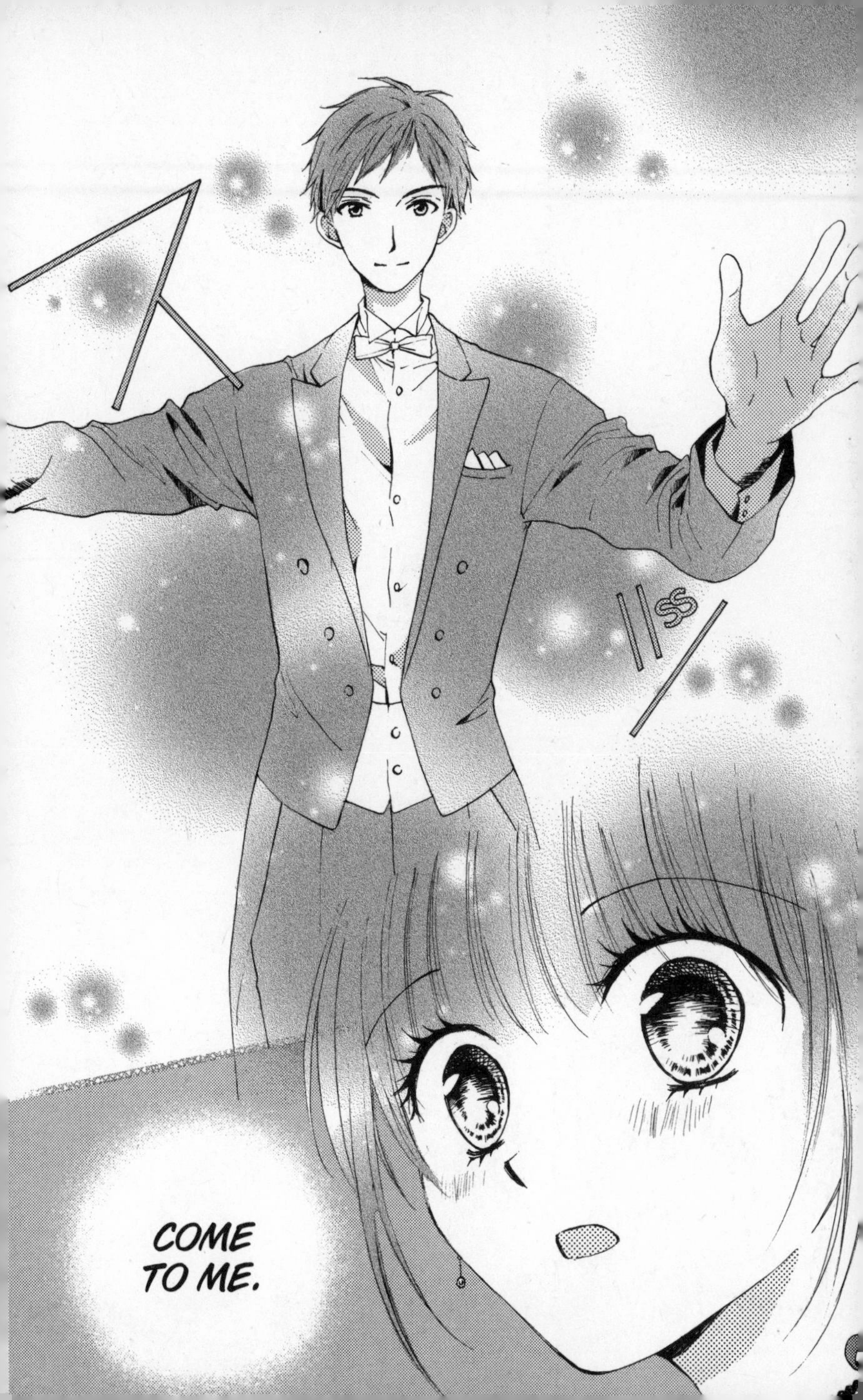
COME TO ME.

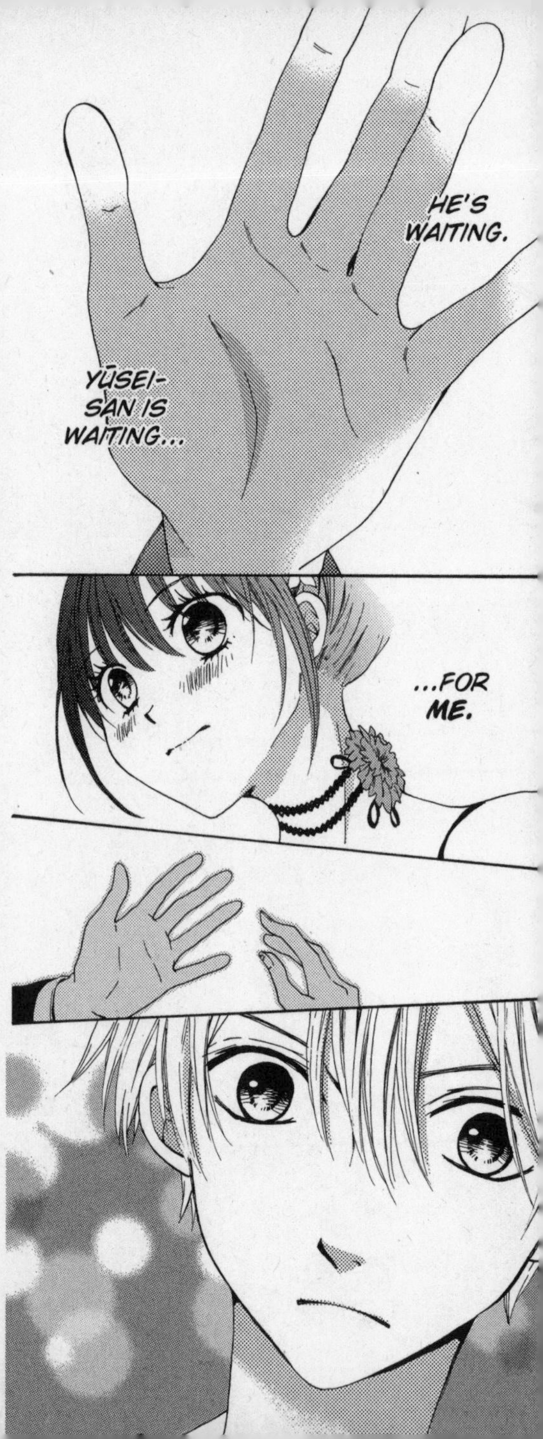
HE'S WAITING.
YŪSEI-SAN IS WAITING...
...FOR ME.

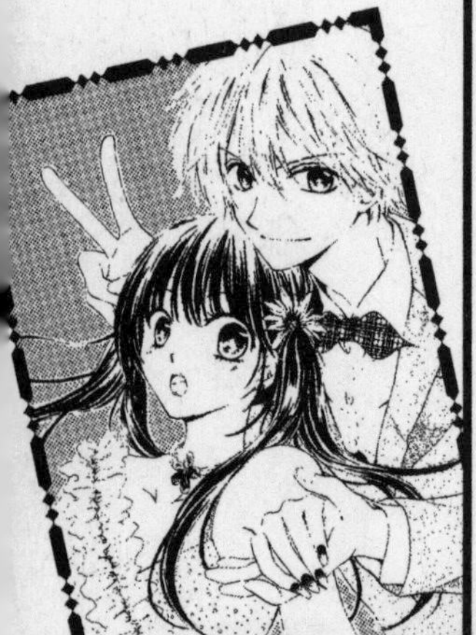

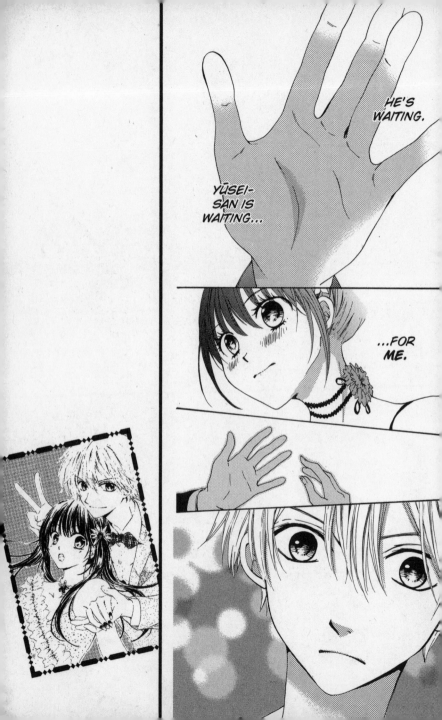

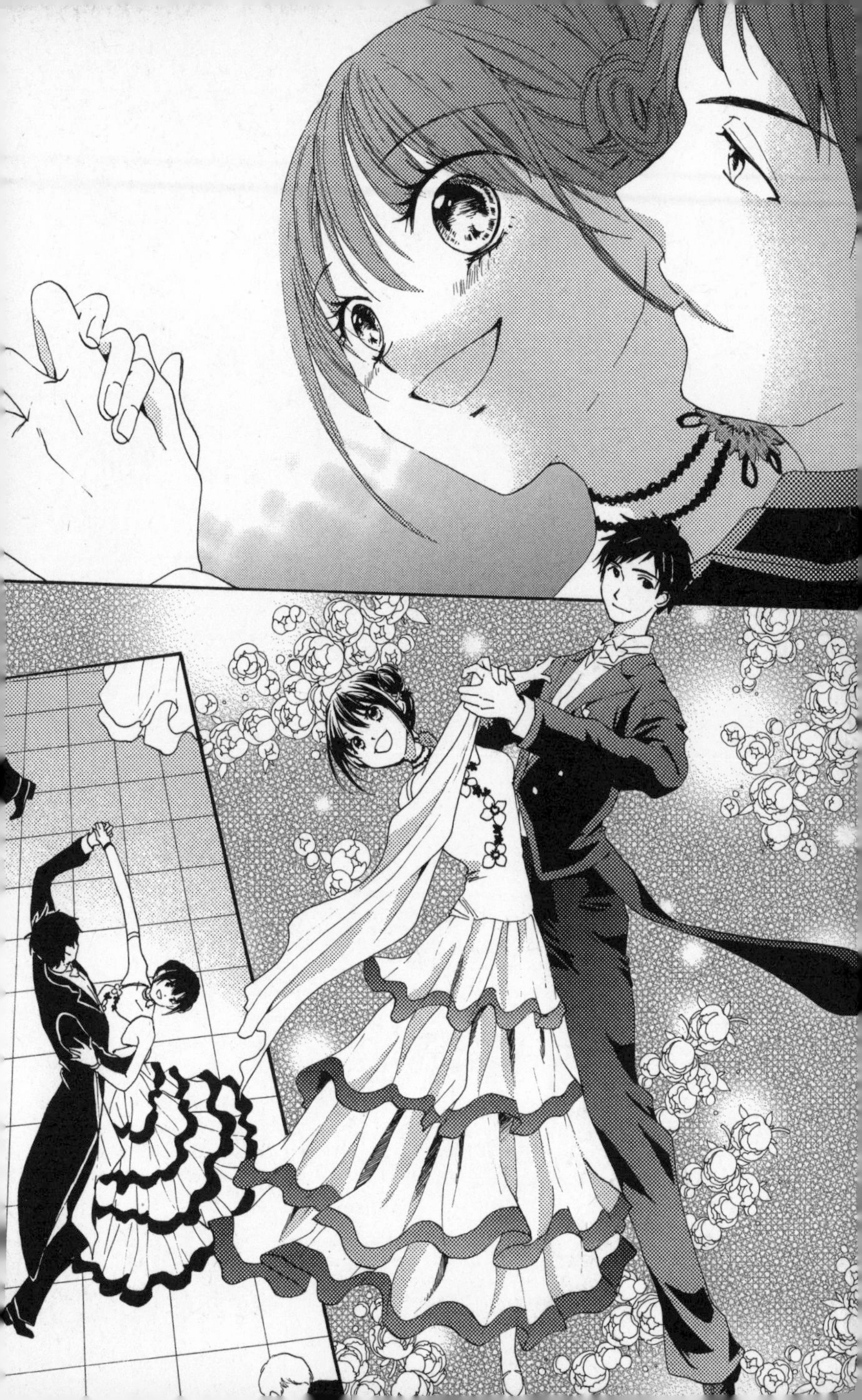

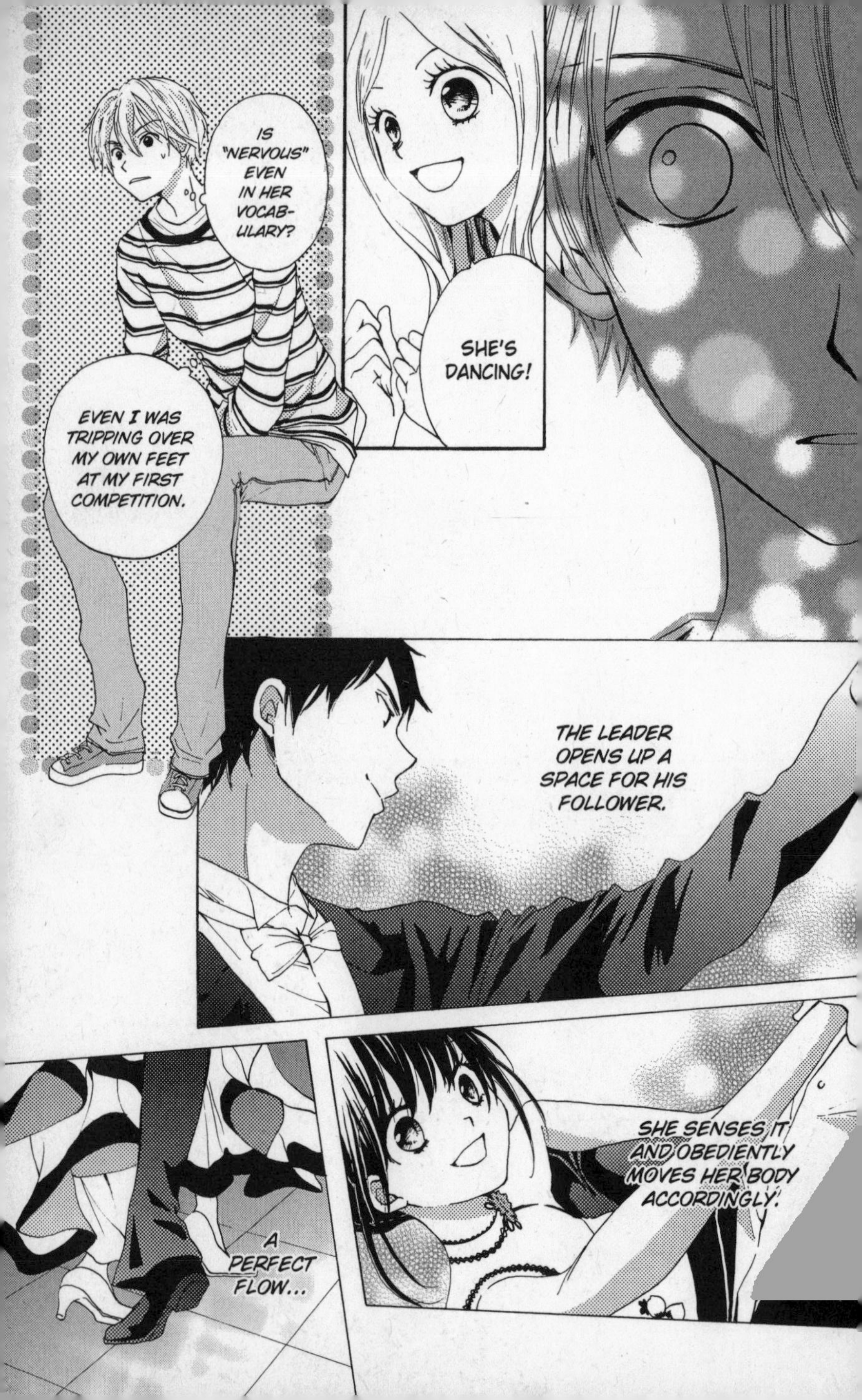
SHE'S DANCING!
IS "NERVOUS" EVEN IN HER VOCABULARY?
EVEN I WAS TRIPPING OVER MY OWN FEET AT MY FIRST COMPETITION.
THE LEADER OPENS UP A SPACE FOR HIS FOLLOWER.
SHE SENSES IT AND OBEDIENTLY MOVES HER BODY ACCORDINGLY.
A PERFECT FLOW...

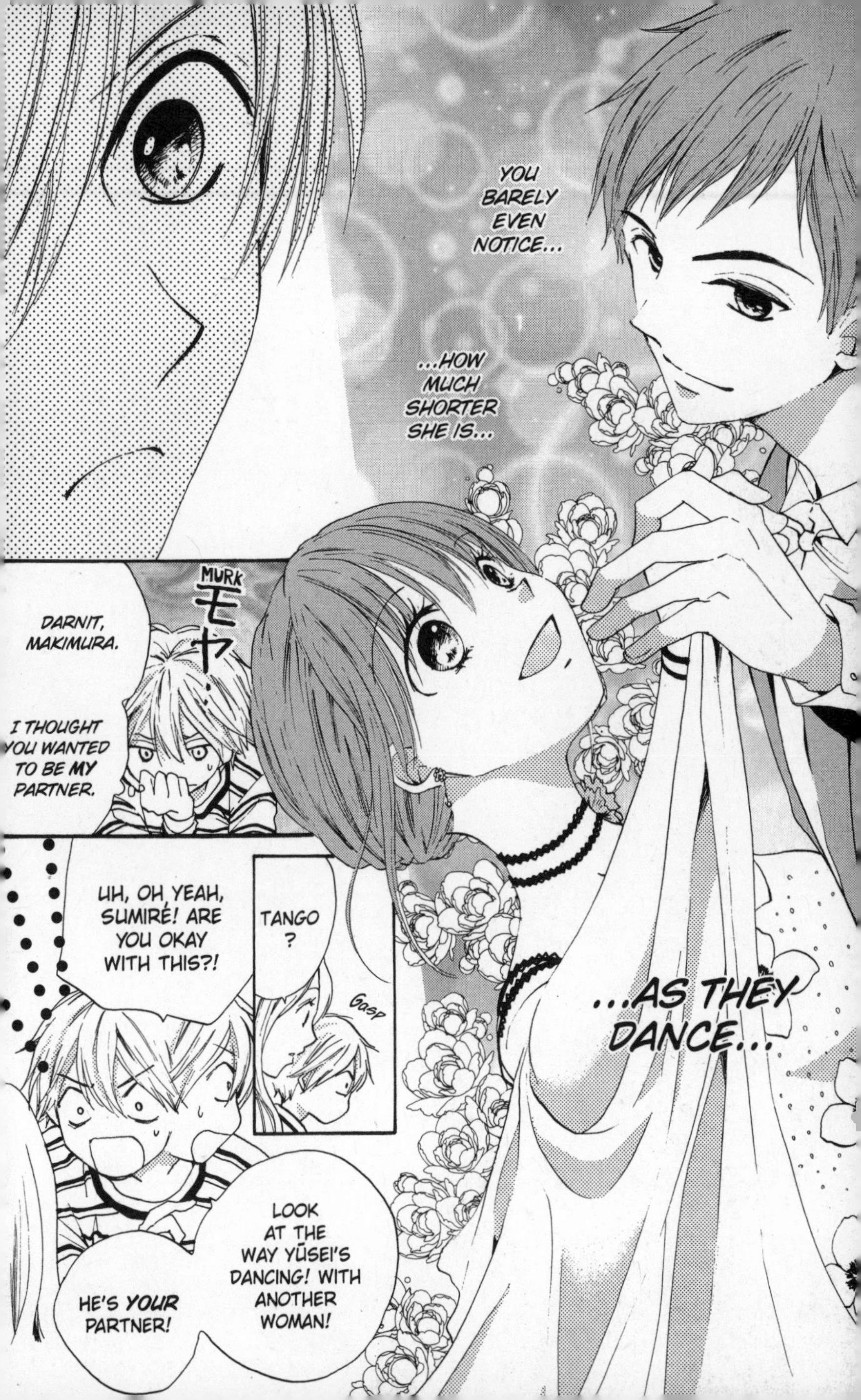
YOU BARELY EVEN NOTICE...
...HOW MUCH SHORTER SHE IS...
...AS THEY DANCE...
MURK
モヤ
DARNIT, MAKIMURA.
I THOUGHT YOU WANTED TO BE *MY* PARTNER.
TANGO?
Gasp
UH, OH YEAH, SUMIRÉ! ARE YOU OKAY WITH THIS?!
LOOK AT THE WAY YŪSEI'S DANCING! WITH ANOTHER WOMAN!
HE'S *YOUR* PARTNER!

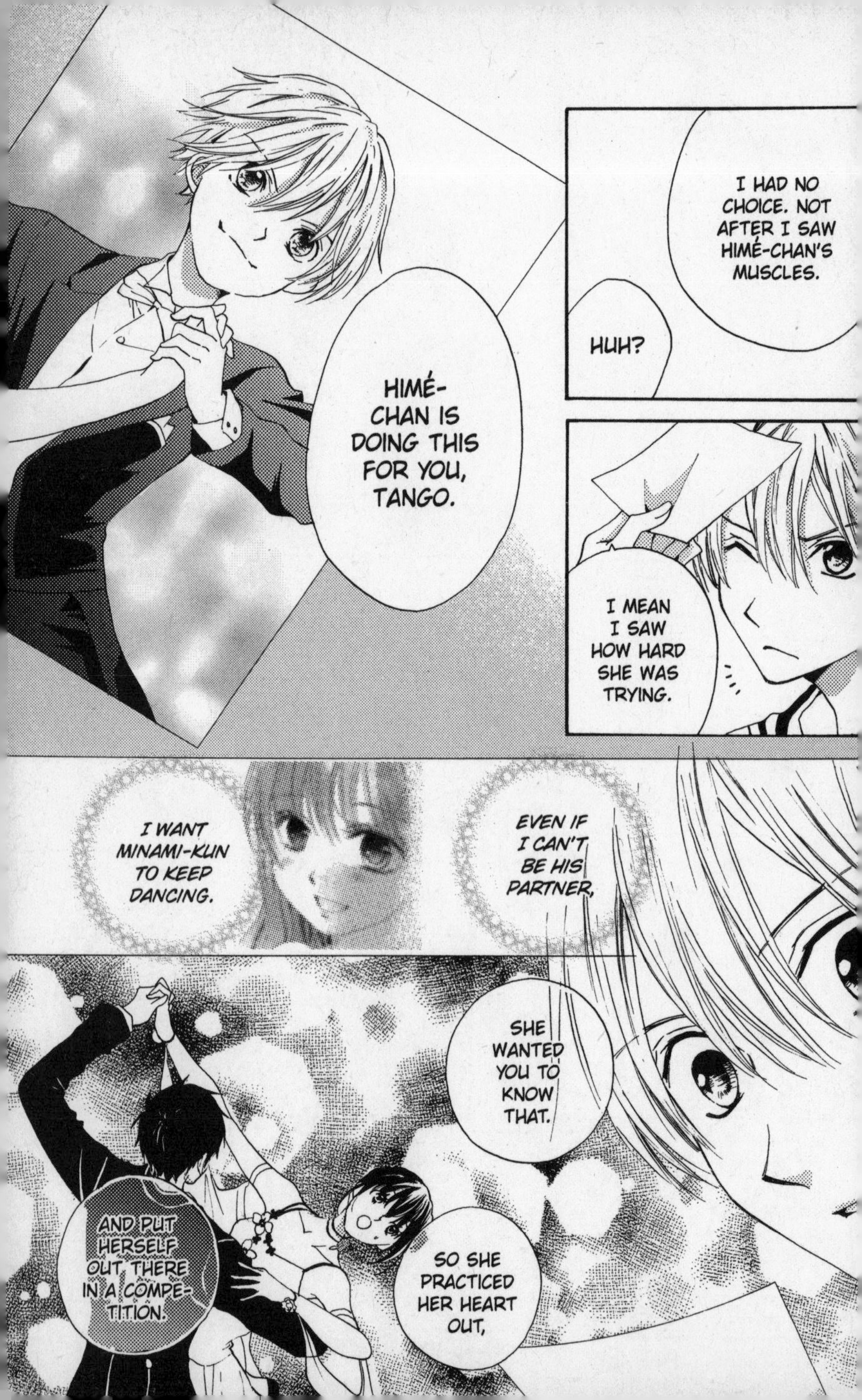
I HAD NO CHOICE. NOT AFTER I SAW HIMÉ-CHAN'S MUSCLES.
HUH?
I MEAN I SAW HOW HARD SHE WAS TRYING.
HIMÉ-CHAN IS DOING THIS FOR YOU, TANGO.
EVEN IF I CAN'T BE HIS PARTNER,
I WANT MINAMI-KUN TO KEEP DANCING.
SO SHE PRACTICED HER HEART OUT,
AND PUT HERSELF OUT THERE IN A COMPETITION.
SHE WANTED YOU TO KNOW THAT.

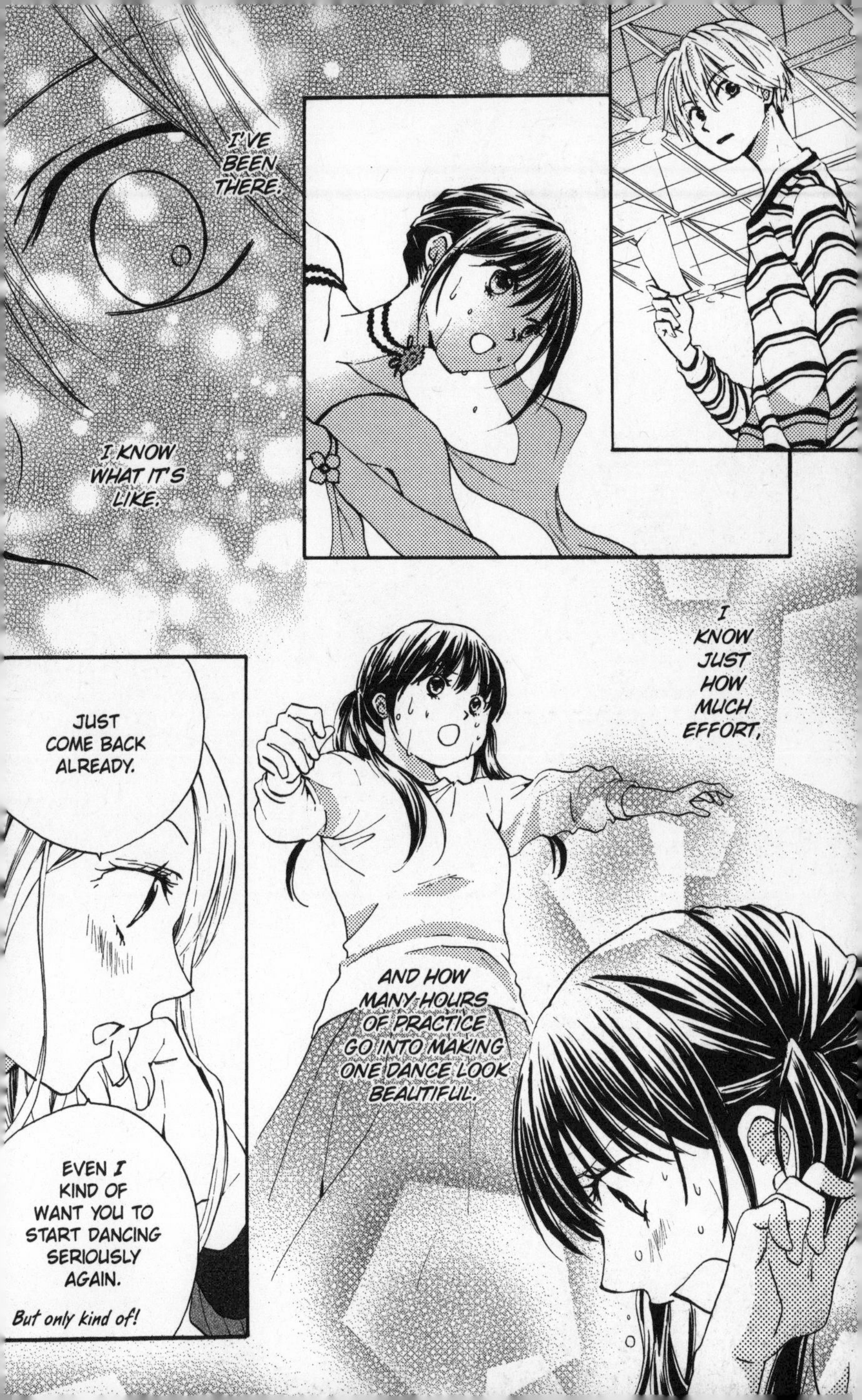

I'VE BEEN THERE.
I KNOW WHAT IT'S LIKE.
I KNOW JUST HOW MUCH EFFORT,
AND HOW MANY HOURS OF PRACTICE GO INTO MAKING ONE DANCE LOOK BEAUTIFUL.
JUST COME BACK ALREADY.
EVEN I KIND OF WANT YOU TO START DANCING SERIOUSLY AGAIN.
But only kind of!

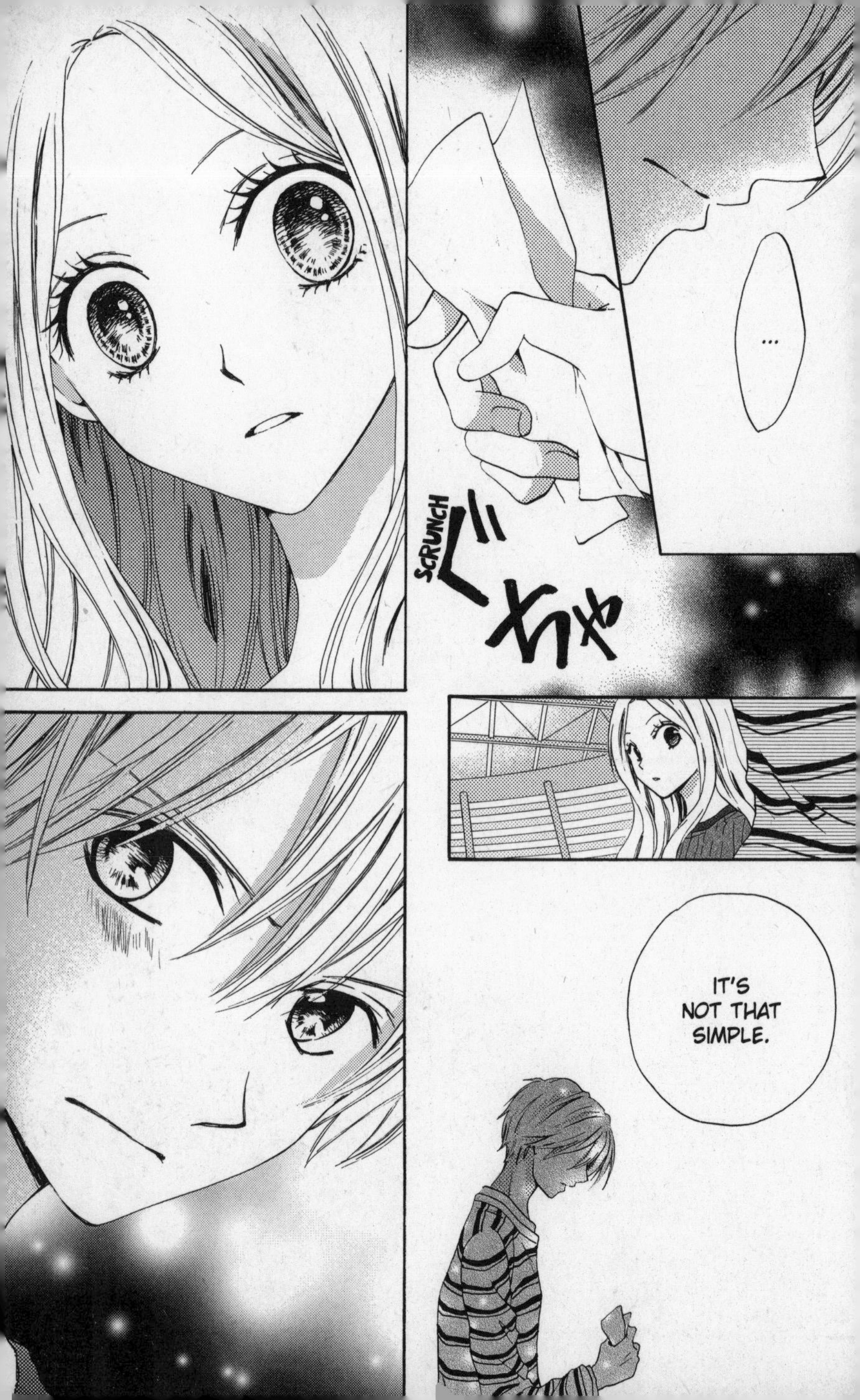
...
SCRUNCH
ぐちゃ
IT'S NOT THAT SIMPLE.

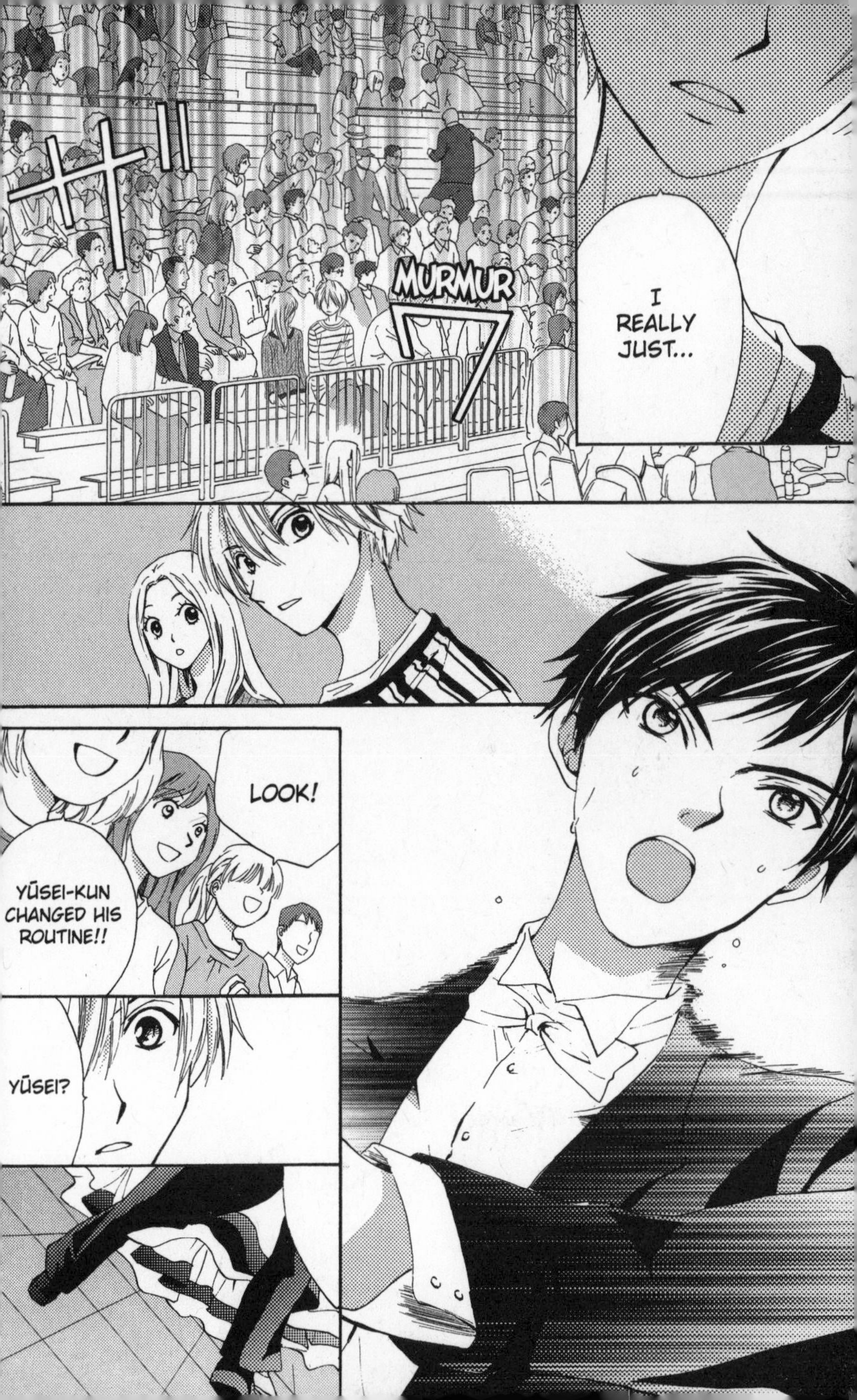
I REALLY JUST...
MURMUR
LOOK!
YŪSEI-KUN CHANGED HIS ROUTINE!!
YŪSEI?

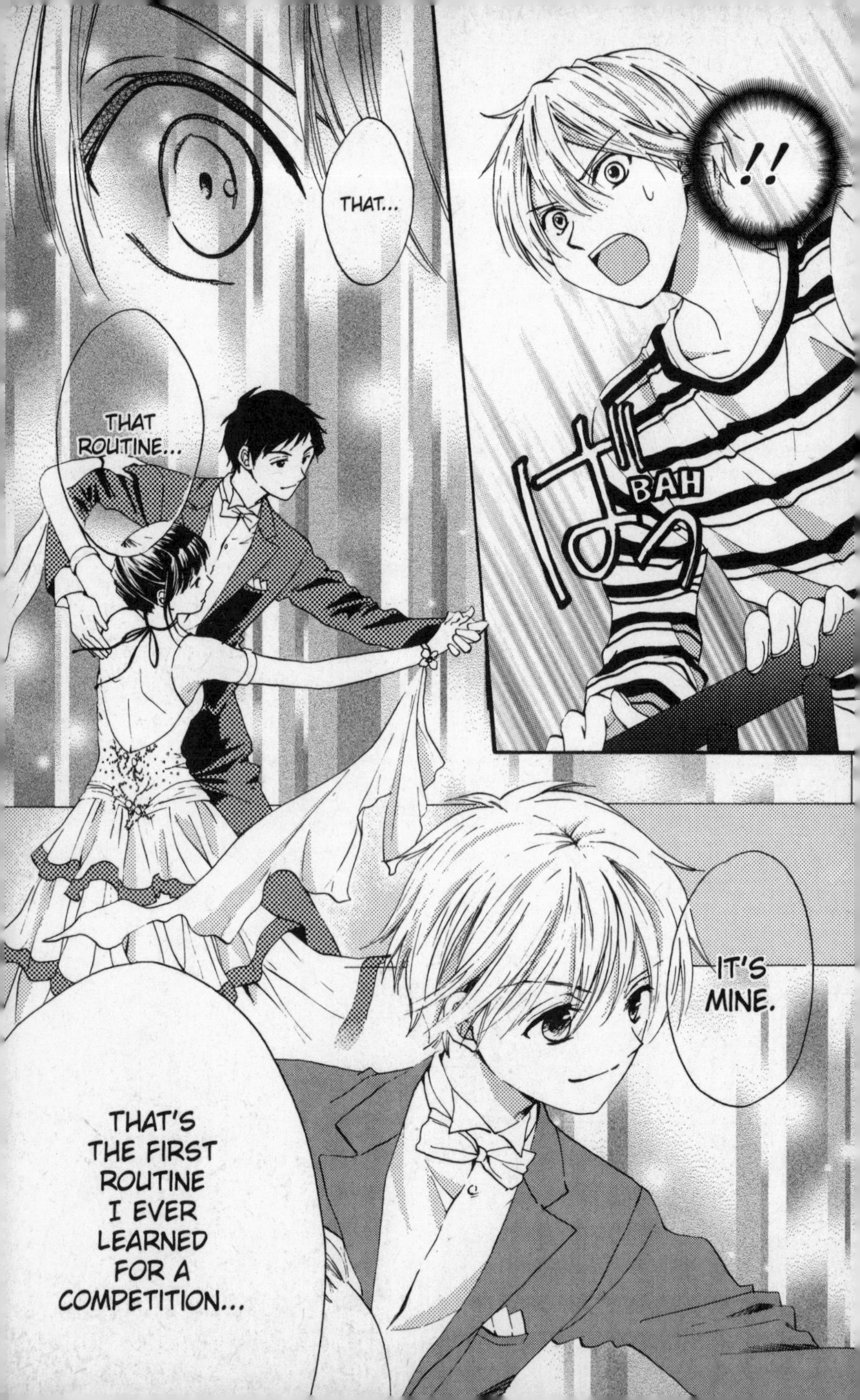
!!
BAH
THAT...
THAT ROUTINE...
IT'S MINE.
THAT'S THE FIRST ROUTINE I EVER LEARNED FOR A COMPETITION...

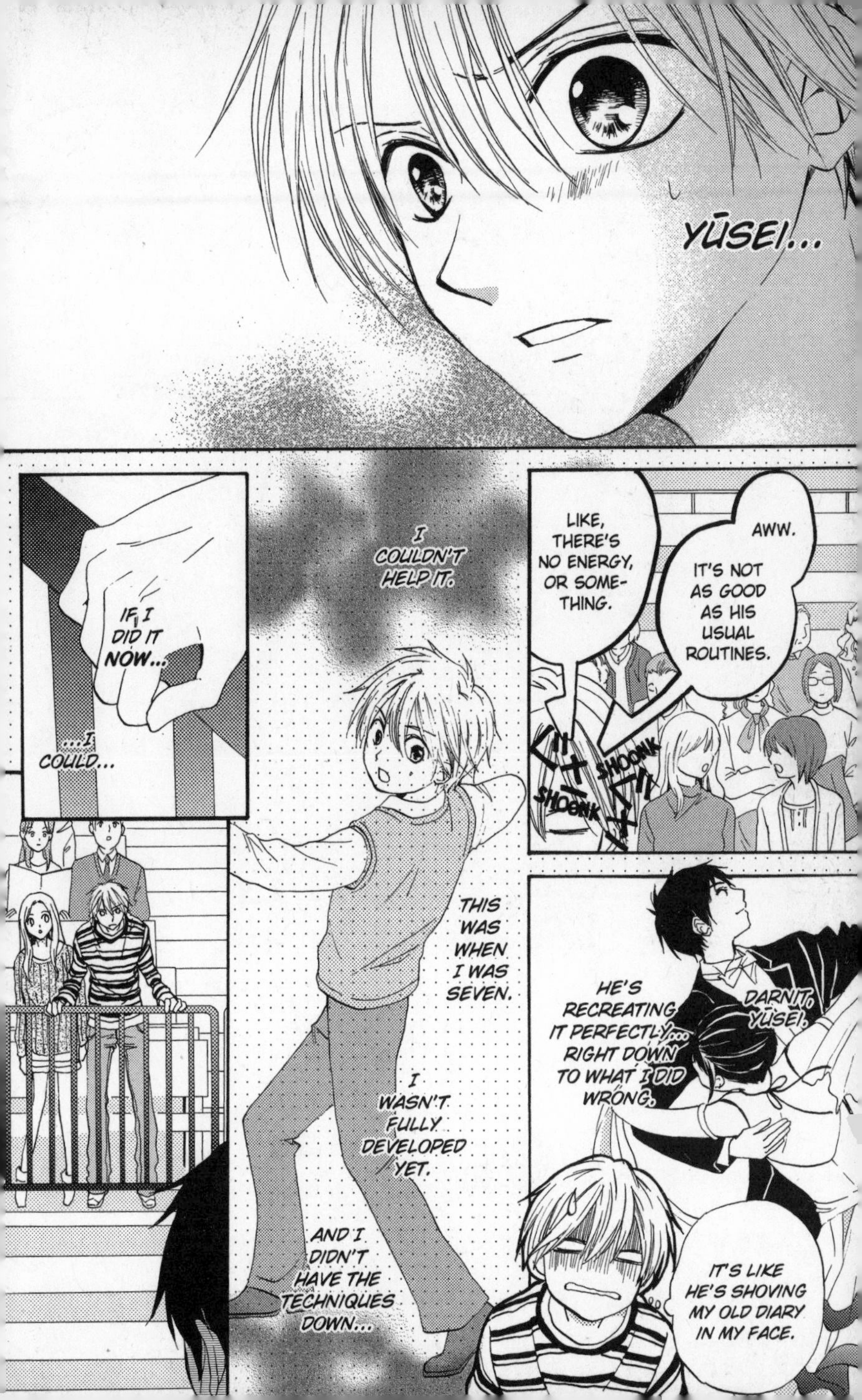
YŪSEI...
AWW.
IT'S NOT AS GOOD AS HIS USUAL ROUTINES.
LIKE, THERE'S NO ENERGY, OR SOME-THING.
SHOONK
SHOONK
DARNIT, YŪSEI.
HE'S RECREATING IT PERFECTLY... RIGHT DOWN TO WHAT I DID WRONG.
IT'S LIKE HE'S SHOVING MY OLD DIARY IN MY FACE.
I COULDN'T HELP IT.
THIS WAS WHEN I WAS SEVEN.
I WASN'T FULLY DEVELOPED YET.
AND I DIDN'T HAVE THE TECHNIQUES DOWN...
IF I DID IT NOW...
...I COULD...

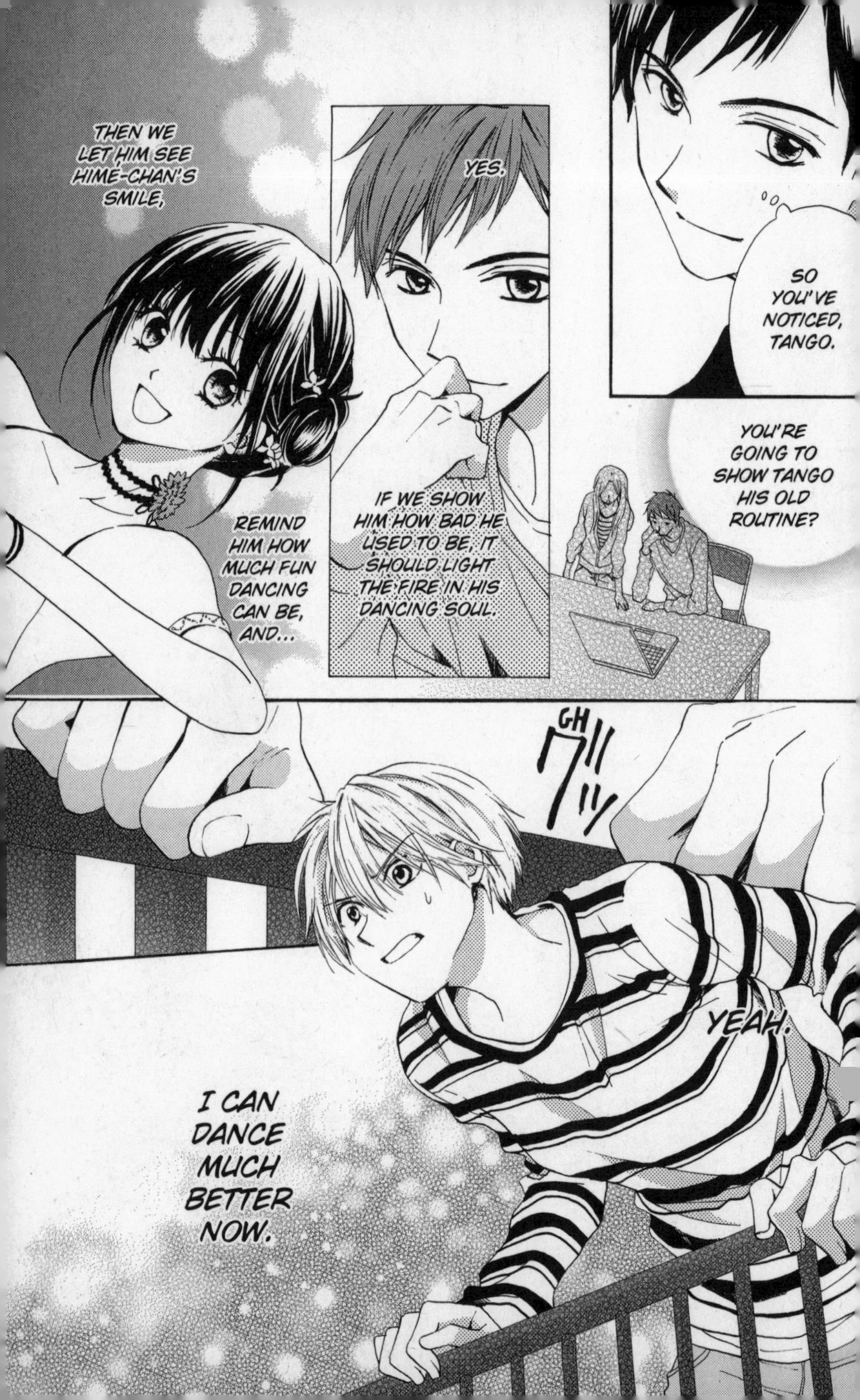
SO YOU'VE NOTICED, TANGO.
YOU'RE GOING TO SHOW TANGO HIS OLD ROUTINE?
YES.
IF WE SHOW HIM HOW BAD HE USED TO BE, IT SHOULD LIGHT THE FIRE IN HIS DANCING SOUL.
THEN WE LET HIM SEE HIME-CHAN'S SMILE,
REMIND HIM HOW MUCH FUN DANCING CAN BE, AND...
GH
YEAH.
I CAN DANCE MUCH BETTER NOW.

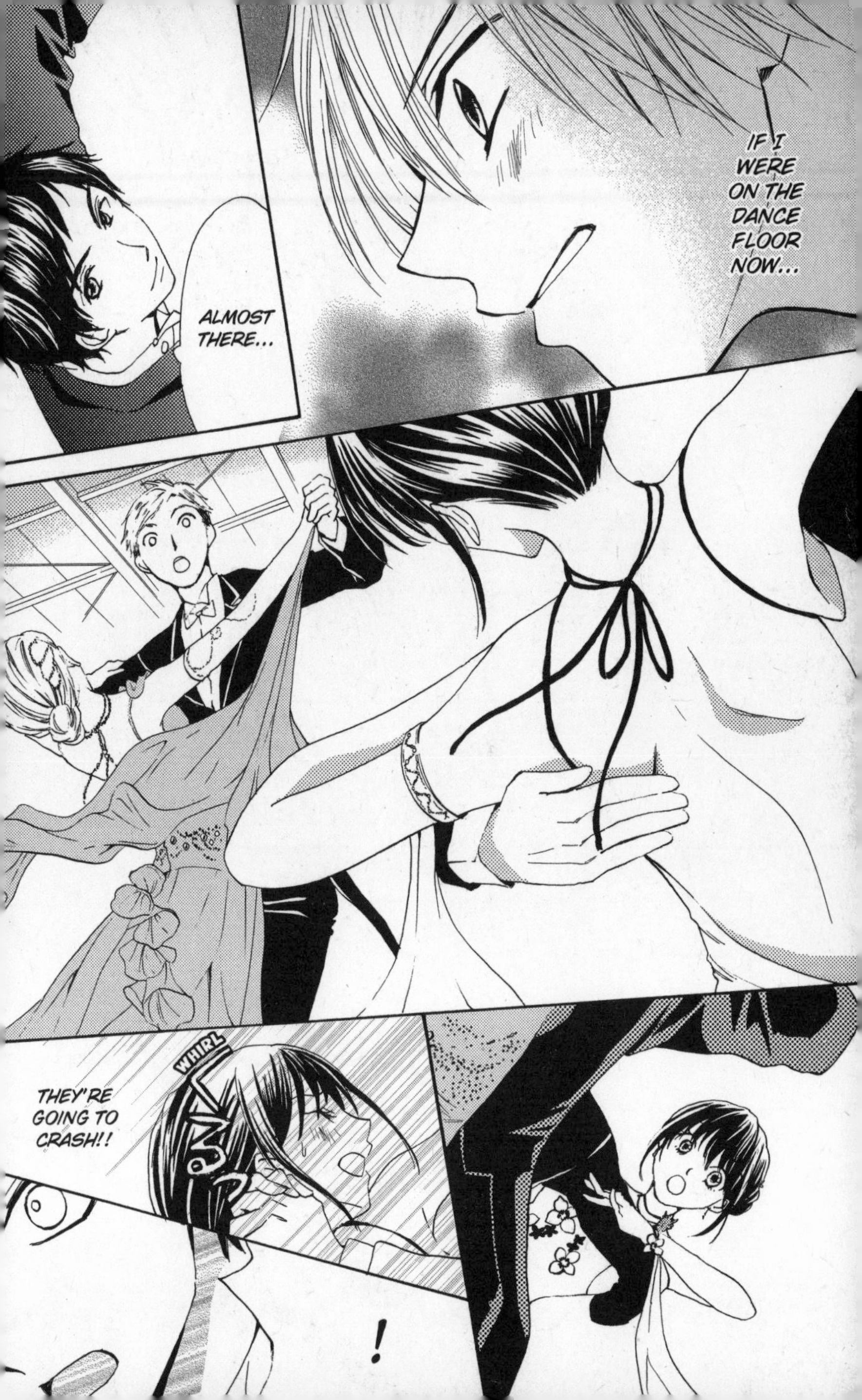
IF I WERE ON THE DANCE FLOOR NOW...
ALMOST THERE...
!
WHIRL
THEY'RE GOING TO CRASH!!

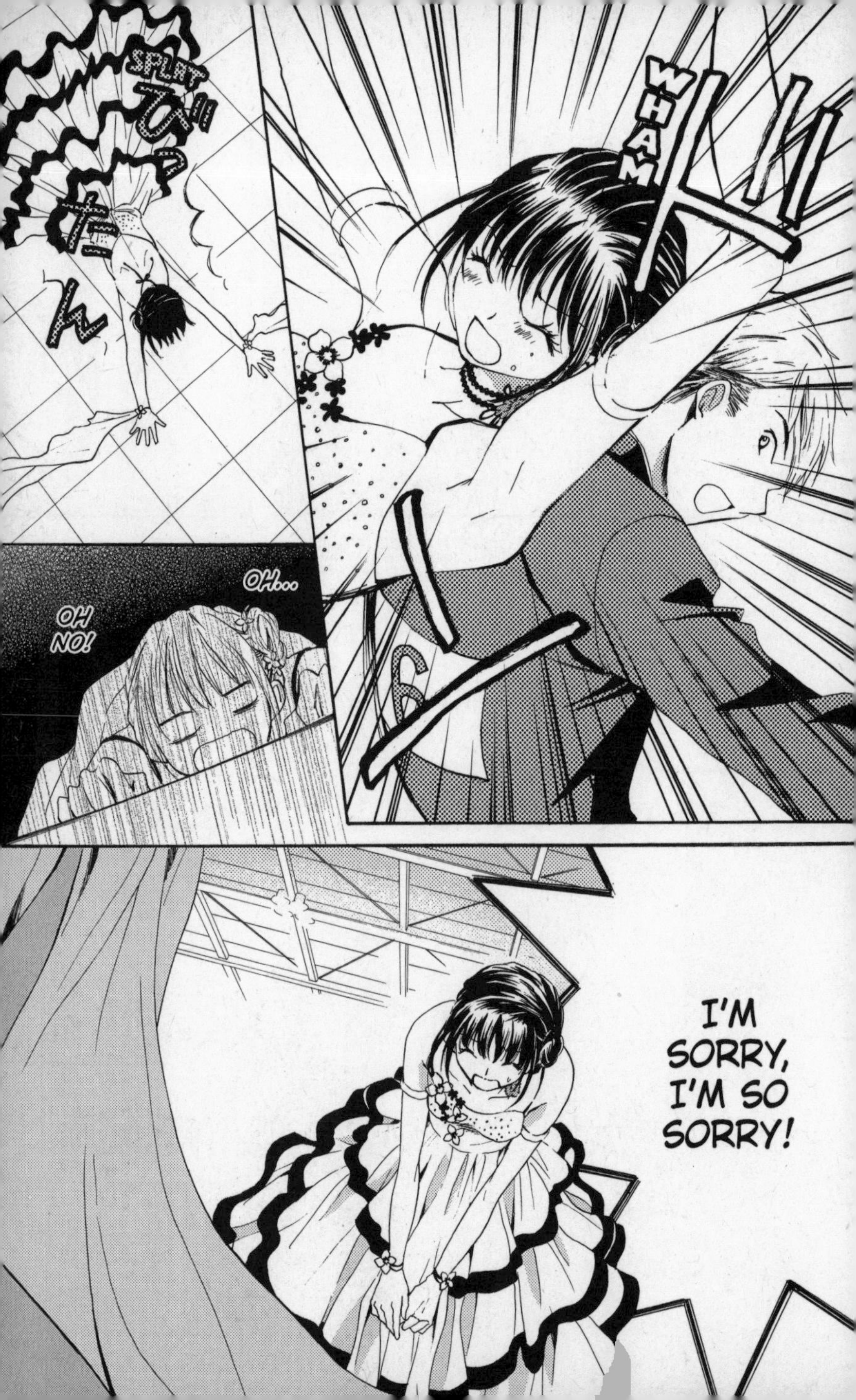
WHAM
SPLAT
OH...
OH NO!
I'M SORRY, I'M SO SORRY!

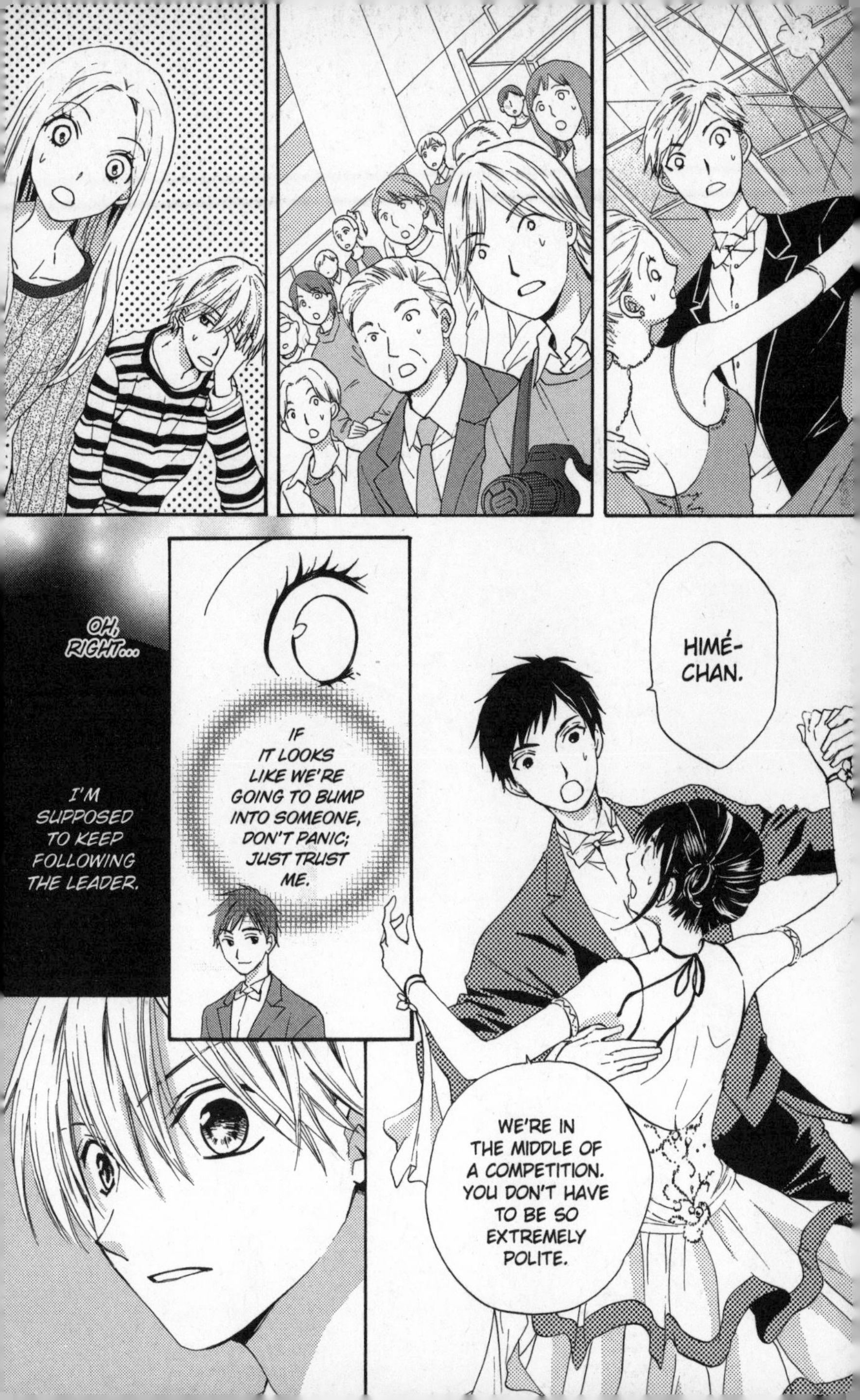
HIMÉ-CHAN.
WE'RE IN THE MIDDLE OF A COMPETITION. YOU DON'T HAVE TO BE SO EXTREMELY POLITE.
IF IT LOOKS LIKE WE'RE GOING TO BUMP INTO SOMEONE, DON'T PANIC; JUST TRUST ME.
OH, RIGHT...
I'M SUPPOSED TO KEEP FOLLOWING THE LEADER.

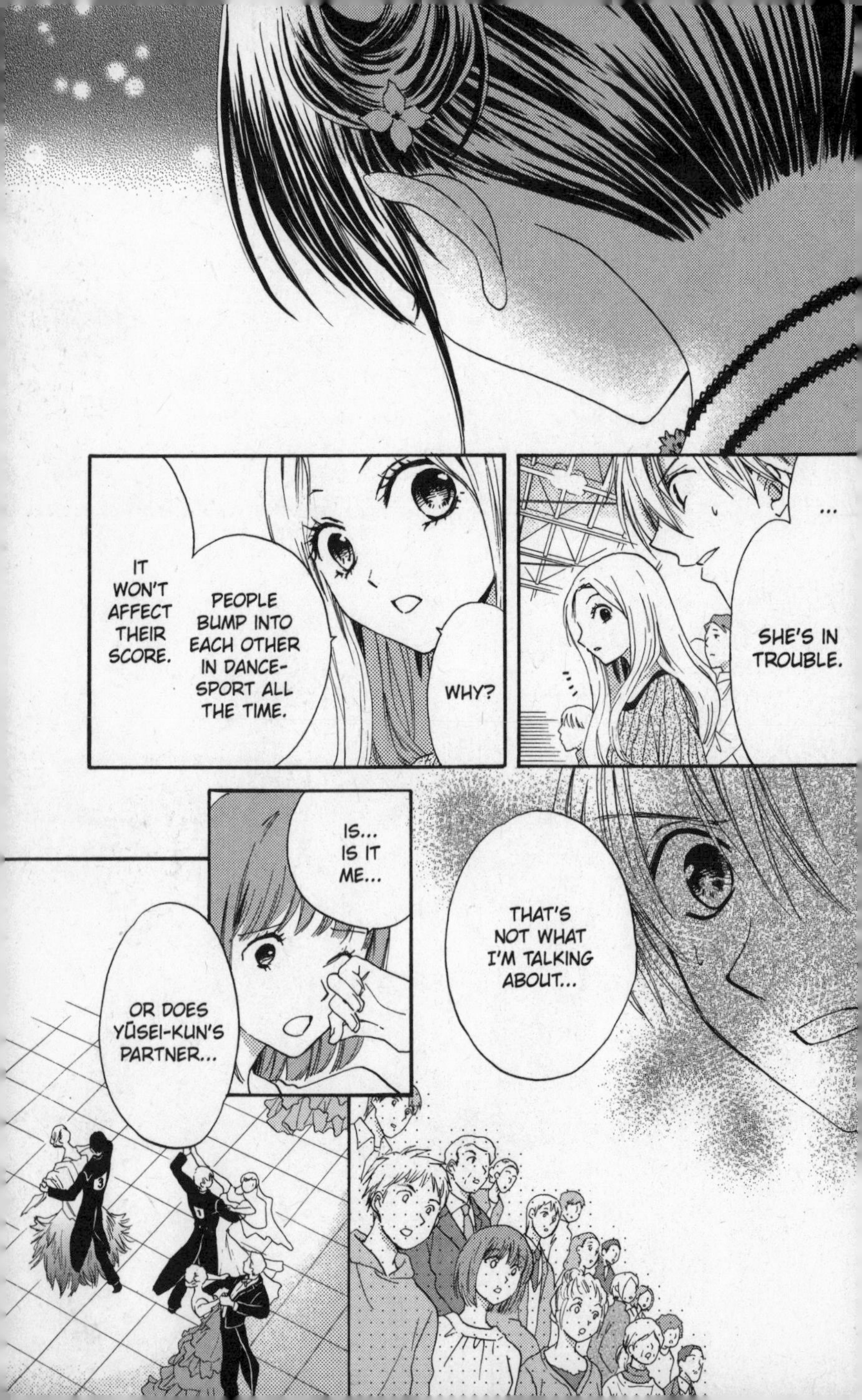
...
SHE'S IN TROUBLE.
WHY?
PEOPLE BUMP INTO EACH OTHER IN DANCE-SPORT ALL THE TIME.
IT WON'T AFFECT THEIR SCORE.
THAT'S NOT WHAT I'M TALKING ABOUT...
IS... IS IT ME...
OR DOES YŪSEI-KUN'S PARTNER...

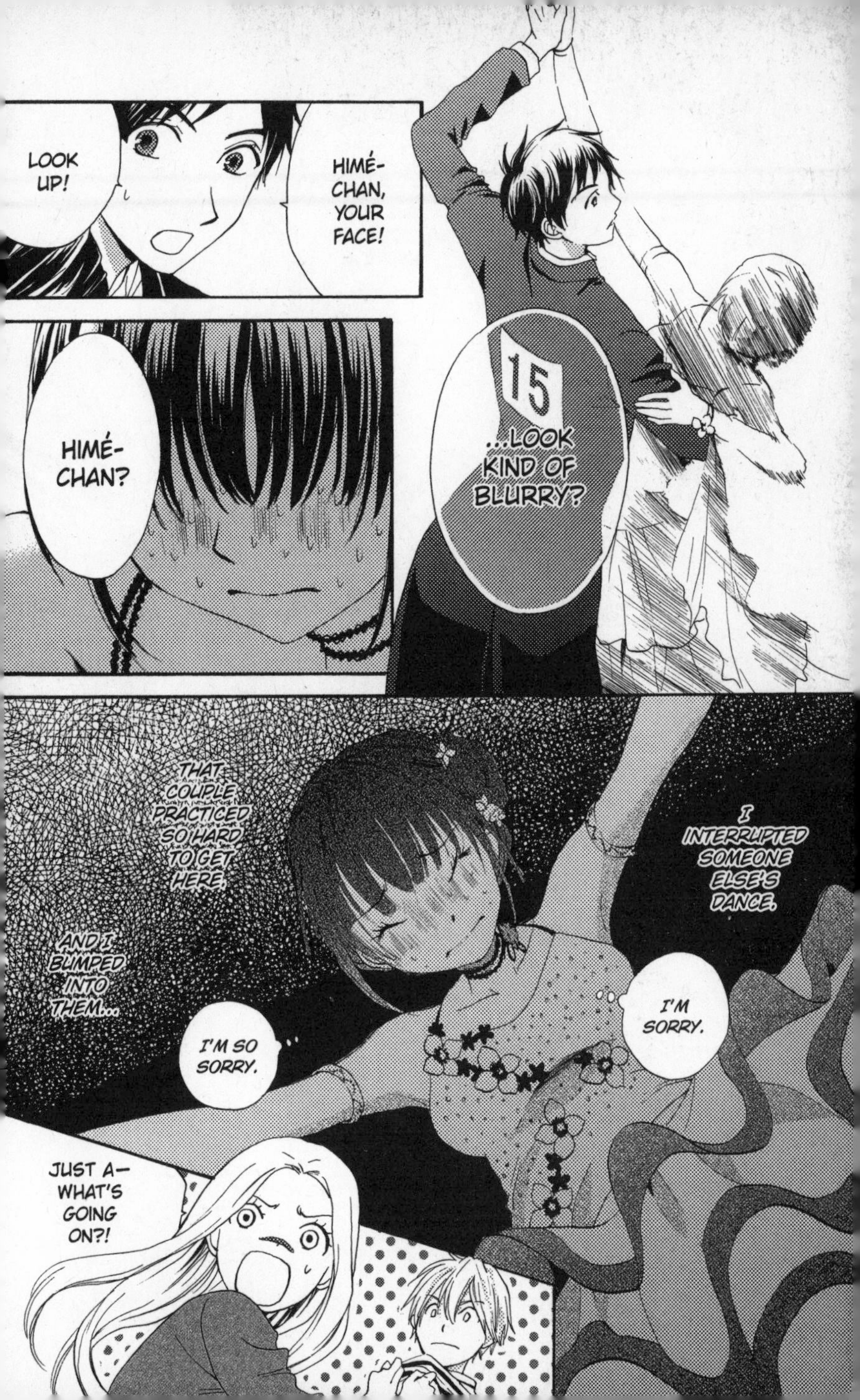
...LOOK KIND OF BLURRY?
HIMÉ-CHAN, YOUR FACE!
LOOK UP!
HIMÉ-CHAN?
I INTERRUPTED SOMEONE ELSE'S DANCE.
THAT COUPLE PRACTICED SO HARD TO GET HERE.
I'M SORRY.
AND I BUMPED INTO THEM...
I'M SO SORRY.
JUST A— WHAT'S GOING ON?!

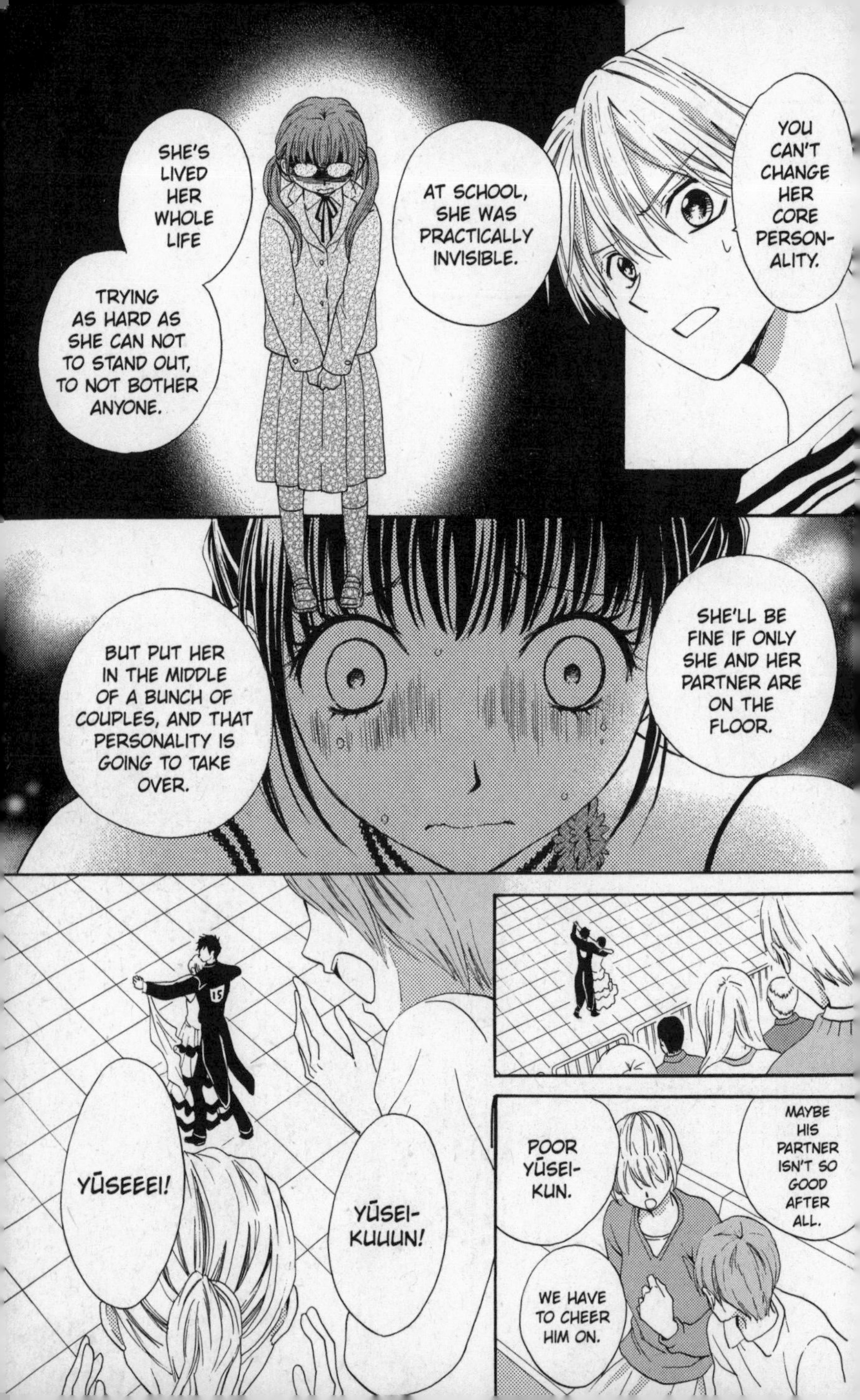
YOU CAN'T CHANGE HER CORE PERSON-ALITY.
AT SCHOOL, SHE WAS PRACTICALLY INVISIBLE.
SHE'S LIVED HER WHOLE LIFE
TRYING AS HARD AS SHE CAN NOT TO STAND OUT, TO NOT BOTHER ANYONE.
SHE'LL BE FINE IF ONLY SHE AND HER PARTNER ARE ON THE FLOOR.
BUT PUT HER IN THE MIDDLE OF A BUNCH OF COUPLES, AND THAT PERSONALITY IS GOING TO TAKE OVER.
MAYBE HIS PARTNER ISN'T SO GOOD AFTER ALL.
POOR YŪSEI-KUN.
WE HAVE TO CHEER HIM ON.
YŪSEI-KUUUN!
YŪSEEEI!

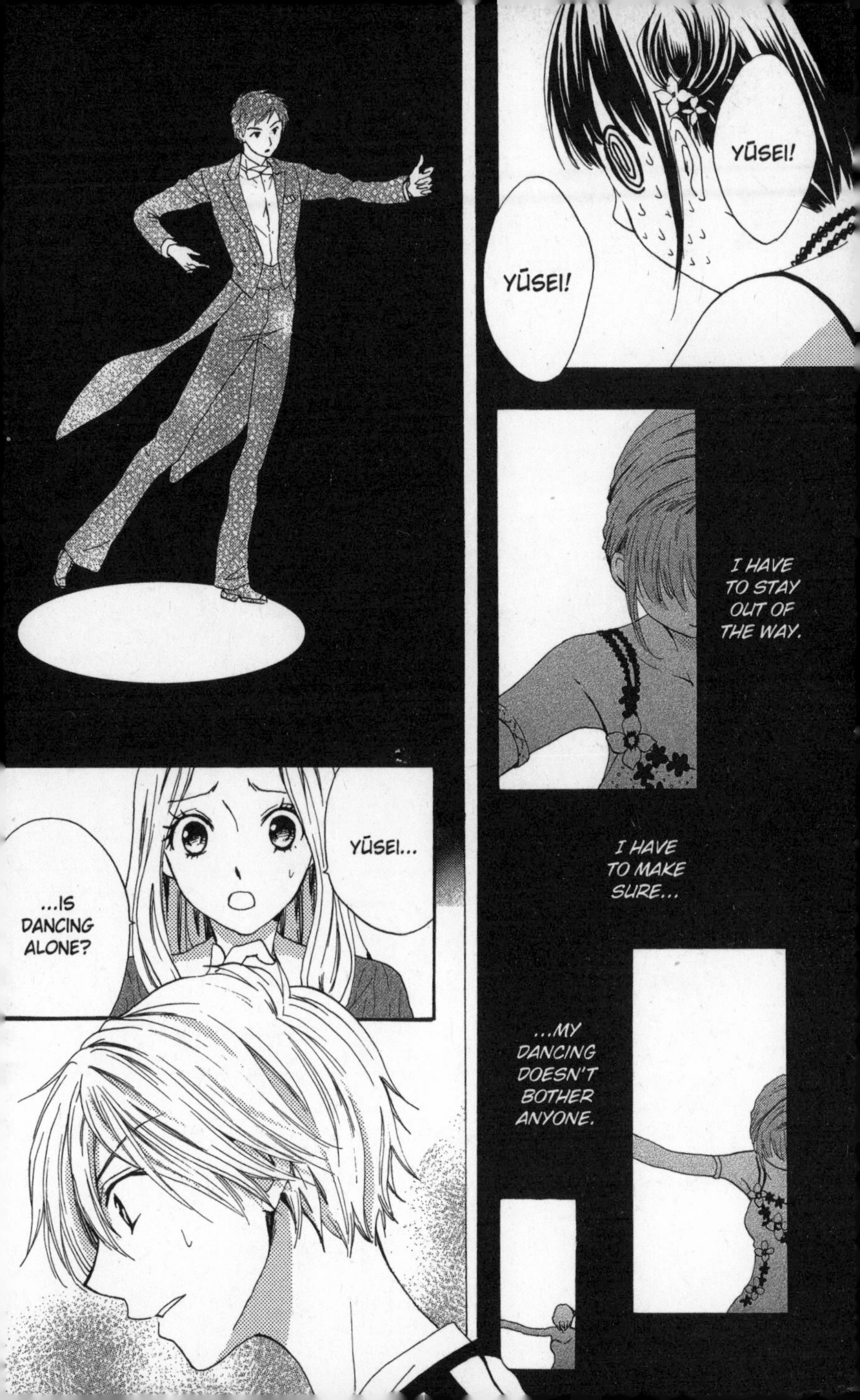
YŪSEI!
YŪSEI!
I HAVE TO STAY OUT OF THE WAY.
I HAVE TO MAKE SURE...
...MY DANCING DOESN'T BOTHER ANYONE.
YŪSEI...
...IS DANCING ALONE?

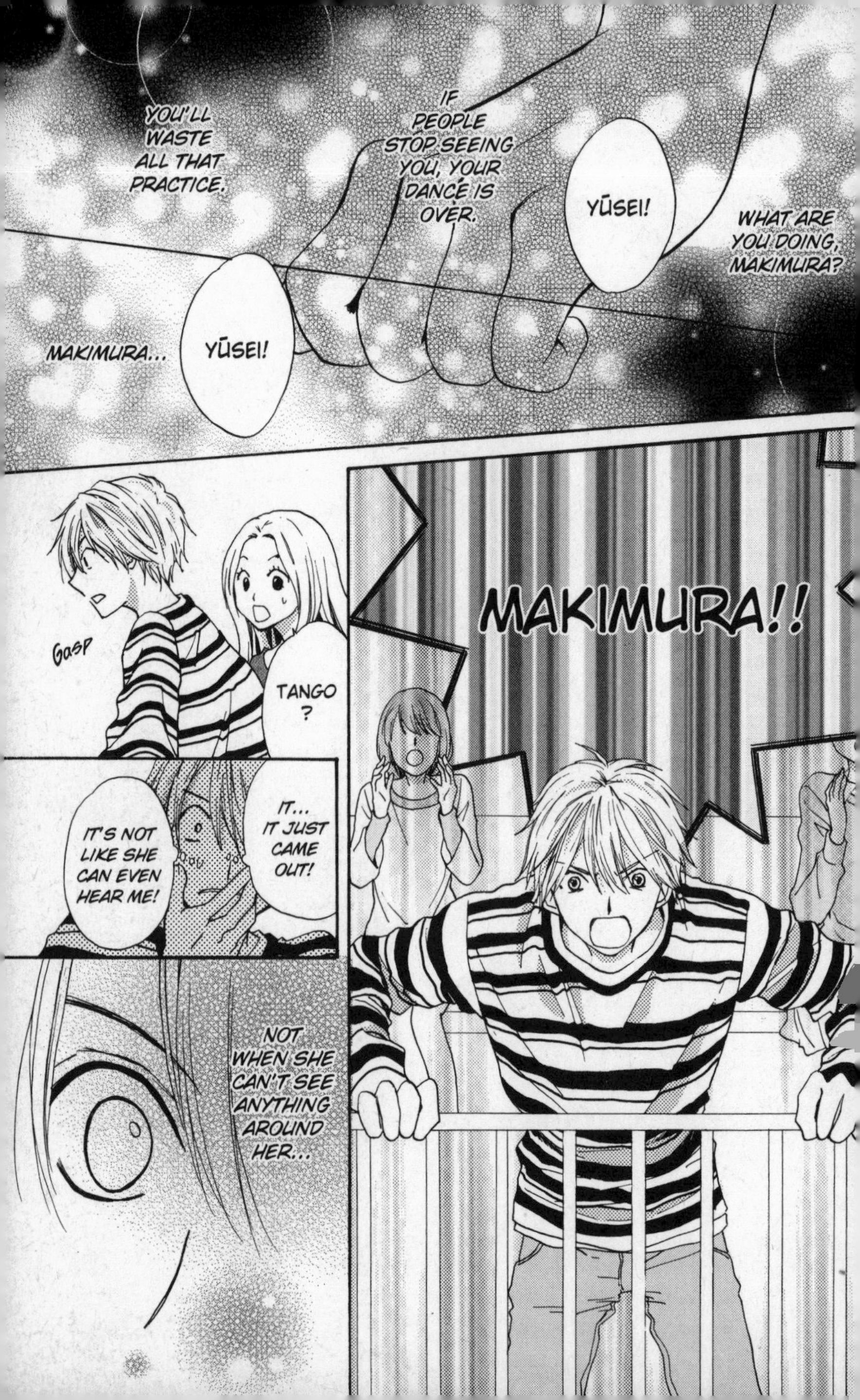
WHAT ARE YOU DOING, MAKIMURA?
YŪSEI!
IF PEOPLE STOP SEEING YOU, YOUR DANCE IS OVER.
YOU'LL WASTE ALL THAT PRACTICE.
YŪSEI!
MAKIMURA...
MAKIMURA!!
TANGO?
Gasp
IT... IT JUST CAME OUT!
IT'S NOT LIKE SHE CAN EVEN HEAR ME!
NOT WHEN SHE CAN'T SEE ANYTHING AROUND HER...

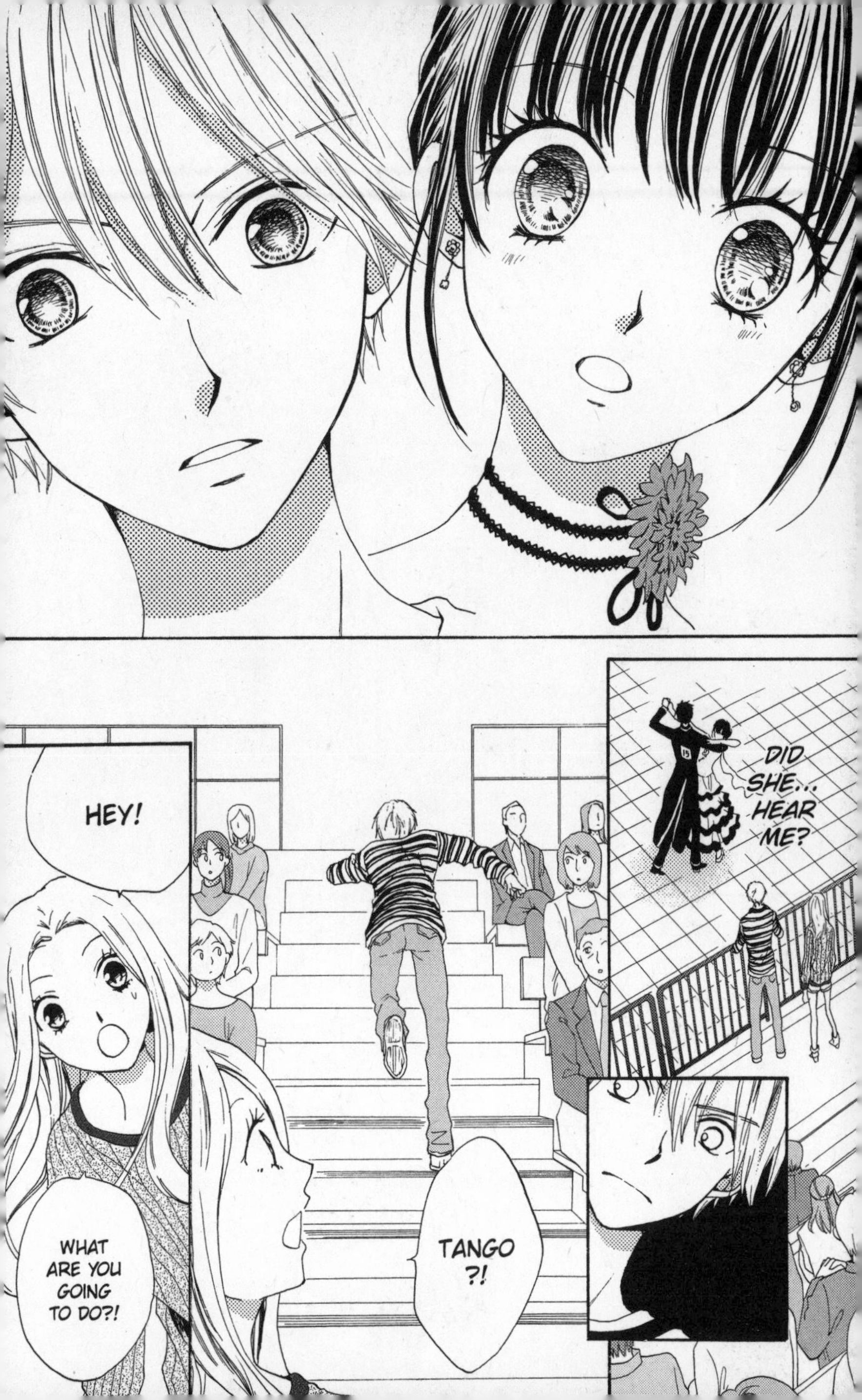
DID SHE... HEAR ME?
HEY!
TANGO ?!
WHAT ARE YOU GOING TO DO?!

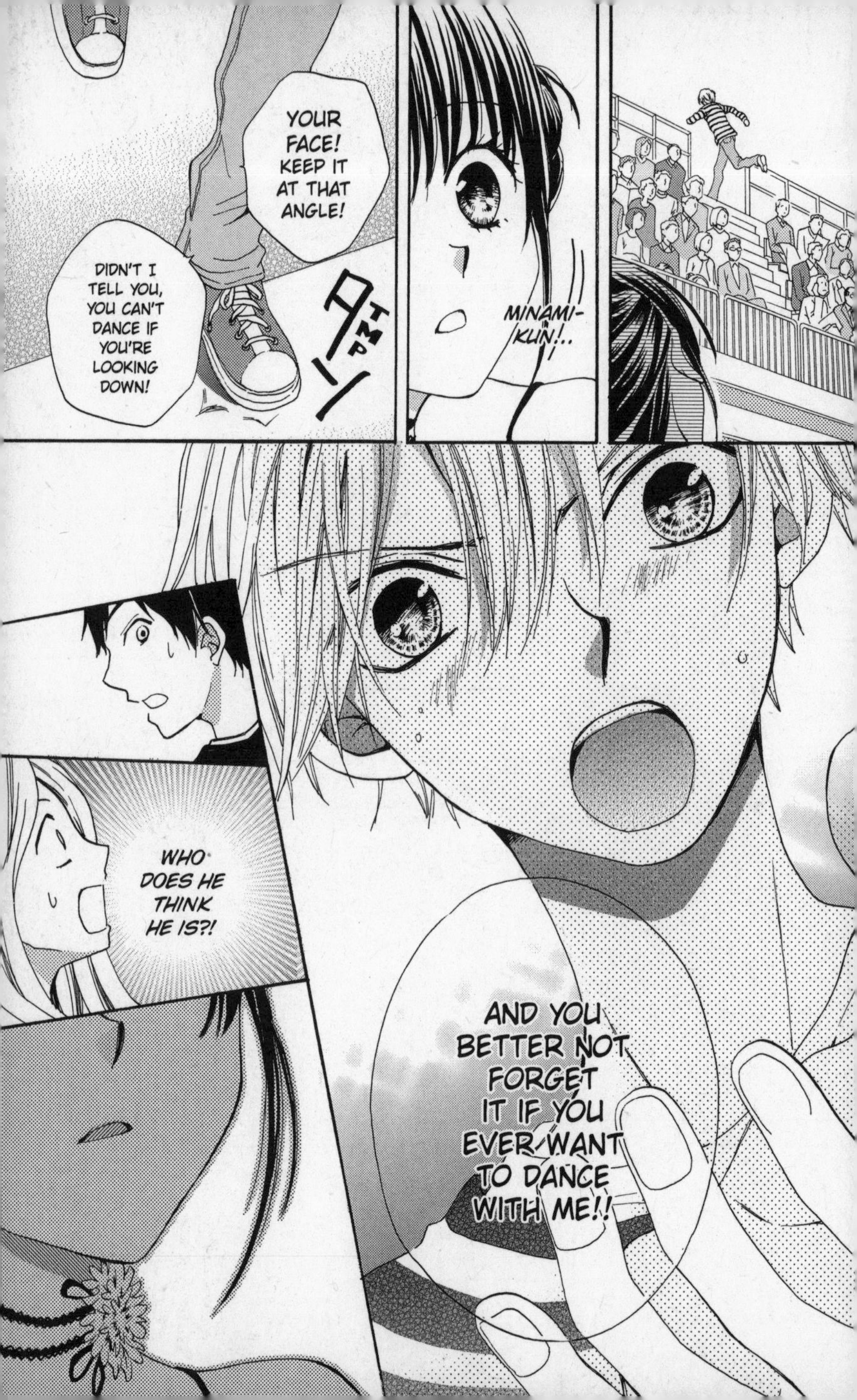
MINAMI-KUN!..
YOUR FACE! KEEP IT AT THAT ANGLE!
DIDN'T I TELL YOU, YOU CAN'T DANCE IF YOU'RE LOOKING DOWN!
TMP
AND YOU BETTER NOT FORGET IT IF YOU EVER WANT TO DANCE WITH ME!!
WHO DOES HE THINK HE IS?!

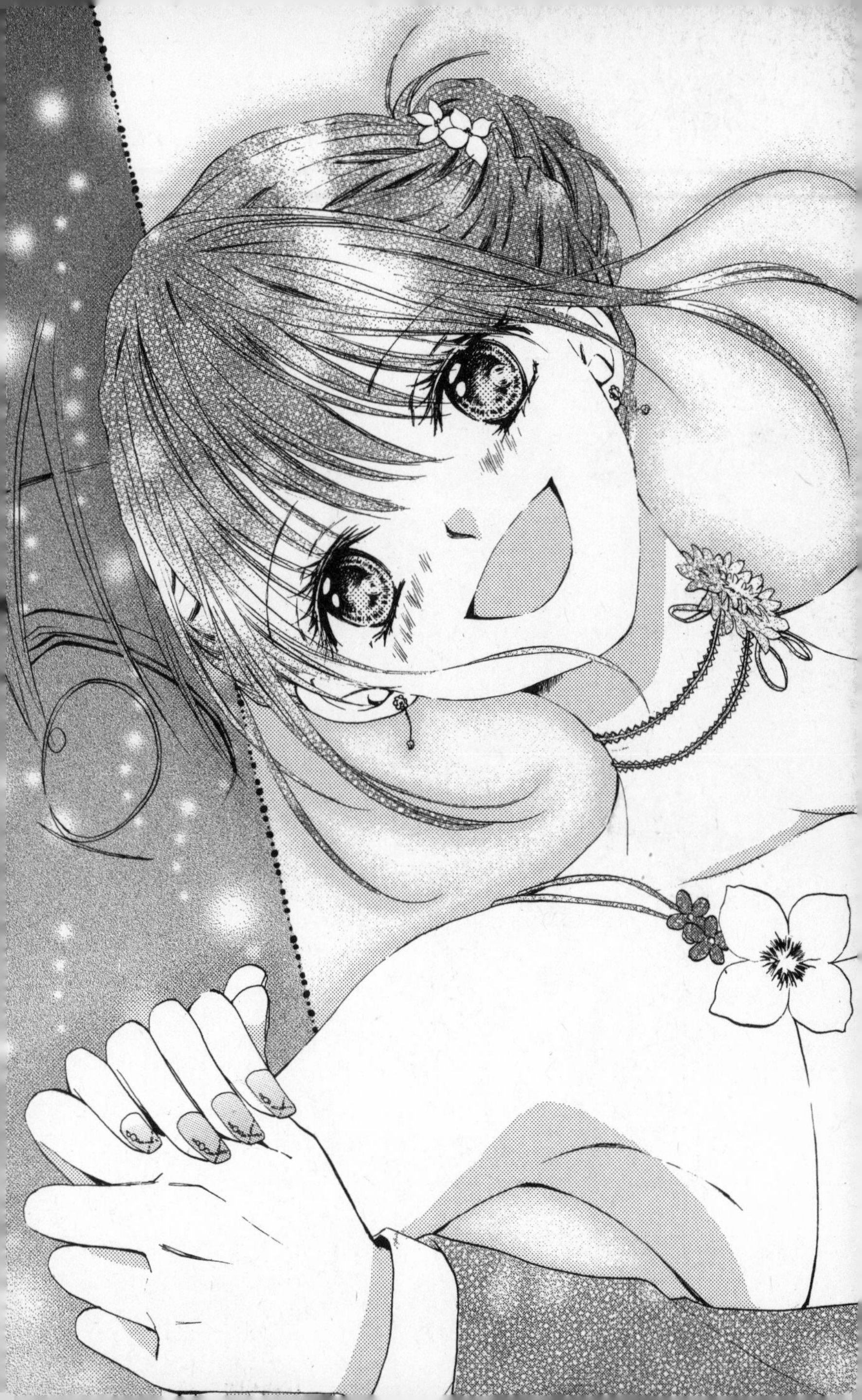

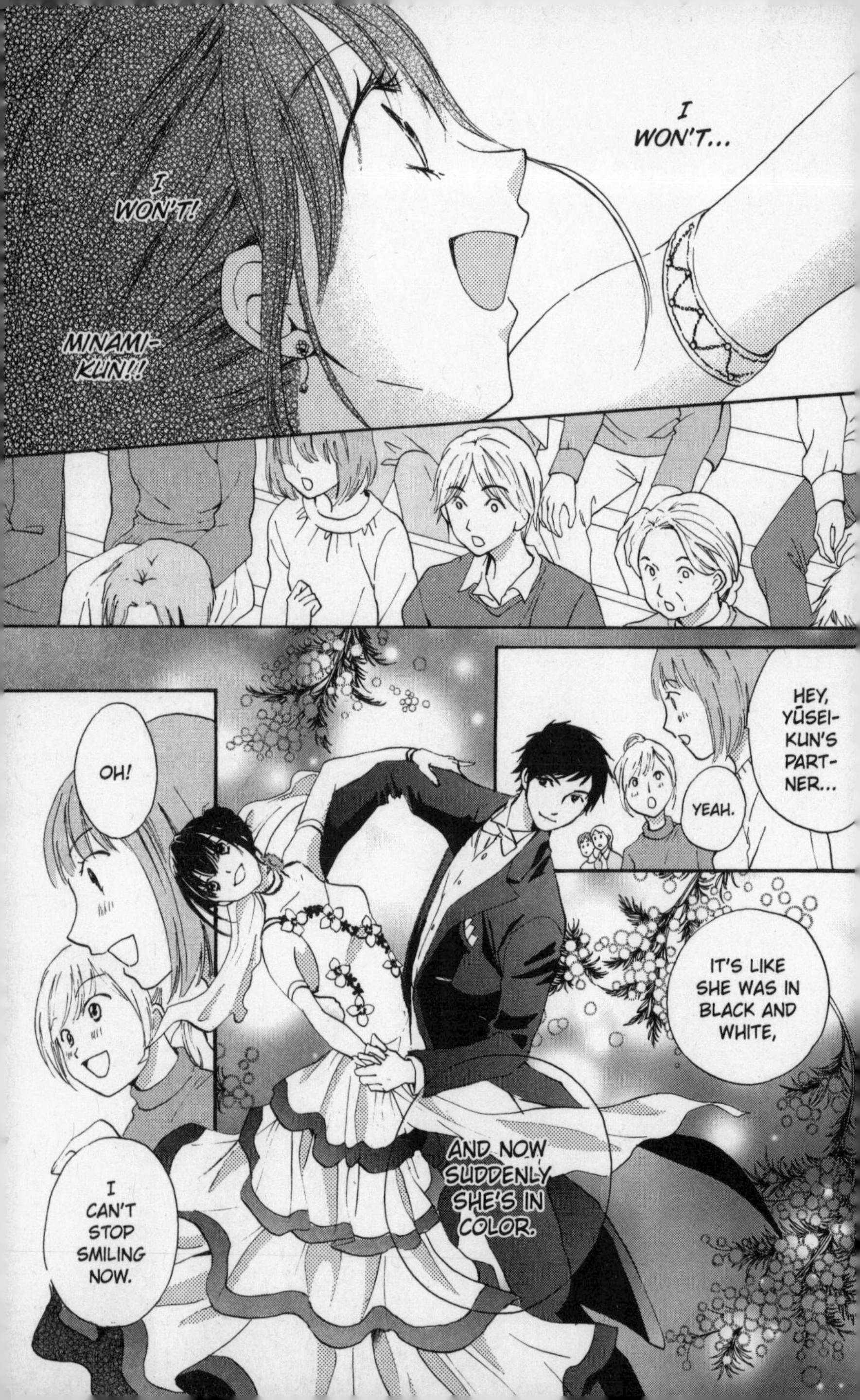
I WON'T...
I WON'T!
MINAMI-KUN!!
HEY, YŪSEI-KUN'S PARTNER...
YEAH.
IT'S LIKE SHE WAS IN BLACK AND WHITE,
AND NOW SUDDENLY SHE'S IN COLOR.
OH!
I CAN'T STOP SMILING NOW.

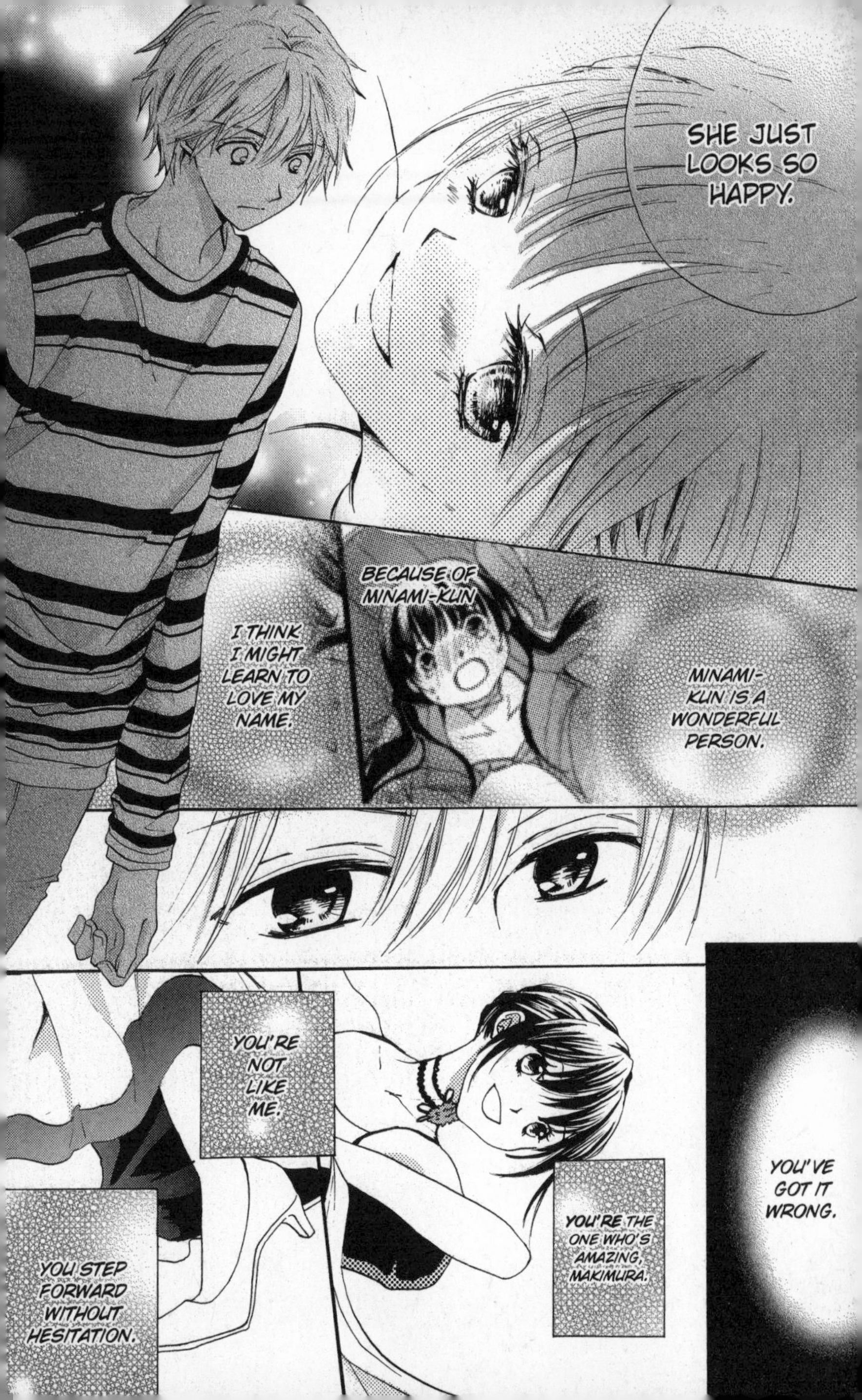
SHE JUST LOOKS SO HAPPY.
MINAMI-KUN IS A WONDERFUL PERSON.
BECAUSE OF MINAMI-KUN
I THINK I MIGHT LEARN TO LOVE MY NAME.
YOU'VE GOT IT WRONG.
YOU'RE NOT LIKE ME.
YOU'RE THE ONE WHO'S AMAZING, MAKIMURA.
YOU STEP FORWARD WITHOUT HESITATION.

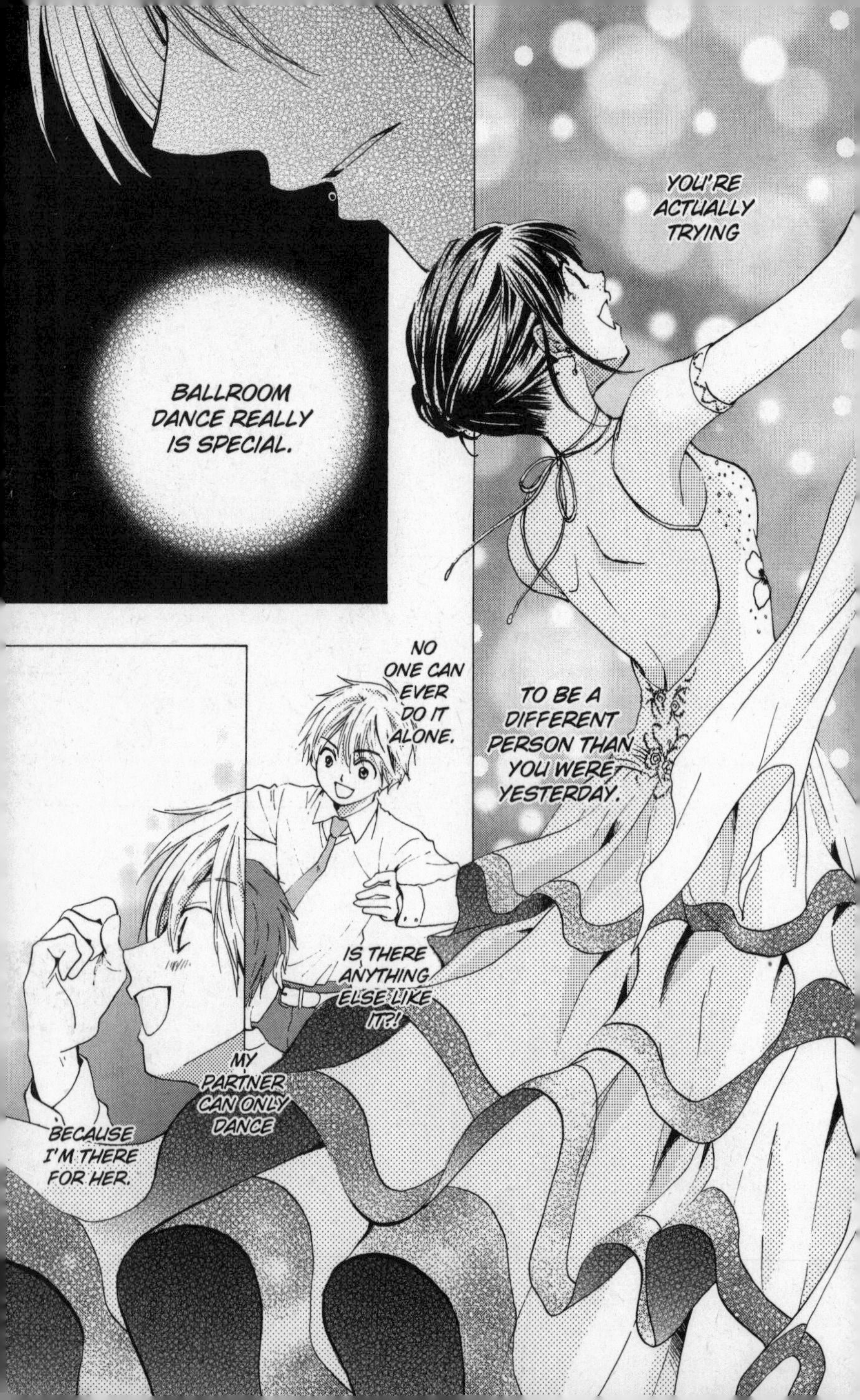
YOU'RE ACTUALLY TRYING
TO BE A DIFFERENT PERSON THAN YOU WERE YESTERDAY.
BALLROOM DANCE REALLY IS SPECIAL.
NO ONE CAN EVER DO IT ALONE.
IS THERE ANYTHING ELSE LIKE IT?!
MY PARTNER CAN ONLY DANCE
BECAUSE I'M THERE FOR HER.

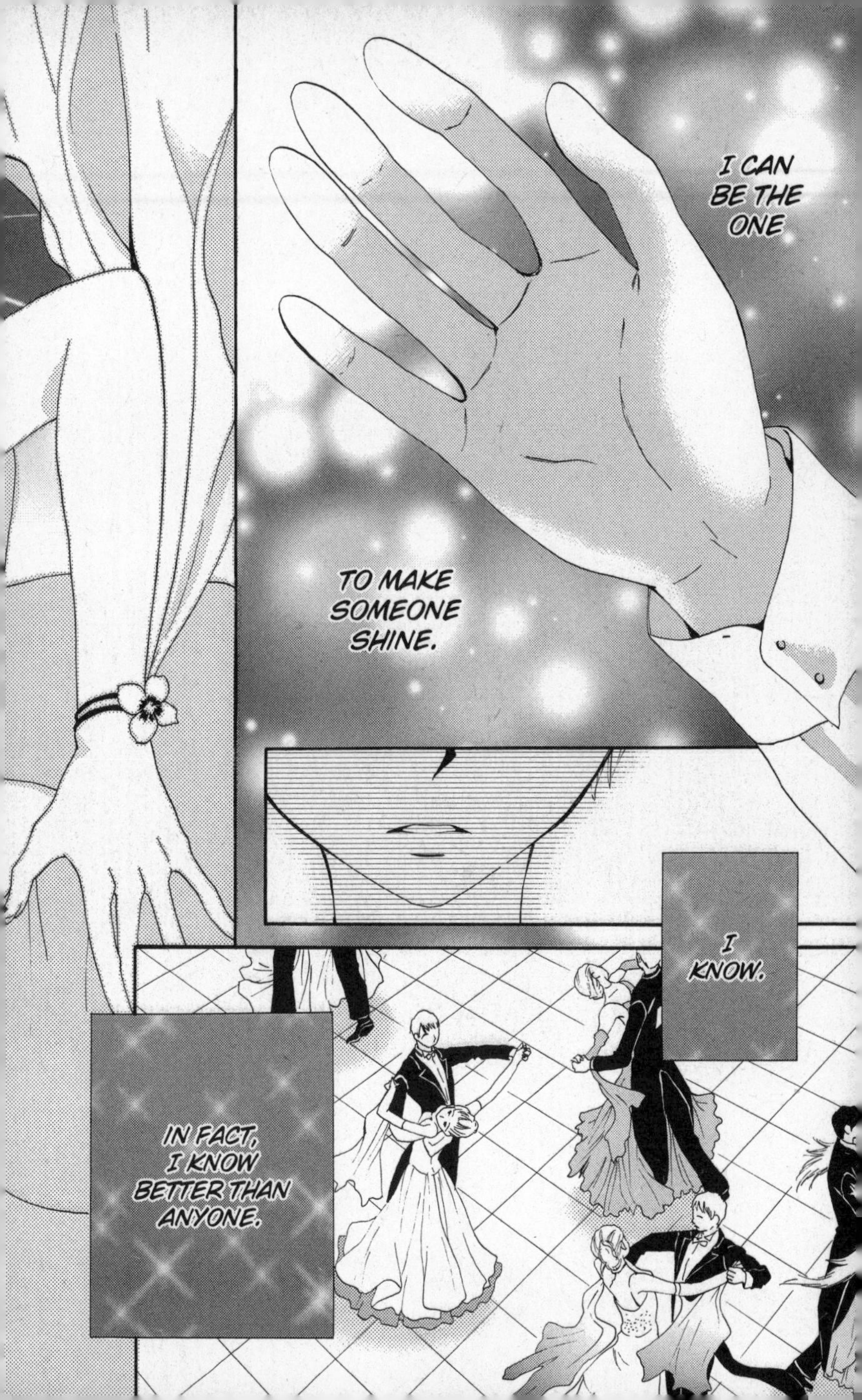
I CAN BE THE ONE
TO MAKE SOMEONE SHINE.
I KNOW.
IN FACT, I KNOW BETTER THAN ANYONE.

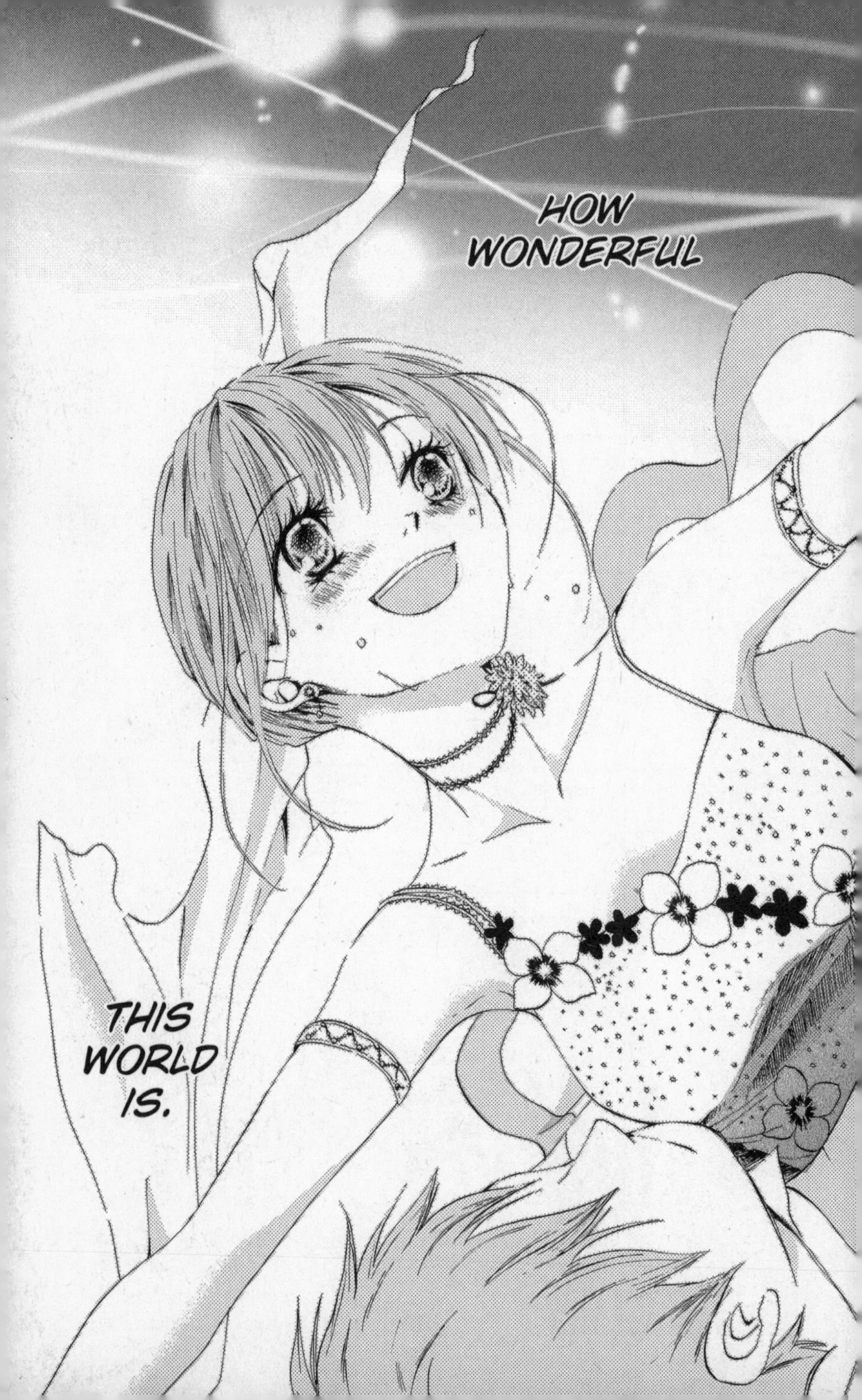
HOW WONDERFUL
THIS WORLD IS.

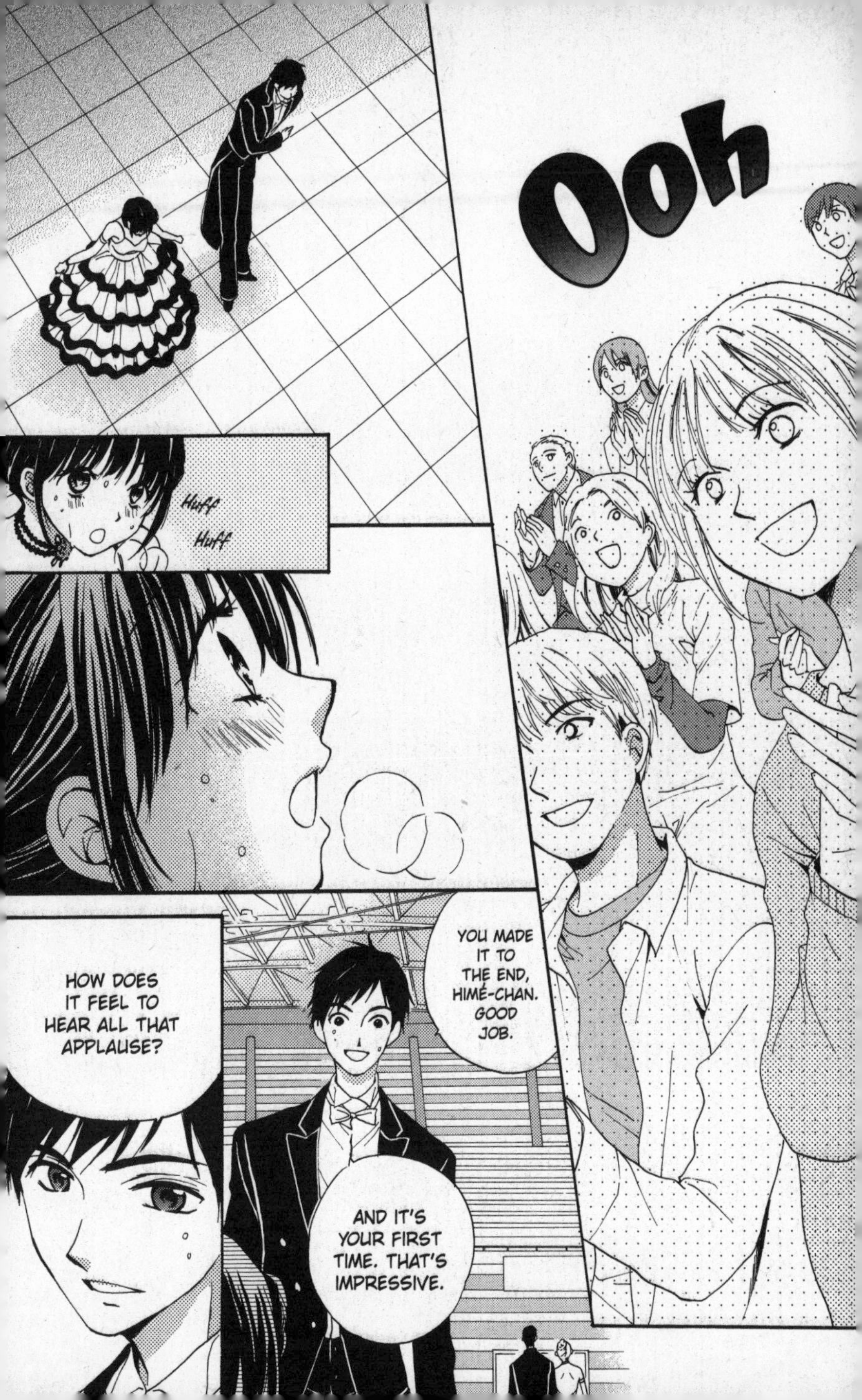
Ooh
Huff Huff
YOU MADE IT TO THE END, HIMÉ-CHAN. GOOD JOB.
AND IT'S YOUR FIRST TIME. THAT'S IMPRESSIVE.
HOW DOES IT FEEL TO HEAR ALL THAT APPLAUSE?

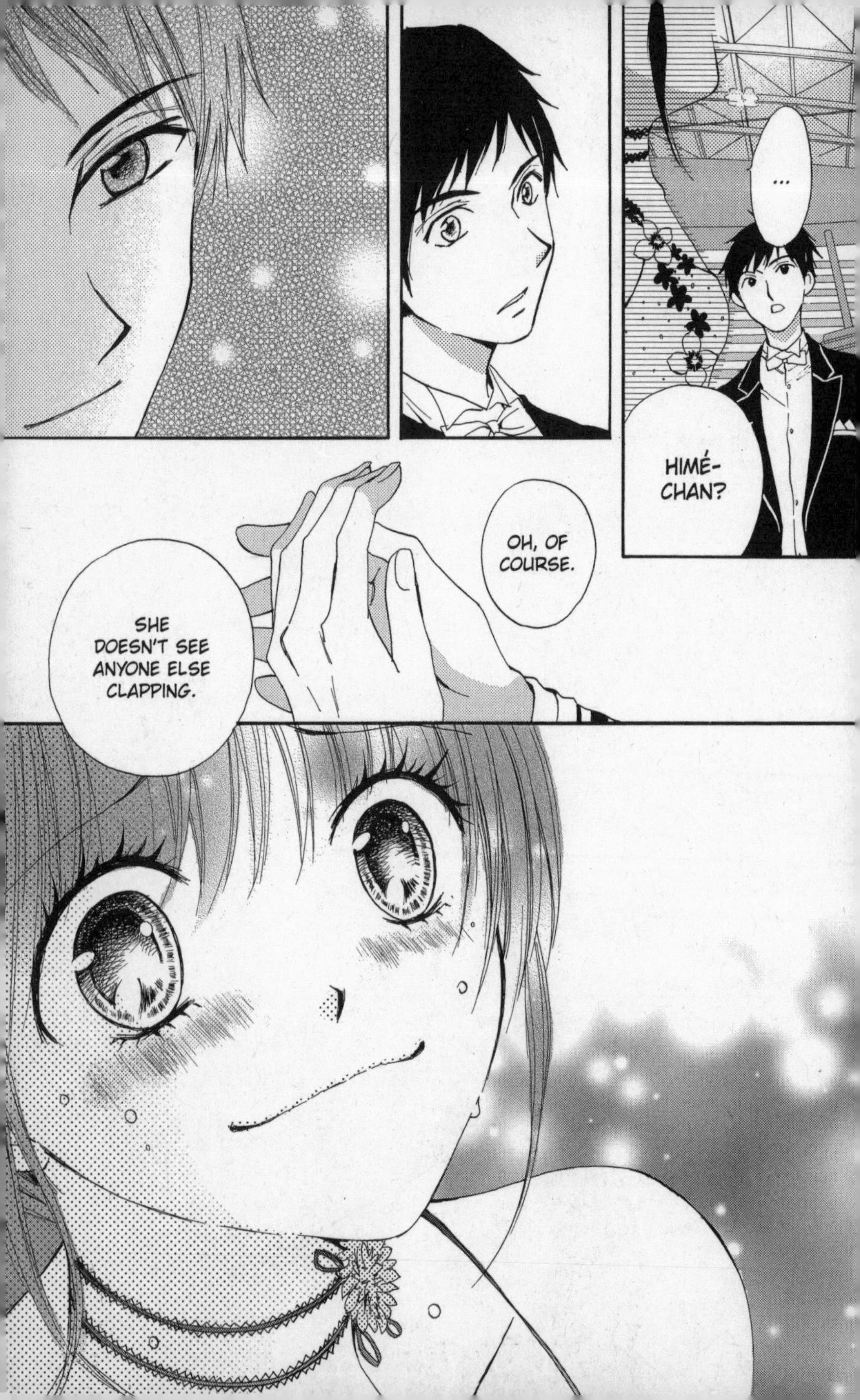
...
HIMÉ-CHAN?
OH, OF COURSE.
SHE DOESN'T SEE ANYONE ELSE CLAPPING.

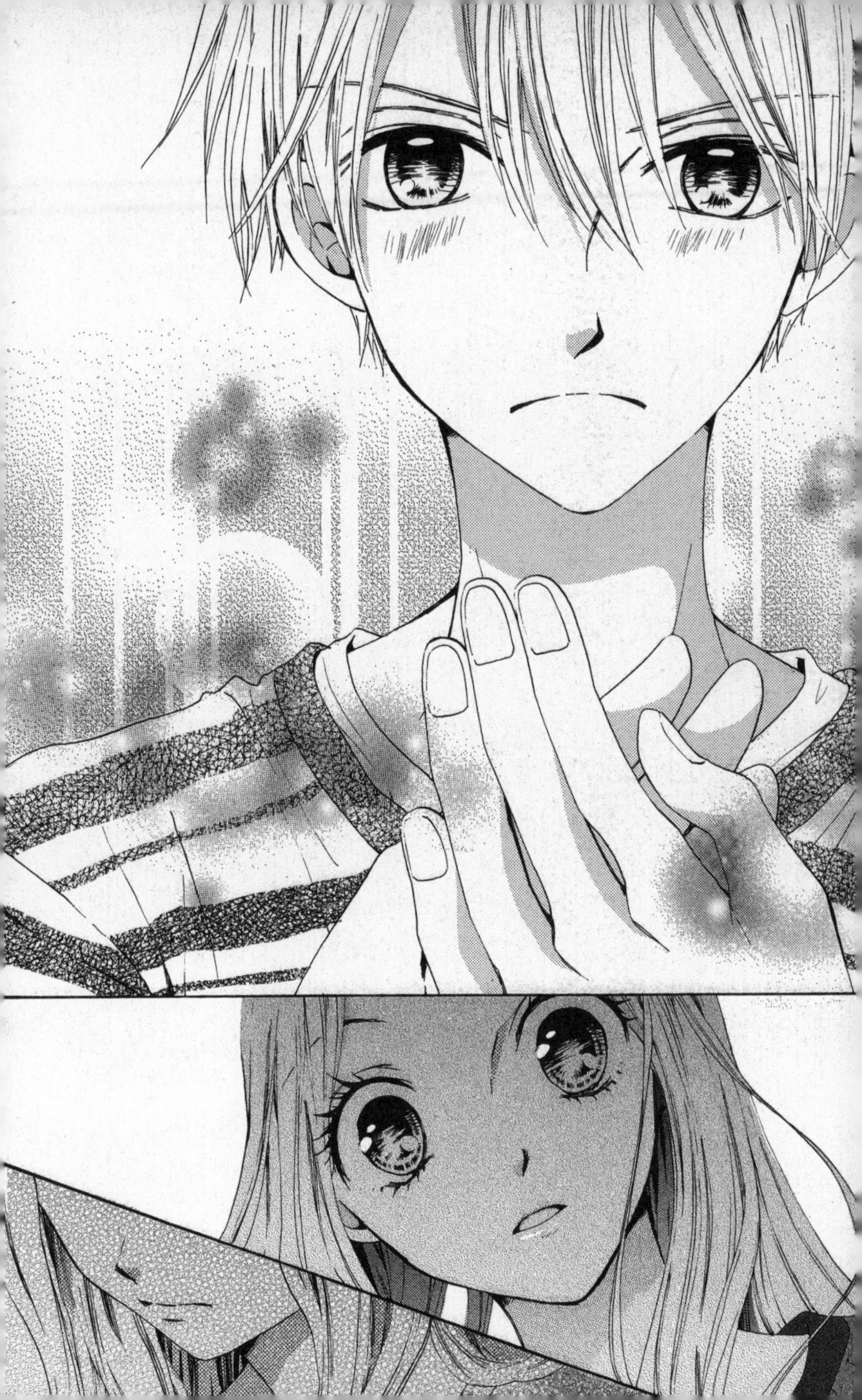

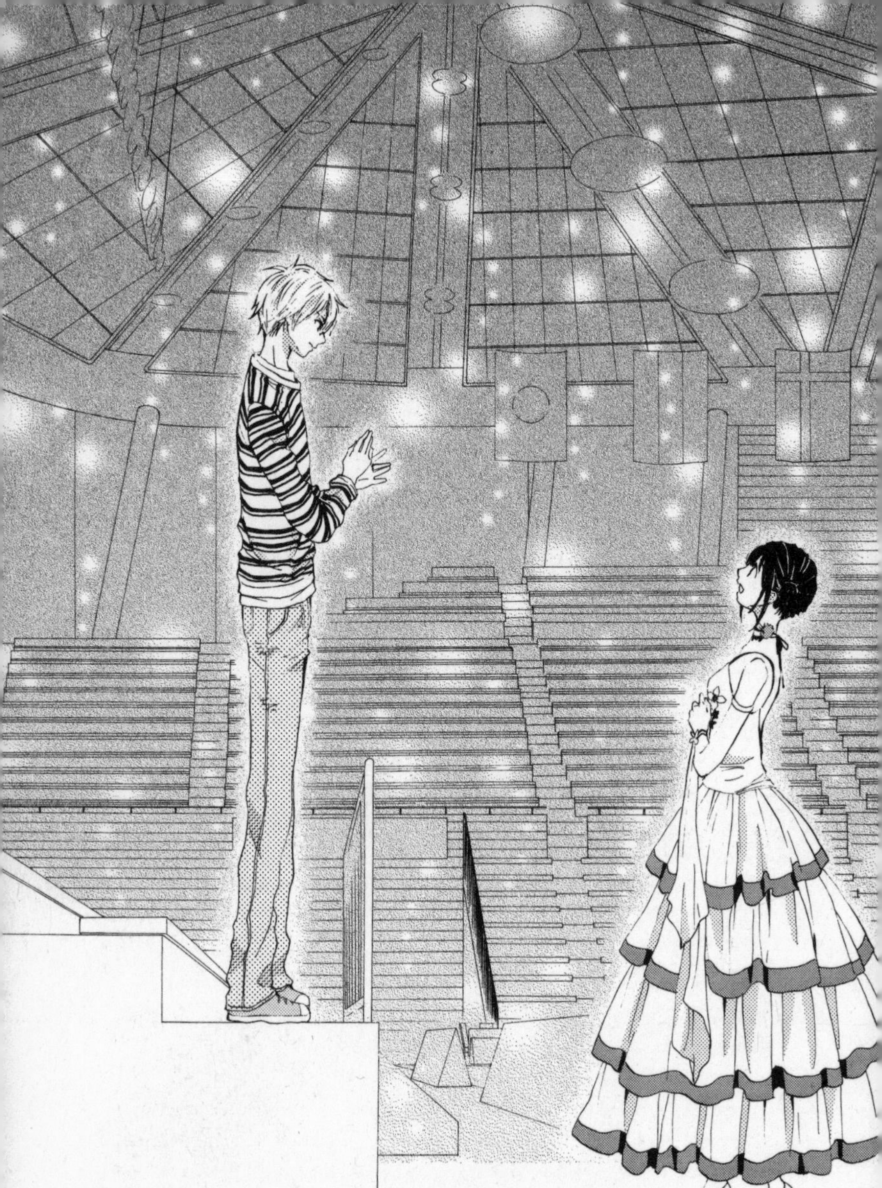

Presenting volume two
of Let's Dance a Waltz ♪

Thank you so much for picking up Let's Dance a Waltz volume two!! This volume is chock-full of dance scenes.

The characters in Waltz are all passionately devoting most of their lives to dance. When I was their age, my passion was for swimming. When the pool was filled with water and the season started, it was... morning practice! Swim meets! Every day, even during summer break!! One hundred 25m laps!! Ten laps of each of the four main strokes!! It really was the training from hell.

And after morning practice, I'd still go to all my classes, including PE... Looking back, I'm seriously confused at the gap between then and now. Where did I get all that energy? And where did it all go?

And of course I drew manga, too. I'd get home from school, and it was manga all evening!! But I was just drawing with pencil in a notebook. I made my own series–after the course of three years. I had an epic masterpiece that filled nearly 20 notebooks. It was about three ninja sisters, and I'm sure I took tons of inspiration from a TV series that was popular at the time. Or actually, the premise was pretty much an exact copy. Anyway, there are lots of things to make fun of, but I treasure that manga to this day.

What are all of you passionate about?

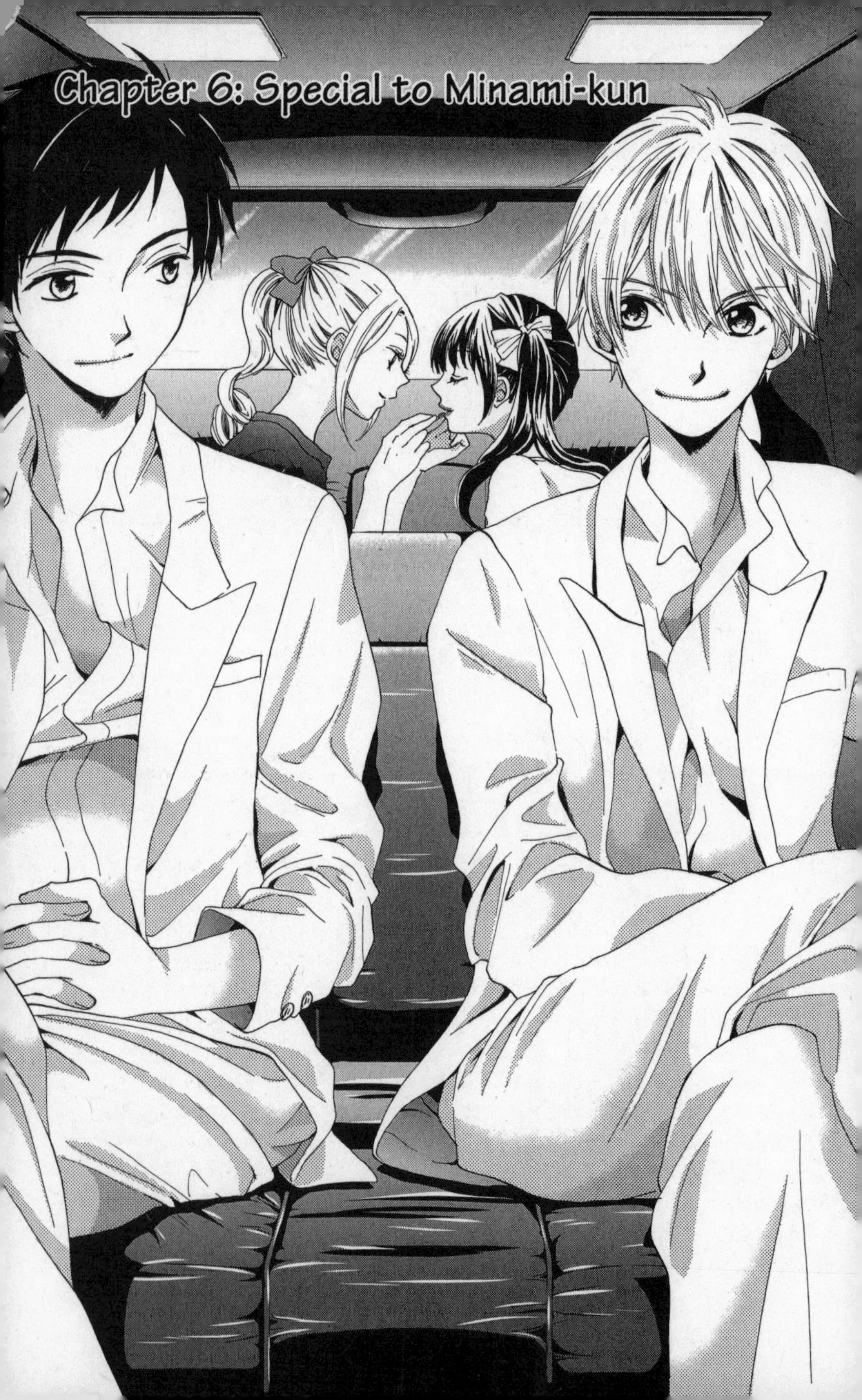
Chapter 6: Special to Minami-kun

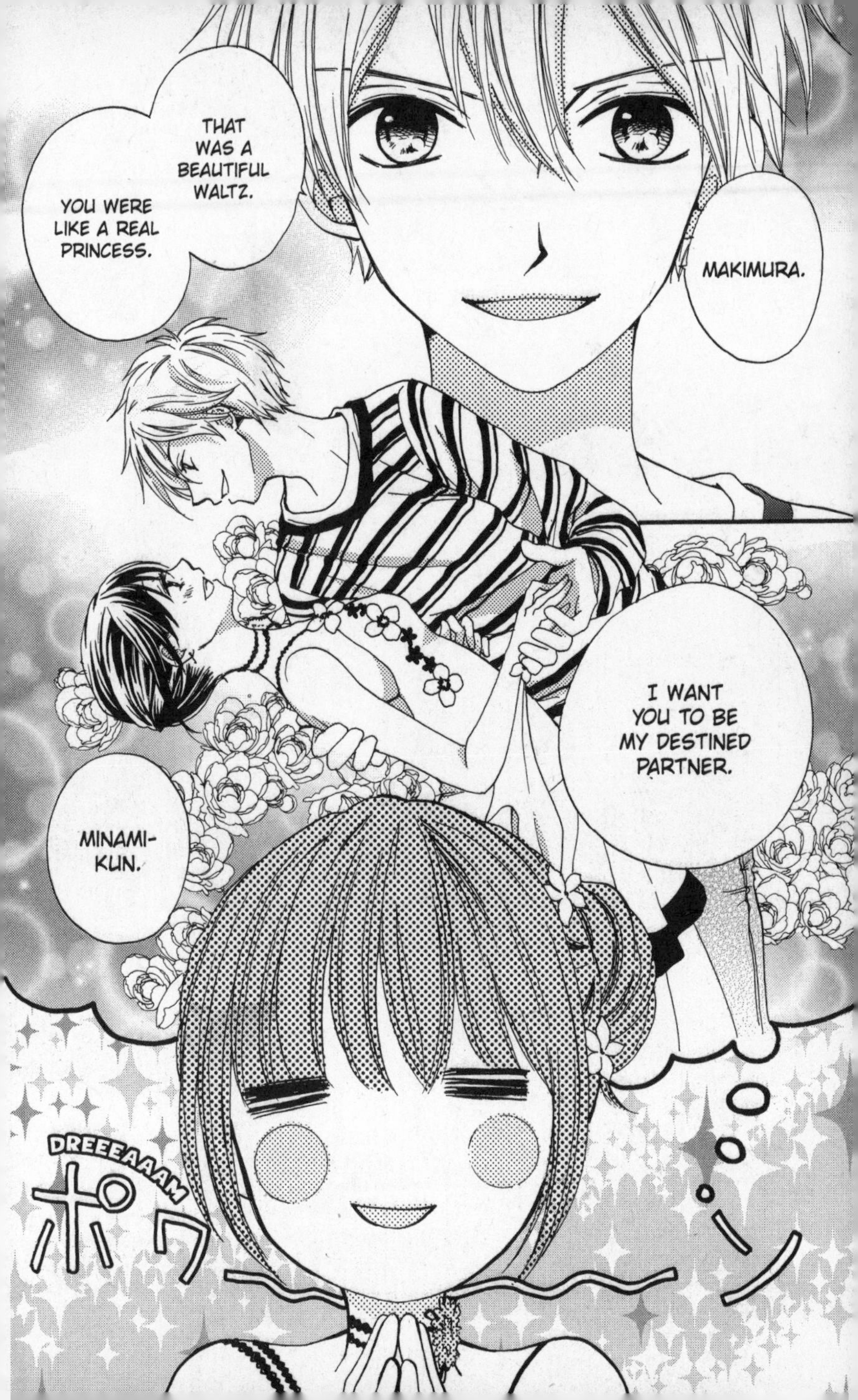
MAKIMURA.
THAT WAS A BEAUTIFUL WALTZ.
YOU WERE LIKE A REAL PRINCESS.
I WANT YOU TO BE MY DESTINED PARTNER.
MINAMI-KUN.
DREEEAAAM
ポワ〜〜ン

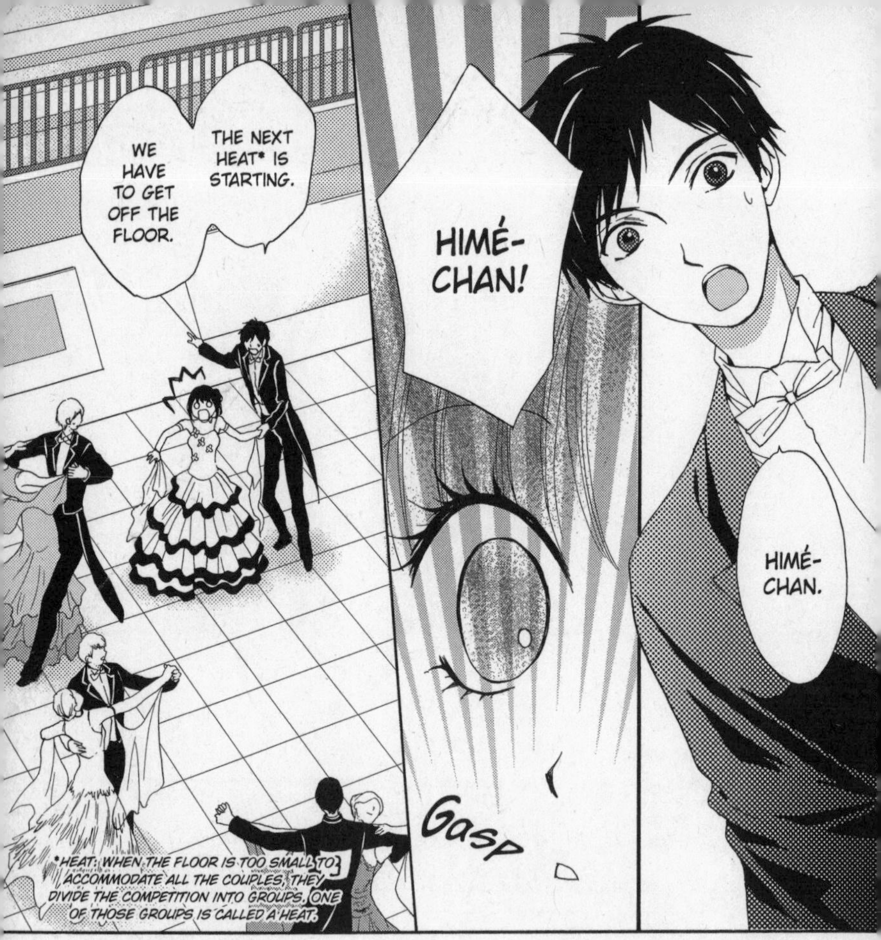
HIMÉ-CHAN!
HIMÉ-CHAN.
Gasp
THE NEXT HEAT* IS STARTING.
WE HAVE TO GET OFF THE FLOOR.
*HEAT: WHEN THE FLOOR IS TOO SMALL TO ACCOMMODATE ALL THE COUPLES, THEY DIVIDE THE COMPETITION INTO GROUPS. ONE OF THOSE GROUPS IS CALLED A HEAT.

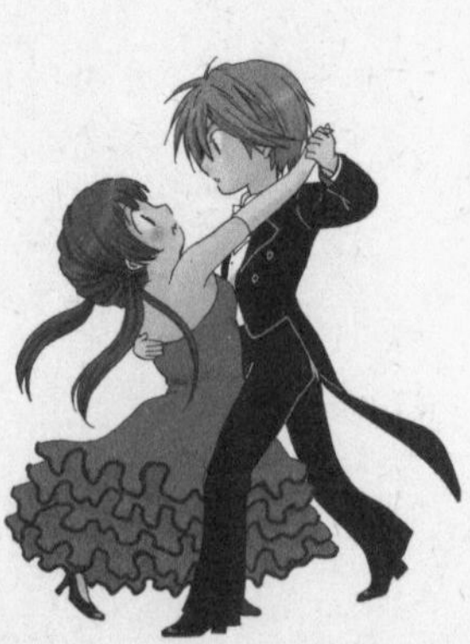

The Tango

A dynamic dance with heavy accents. It is danced in 2/4 or 4/8 time. The dancers keep pace with the staccato notes as they move powerfully across the floor. It doesn't have the same up and down motion of the waltz, but is known for its sharp, distinct movements!

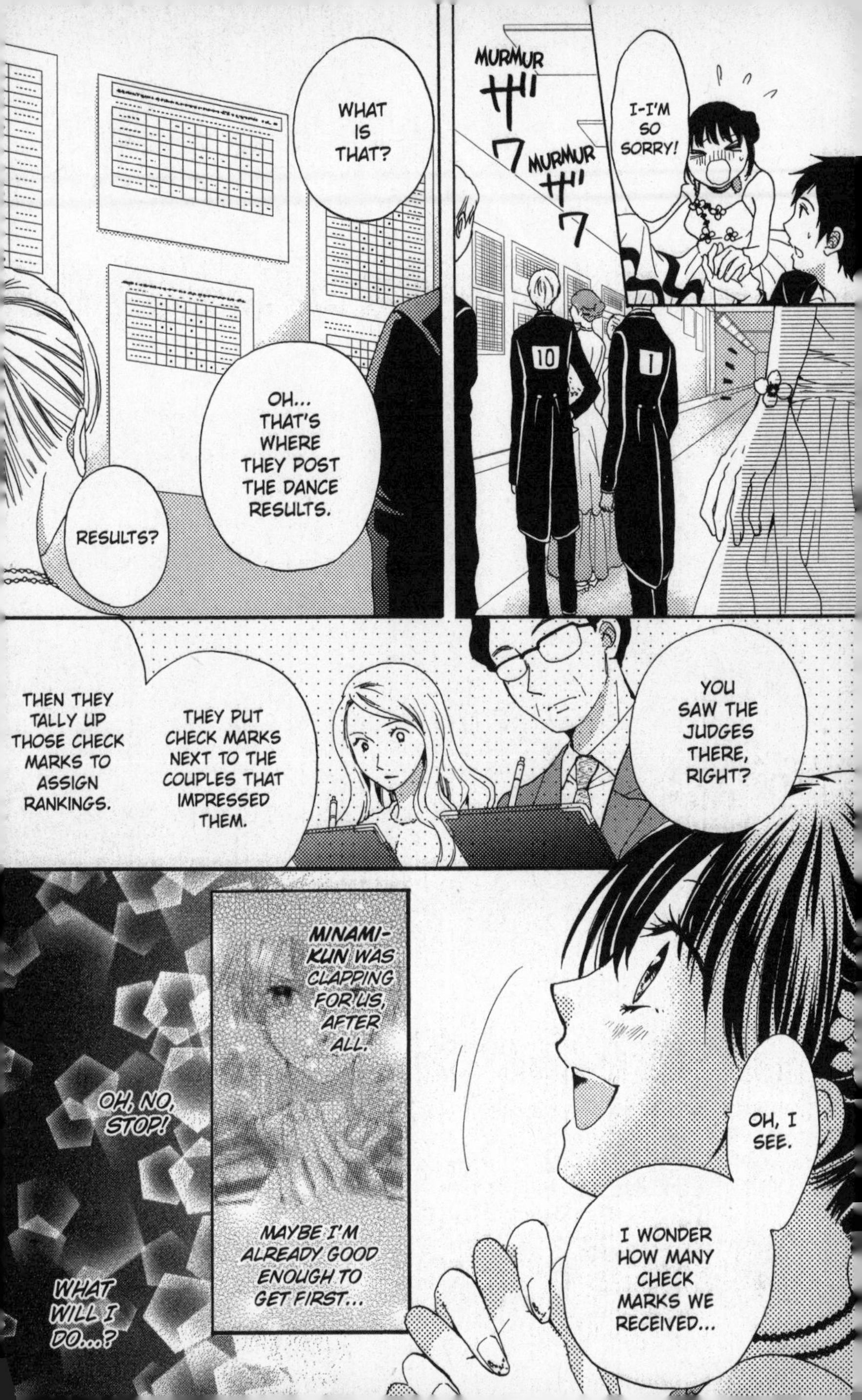
I-I'M SO SORRY!
MURMUR
ザワ
MURMUR
ザワ
WHAT IS THAT?
OH... THAT'S WHERE THEY POST THE DANCE RESULTS.
RESULTS?
YOU SAW THE JUDGES THERE, RIGHT?
THEY PUT CHECK MARKS NEXT TO THE COUPLES THAT IMPRESSED THEM.
THEN THEY TALLY UP THOSE CHECK MARKS TO ASSIGN RANKINGS.
OH, I SEE.
I WONDER HOW MANY CHECK MARKS WE RECEIVED...
MINAMI-KUN WAS CLAPPING FOR US, AFTER ALL.
MAYBE I'M ALREADY GOOD ENOUGH TO GET FIRST...
OH, NO, STOP!
WHAT WILL I DO...?

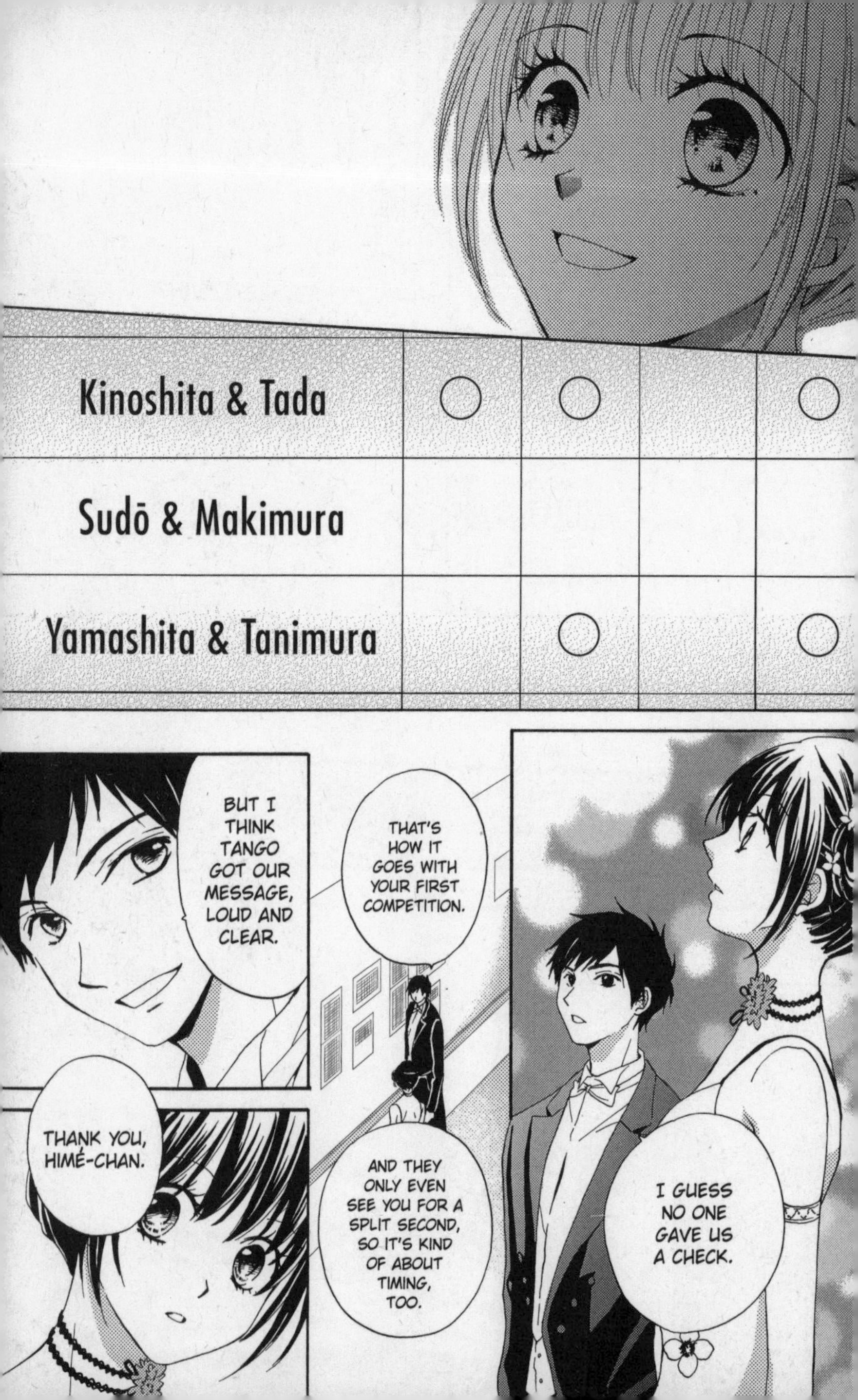
Kinoshita & Tada
Sudō & Makimura
Yamashita & Tanimura
I GUESS NO ONE GAVE US A CHECK.
THAT'S HOW IT GOES WITH YOUR FIRST COMPETITION.
AND THEY ONLY EVEN SEE YOU FOR A SPLIT SECOND, SO IT'S KIND OF ABOUT TIMING, TOO.
BUT I THINK TANGO GOT OUR MESSAGE, LOUD AND CLEAR.
THANK YOU, HIMÉ-CHAN.

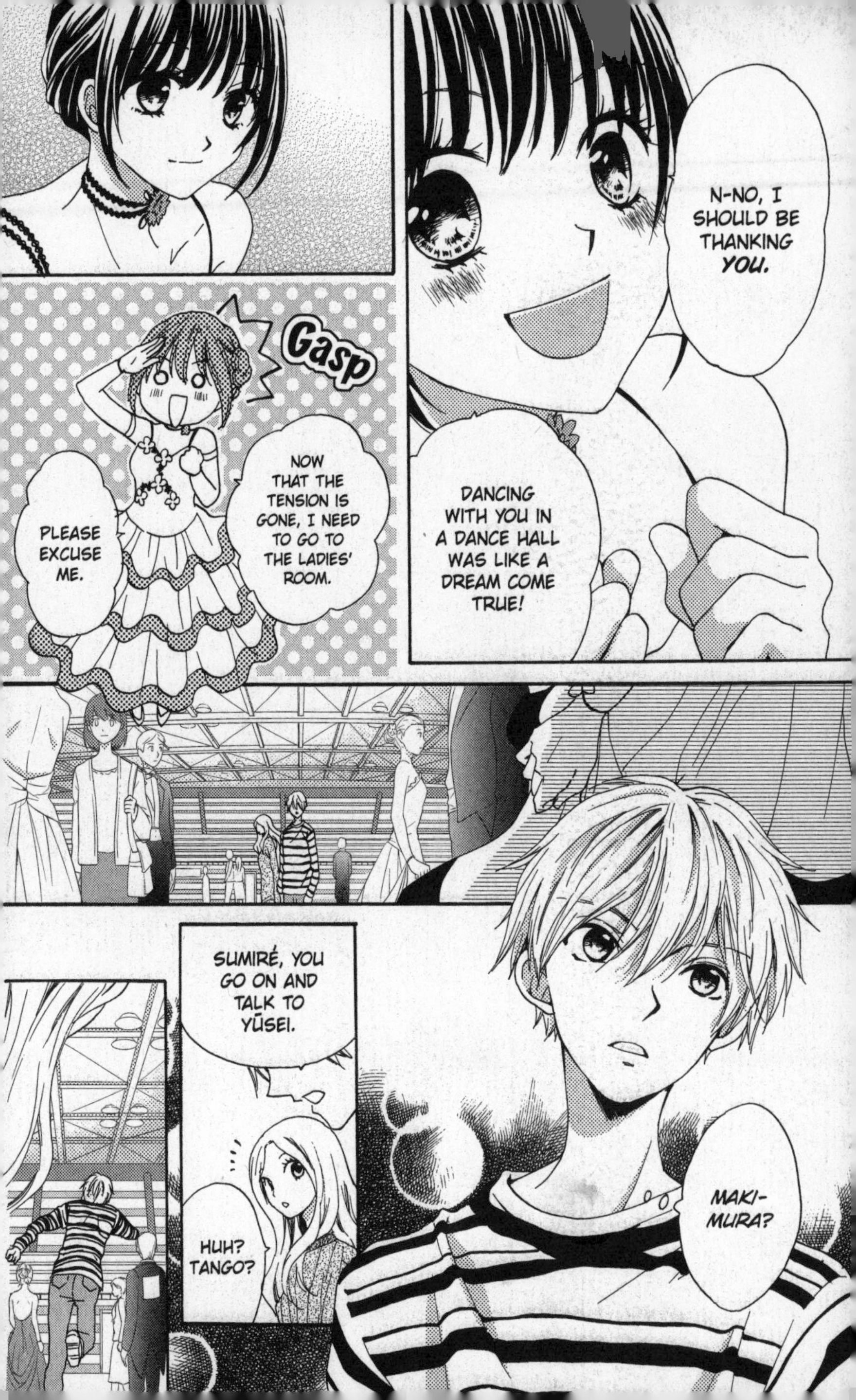
N-NO, I SHOULD BE THANKING YOU.
DANCING WITH YOU IN A DANCE HALL WAS LIKE A DREAM COME TRUE!
Gasp
NOW THAT THE TENSION IS GONE, I NEED TO GO TO THE LADIES' ROOM.
PLEASE EXCUSE ME.
MAKI-MURA?
SUMIRÉ, YOU GO ON AND TALK TO YŪSEI.
HUH? TANGO?

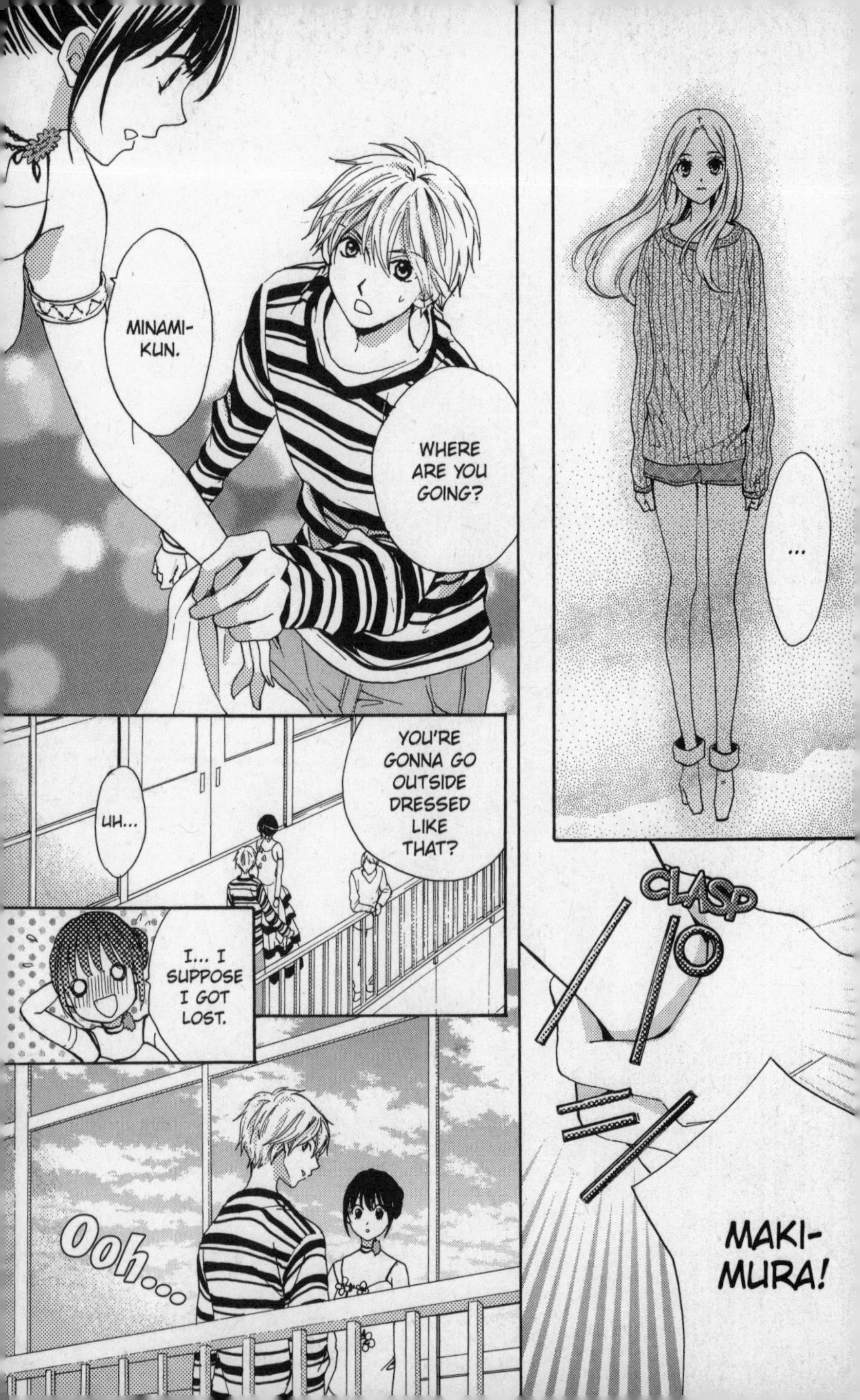
...
CLASP
MAKI-MURA!
MINAMI-KUN.
WHERE ARE YOU GOING?
YOU'RE GONNA GO OUTSIDE DRESSED LIKE THAT?
UH...
I... I SUPPOSE I GOT LOST.
Ooh...

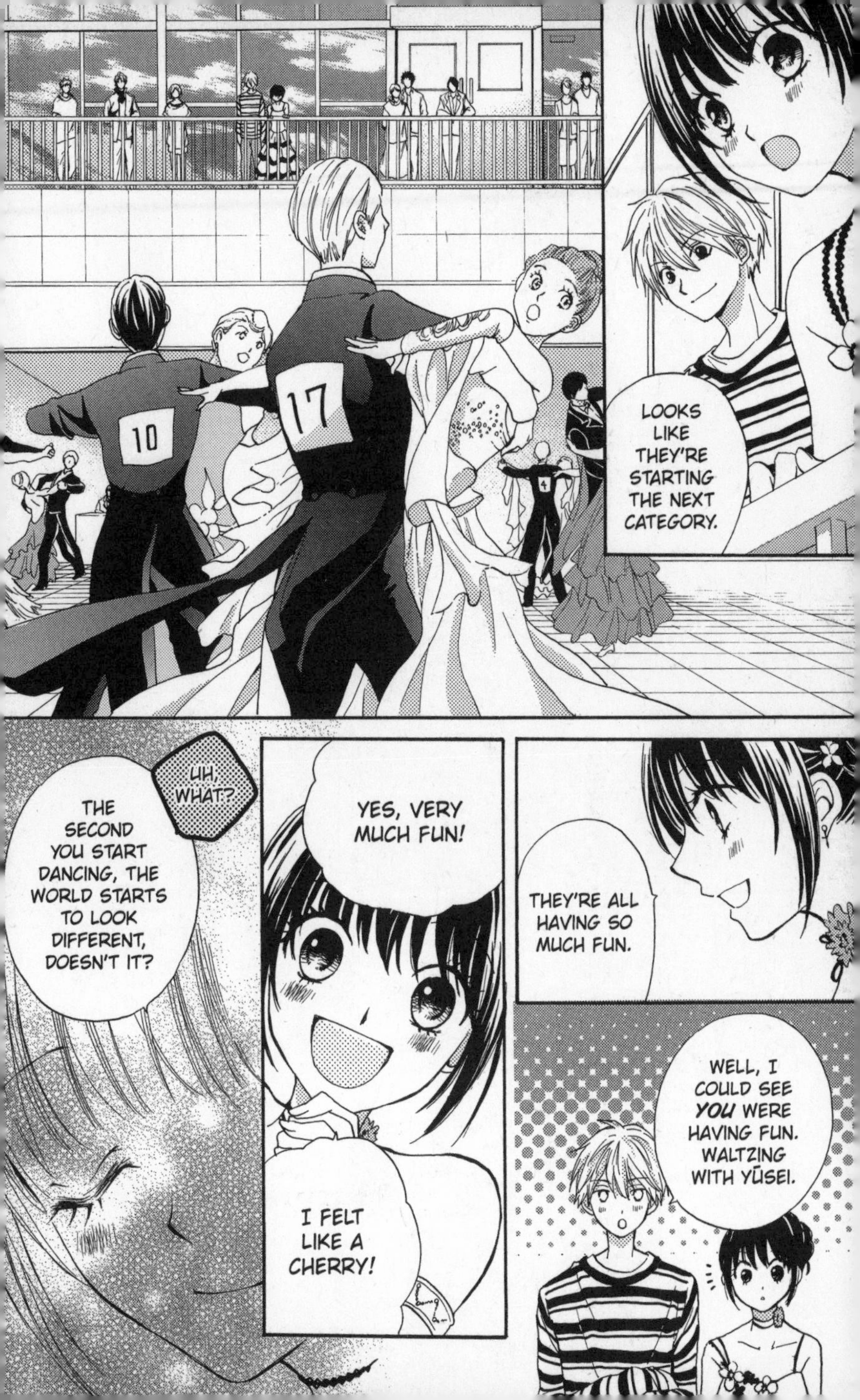
LOOKS LIKE THEY'RE STARTING THE NEXT CATEGORY.
THEY'RE ALL HAVING SO MUCH FUN.
YES, VERY MUCH FUN!
I FELT LIKE A CHERRY!
WELL, I COULD SEE *YOU* WERE HAVING FUN. WALTZING WITH YŪSEI.
THE SECOND YOU START DANCING, THE WORLD STARTS TO LOOK DIFFERENT, DOESN'T IT?
UH, WHAT?

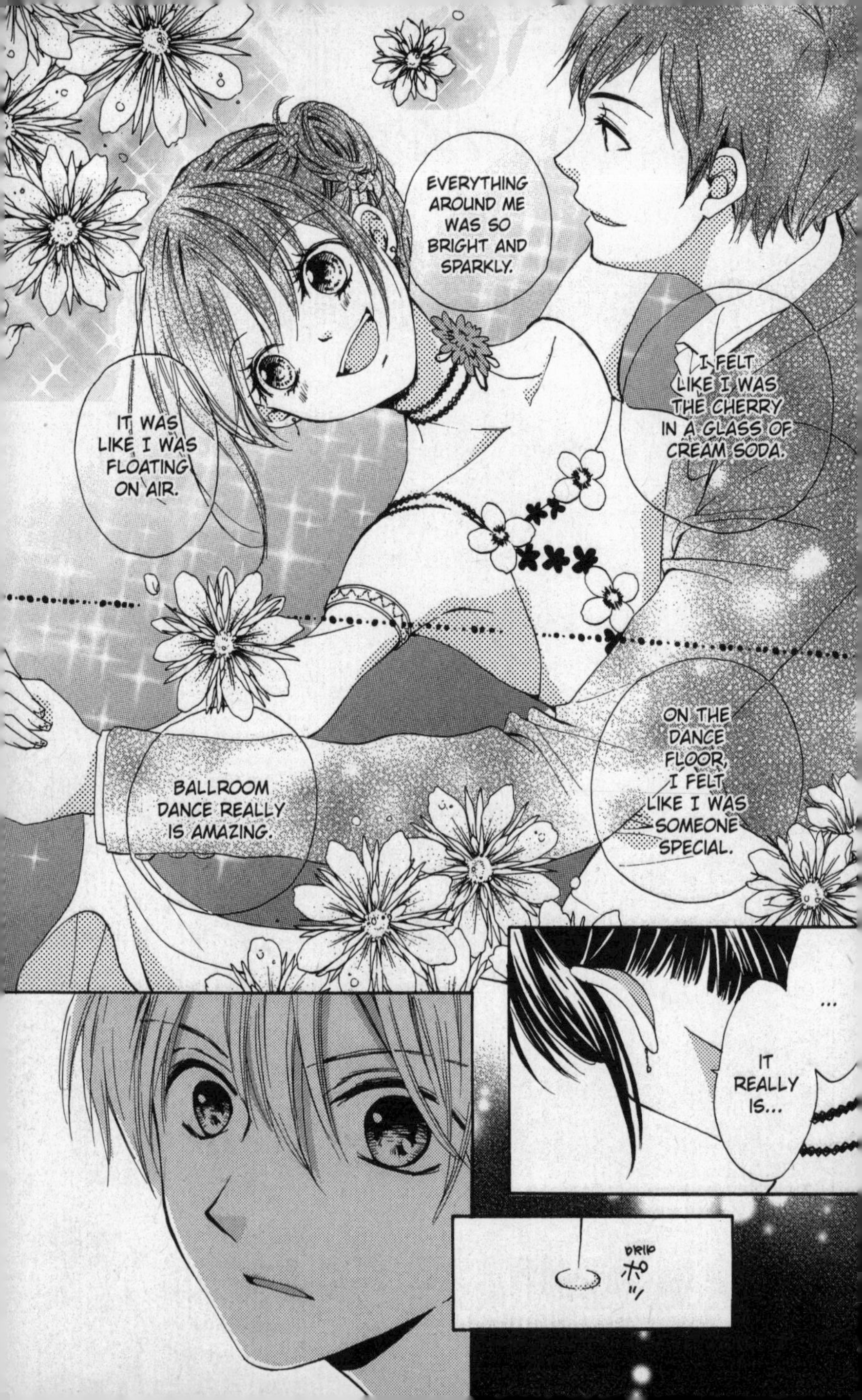
EVERYTHING AROUND ME WAS SO BRIGHT AND SPARKLY.
I FELT LIKE I WAS THE CHERRY IN A GLASS OF CREAM SODA.
IT WAS LIKE I WAS FLOATING ON AIR.
ON THE DANCE FLOOR, I FELT LIKE I WAS SOMEONE SPECIAL.
BALLROOM DANCE REALLY IS AMAZING.
...
IT REALLY IS...
DRIP
ポツ

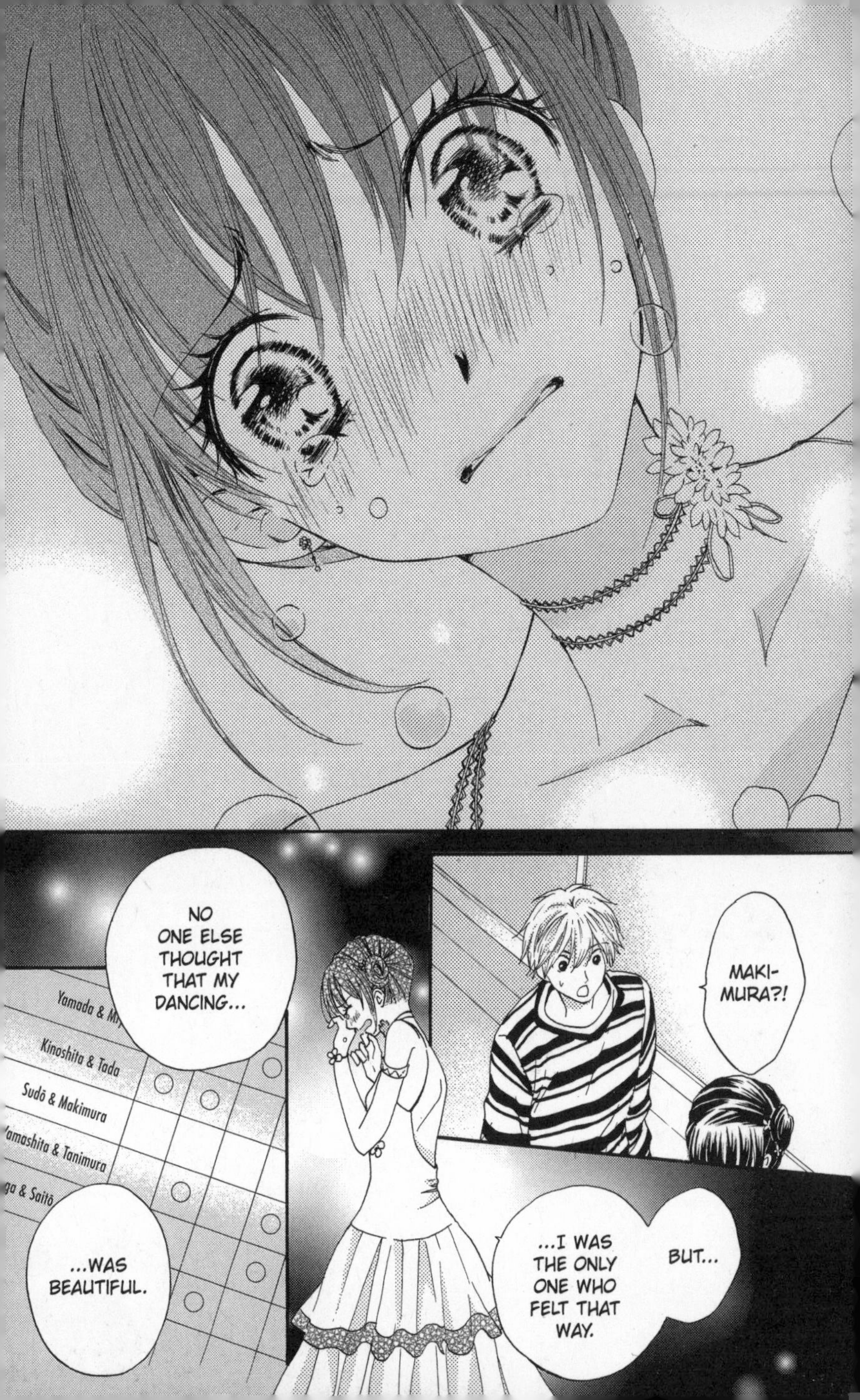
MAKI-MURA?!
BUT...
...I WAS THE ONLY ONE WHO FELT THAT WAY.
NO ONE ELSE THOUGHT THAT MY DANCING...
...WAS BEAUTIFUL.
Yamada & M
Kinoshita & Tada
Sudō & Makimura
amashita & Tanimura
ga & Saitō

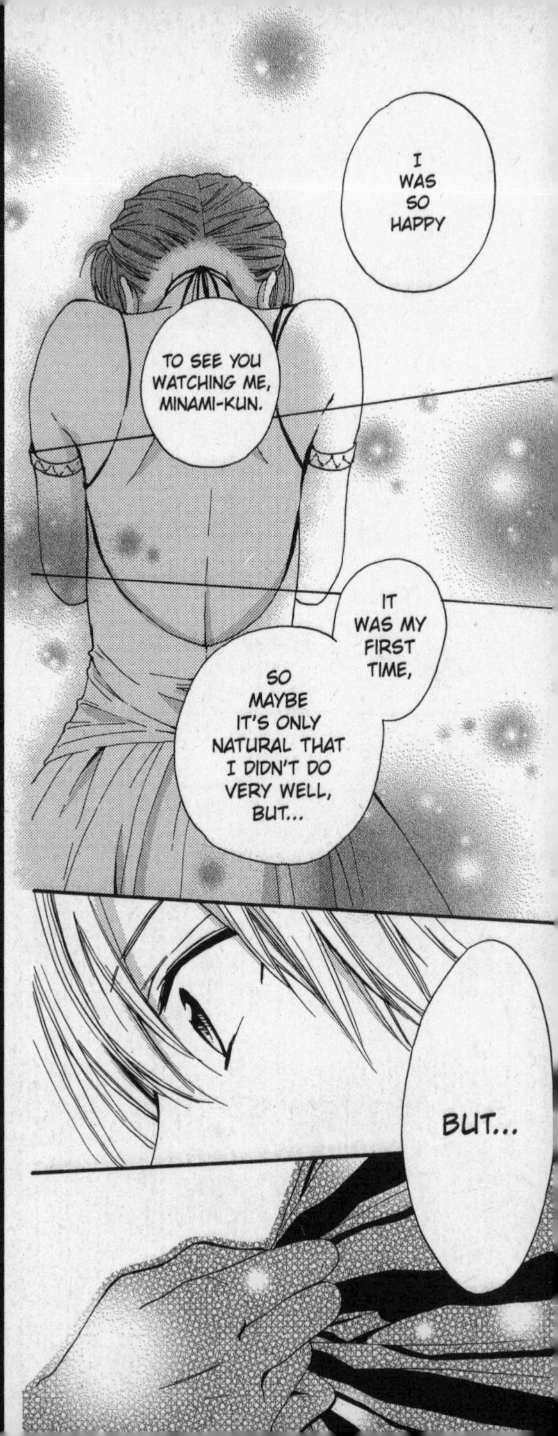
I WAS SO HAPPY
TO SEE YOU WATCHING ME, MINAMI-KUN.
IT WAS MY FIRST TIME,
SO MAYBE IT'S ONLY NATURAL THAT I DIDN'T DO VERY WELL, BUT...
BUT...

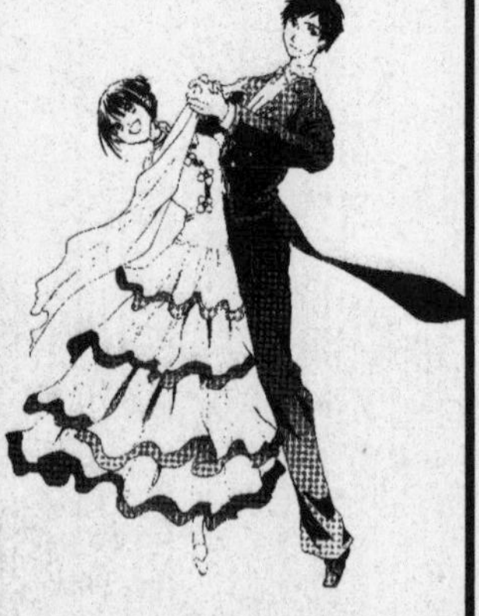

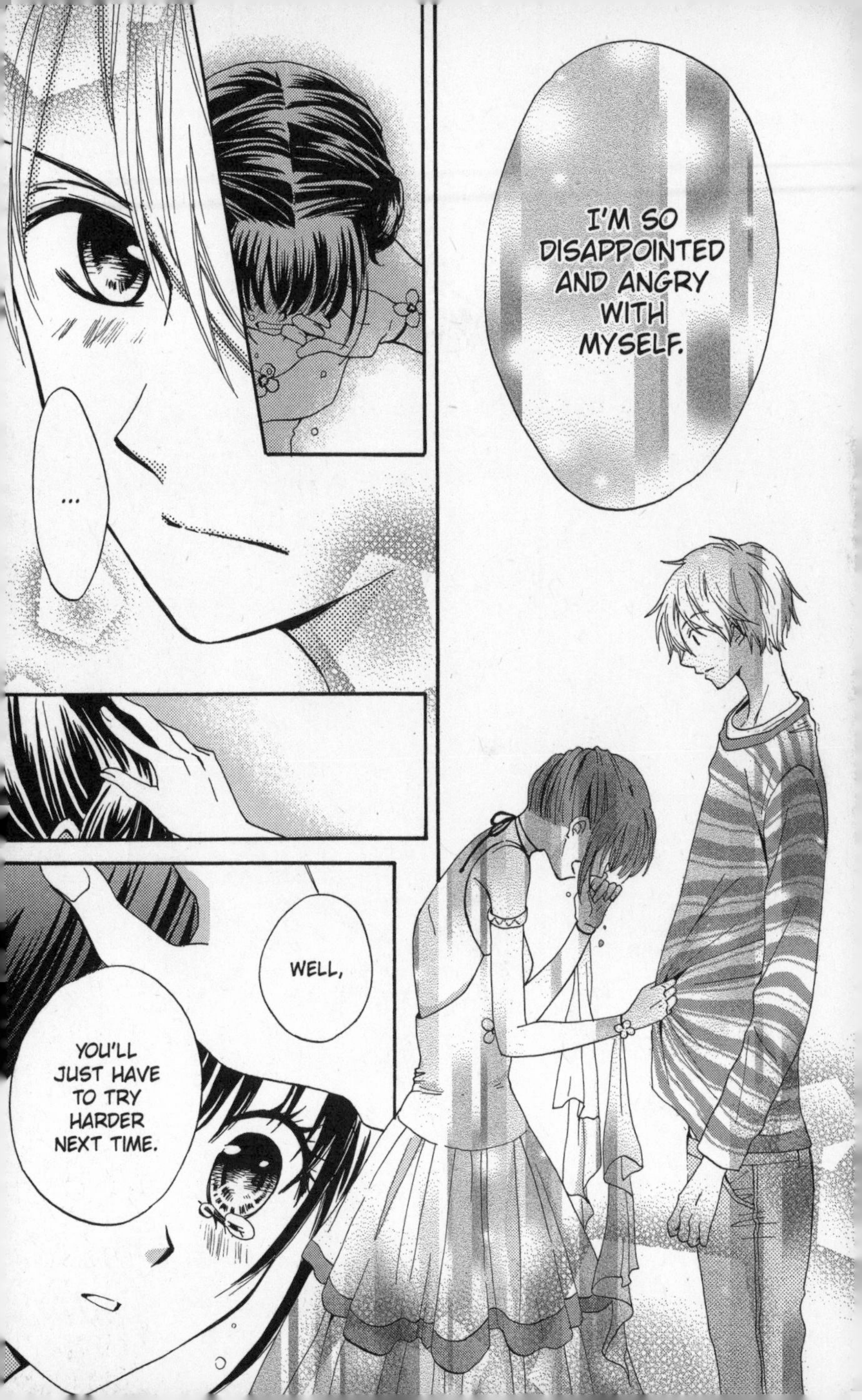
I'M SO DISAPPOINTED AND ANGRY WITH MYSELF.
...
WELL,
YOU'LL JUST HAVE TO TRY HARDER NEXT TIME.

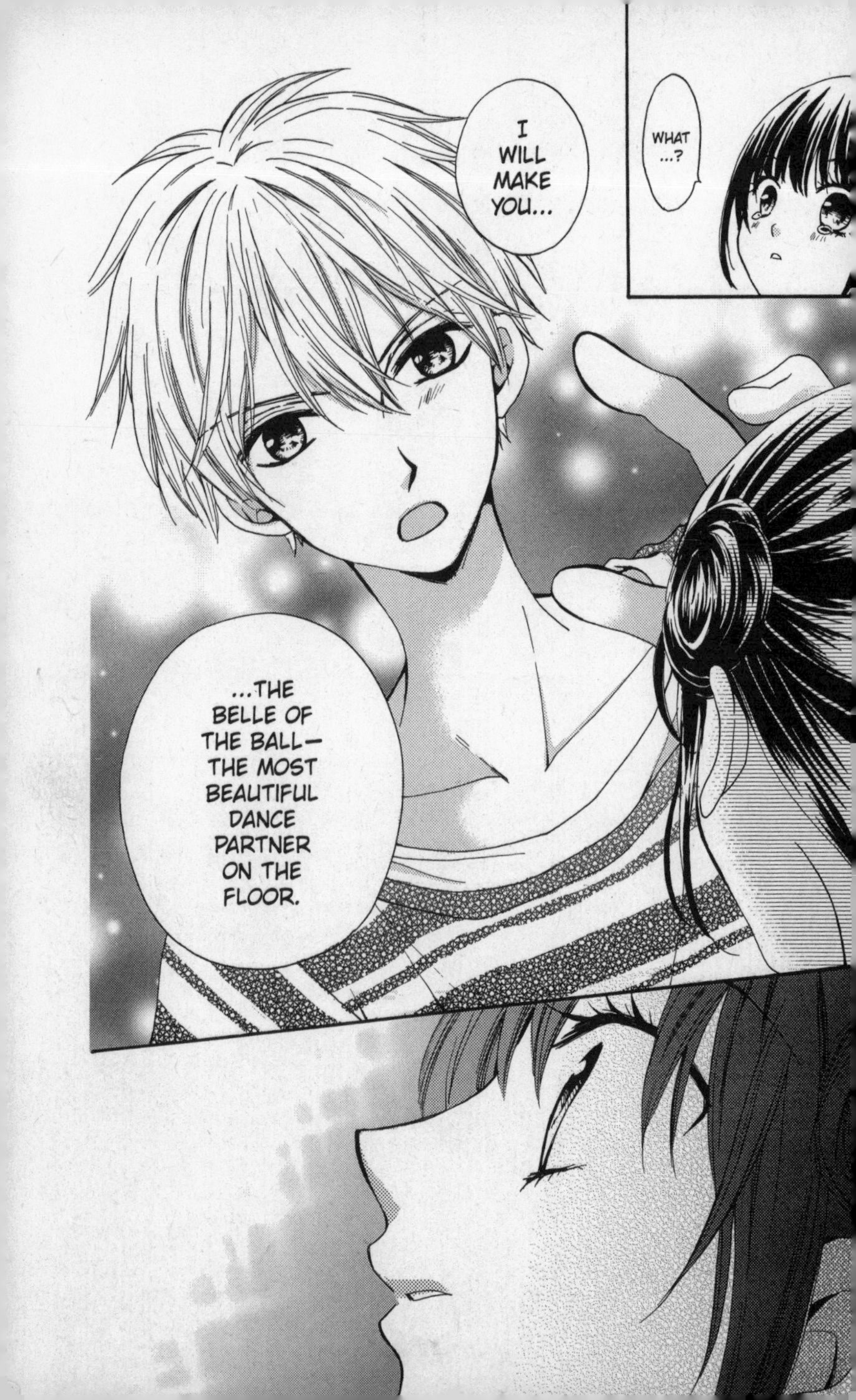
WHAT ...?
I WILL MAKE YOU...
...THE BELLE OF THE BALL—THE MOST BEAUTIFUL DANCE PARTNER ON THE FLOOR.

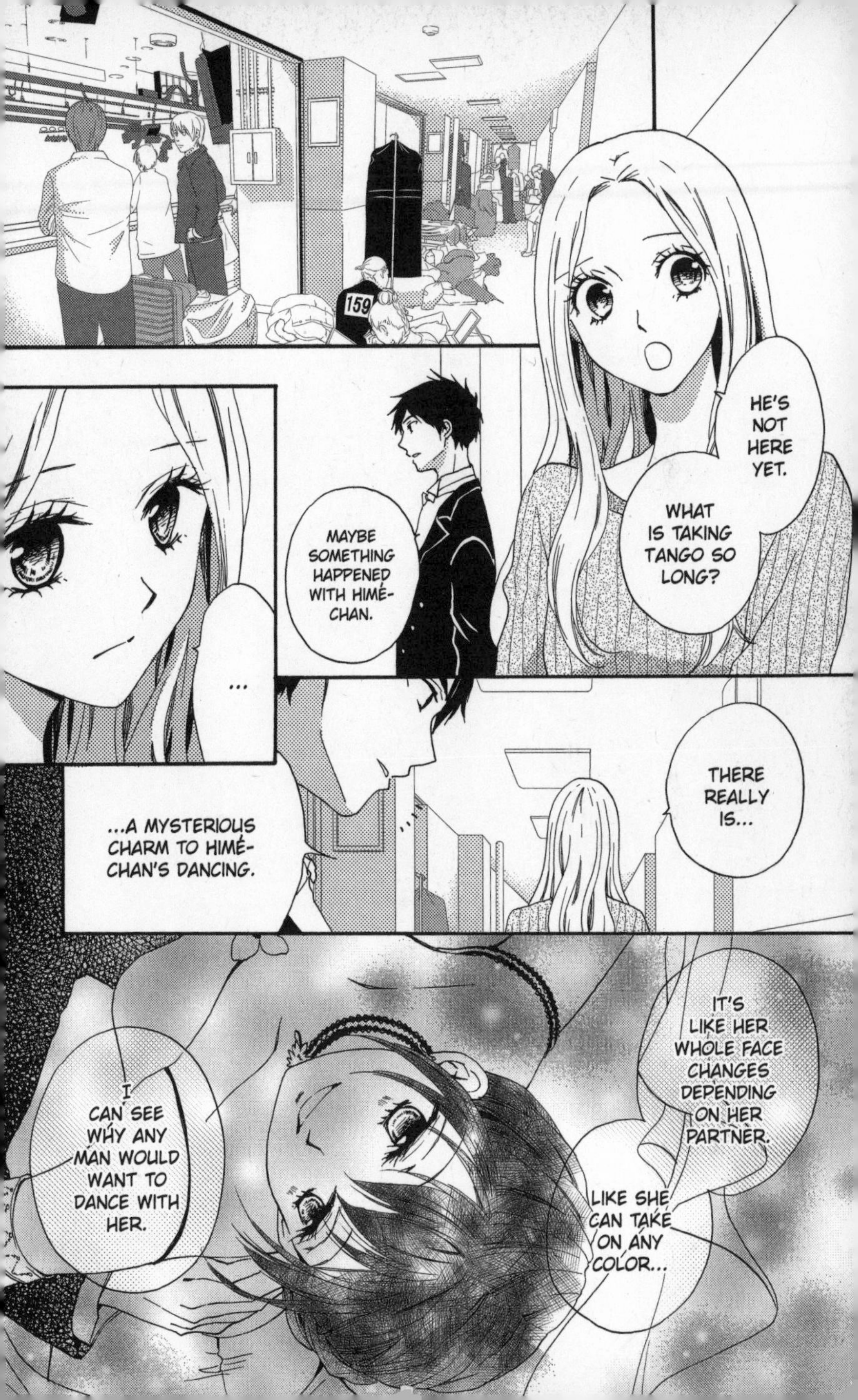
159
HE'S NOT HERE YET.
WHAT IS TAKING TANGO SO LONG?
MAYBE SOMETHING HAPPENED WITH HIMÉ-CHAN.
...
THERE REALLY IS...
...A MYSTERIOUS CHARM TO HIMÉ-CHAN'S DANCING.
IT'S LIKE HER WHOLE FACE CHANGES DEPENDING ON HER PARTNER.
LIKE SHE CAN TAKE ON ANY COLOR...
I CAN SEE WHY ANY MAN WOULD WANT TO DANCE WITH HER.

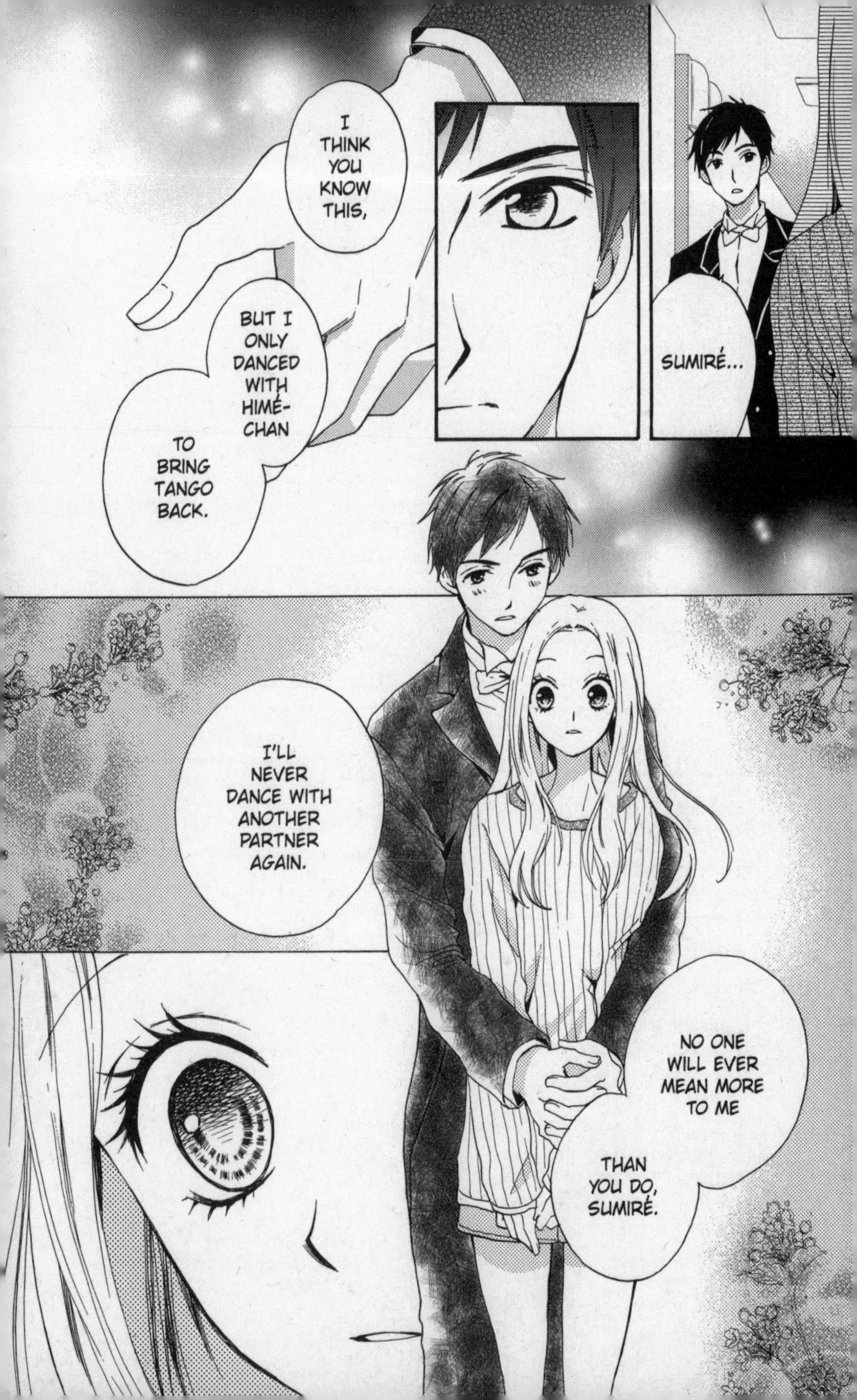
SUMIRÉ...
I THINK YOU KNOW THIS,
BUT I ONLY DANCED WITH HIMÉ-CHAN
TO BRING TANGO BACK.
I'LL NEVER DANCE WITH ANOTHER PARTNER AGAIN.
NO ONE WILL EVER MEAN MORE TO ME
THAN YOU DO, SUMIRÉ.

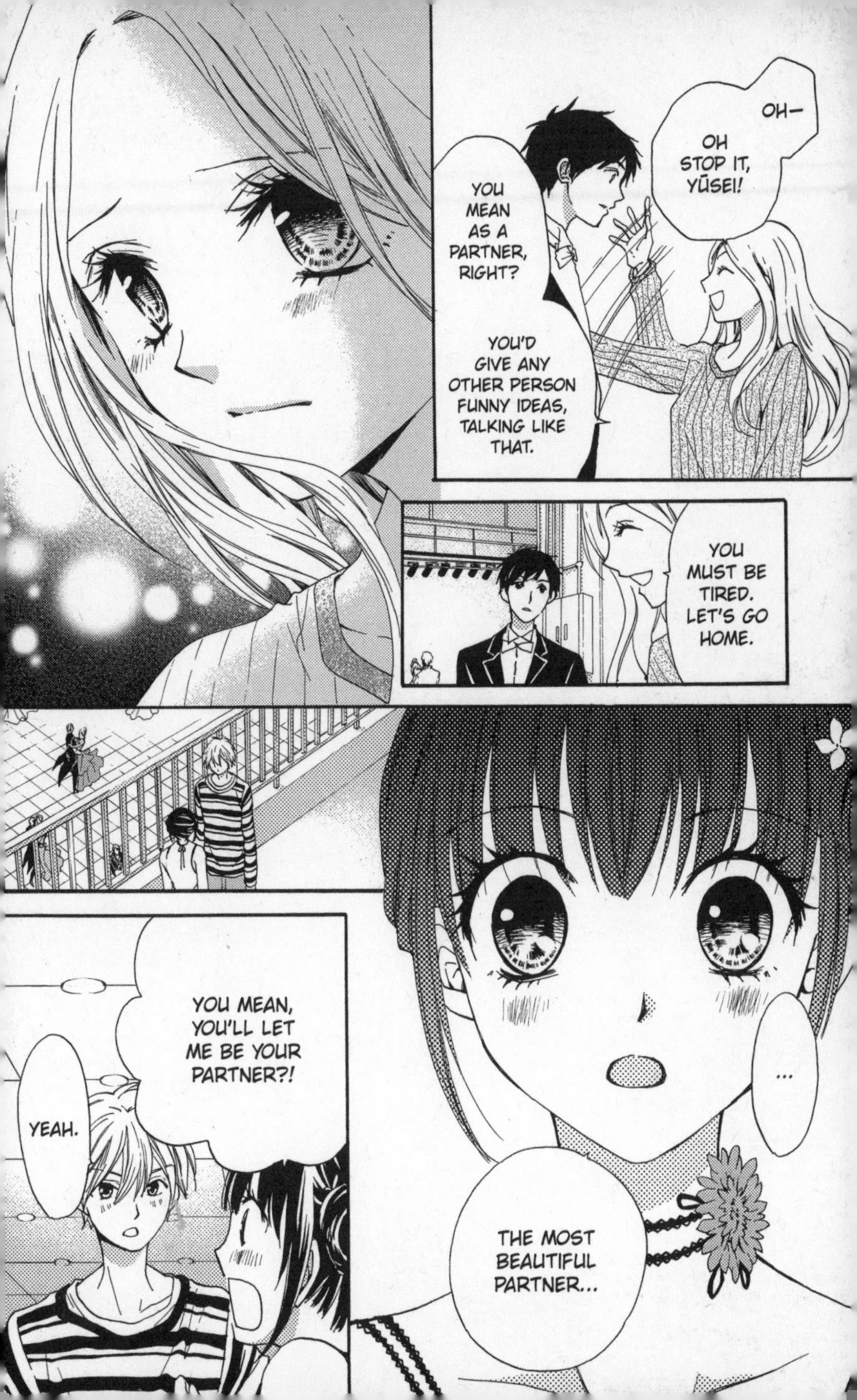
OH—
OH STOP IT, YŪSEI!
YOU MEAN AS A PARTNER, RIGHT?
YOU'D GIVE ANY OTHER PERSON FUNNY IDEAS, TALKING LIKE THAT.
YOU MUST BE TIRED. LET'S GO HOME.
...
THE MOST BEAUTIFUL PARTNER...
YOU MEAN, YOU'LL LET ME BE YOUR PARTNER?!
YEAH.

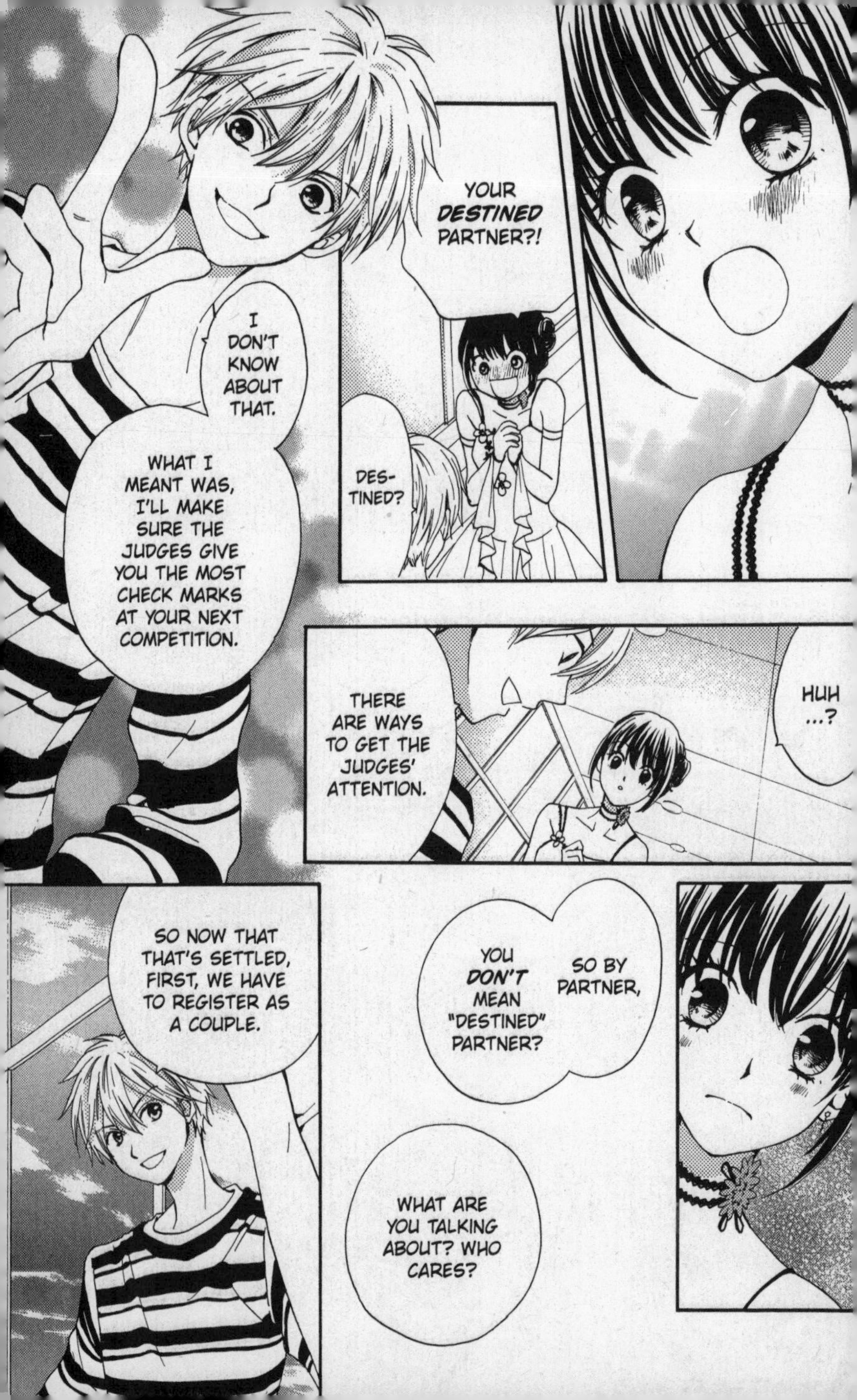
YOUR *DESTINED* PARTNER?!
DES-TINED?
I DON'T KNOW ABOUT THAT.
WHAT I MEANT WAS, I'LL MAKE SURE THE JUDGES GIVE YOU THE MOST CHECK MARKS AT YOUR NEXT COMPETITION.
THERE ARE WAYS TO GET THE JUDGES' ATTENTION.
HUH ...?
SO BY PARTNER,
YOU *DON'T* MEAN "DESTINED" PARTNER?
WHAT ARE YOU TALKING ABOUT? WHO CARES?
SO NOW THAT THAT'S SETTLED, FIRST, WE HAVE TO REGISTER AS A COUPLE.

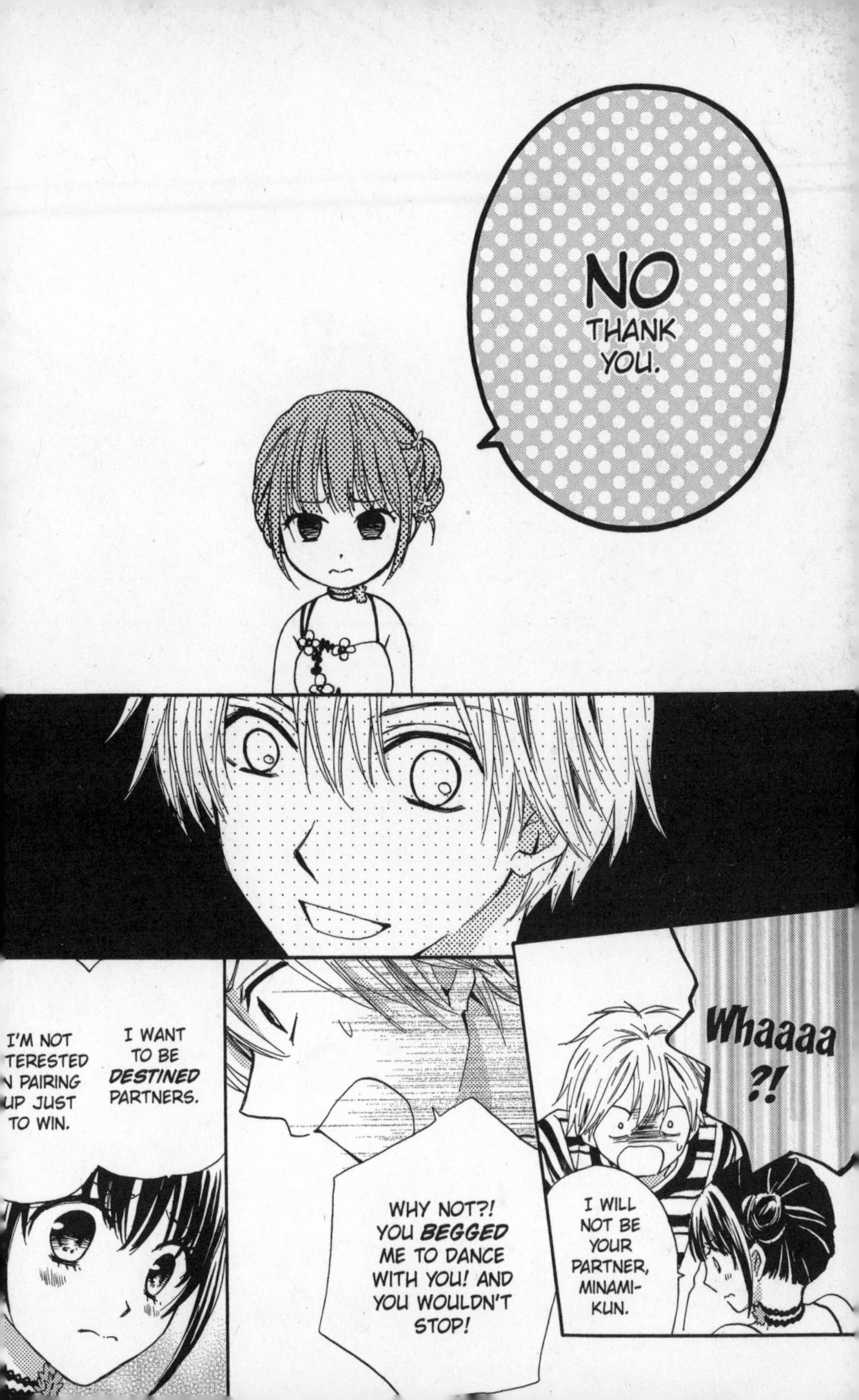
NO THANK YOU.
Whaaaa ?!
I WILL NOT BE YOUR PARTNER, MINAMI-KUN.
WHY NOT?! YOU BEGGED ME TO DANCE WITH YOU! AND YOU WOULDN'T STOP!
I WANT TO BE DESTINED PARTNERS.
I'M NOT TERESTED N PAIRING UP JUST TO WIN.

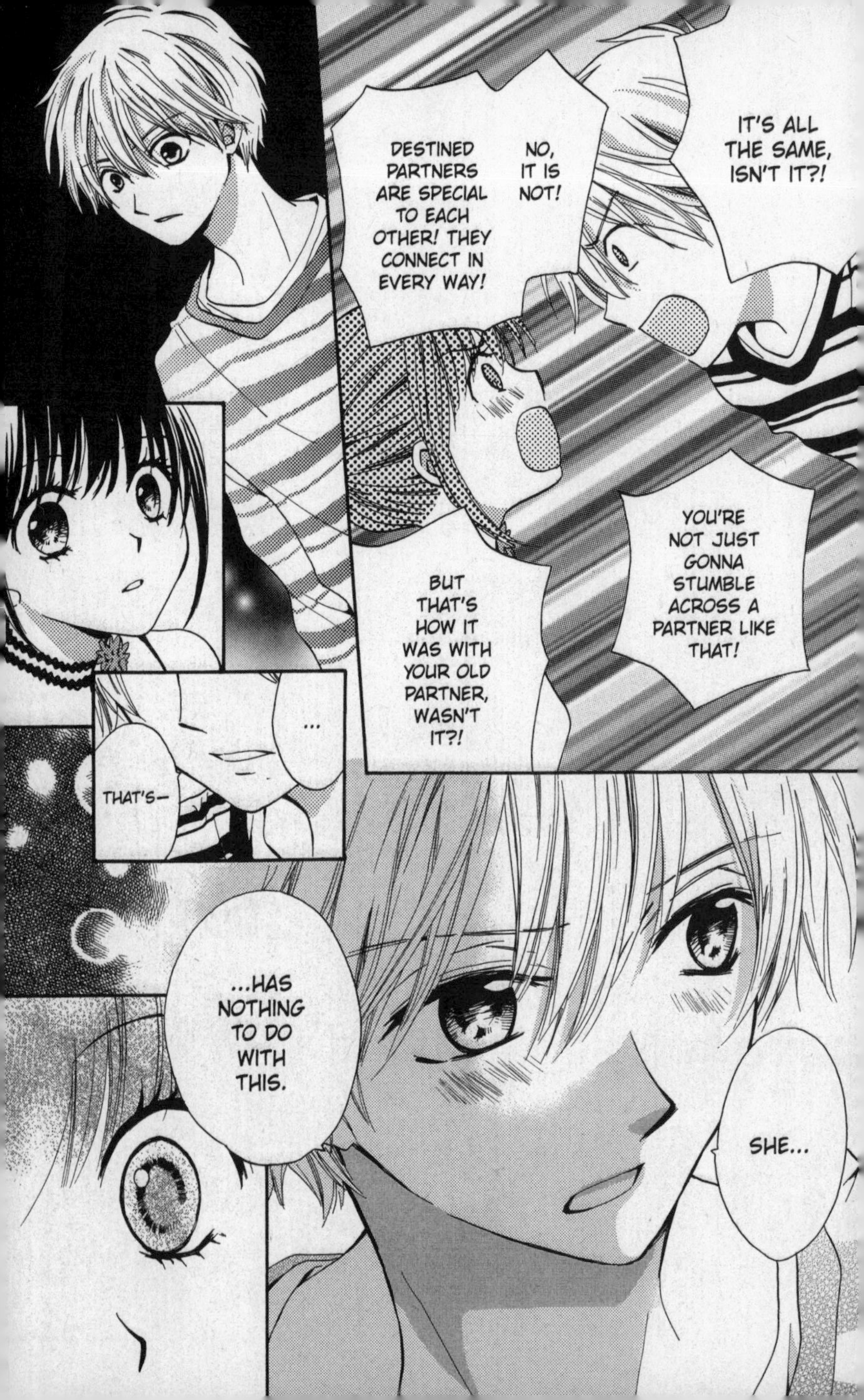
IT'S ALL THE SAME, ISN'T IT?!
NO, IT IS NOT!
DESTINED PARTNERS ARE SPECIAL TO EACH OTHER! THEY CONNECT IN EVERY WAY!
YOU'RE NOT JUST GONNA STUMBLE ACROSS A PARTNER LIKE THAT!
BUT THAT'S HOW IT WAS WITH YOUR OLD PARTNER, WASN'T IT?!
...
THAT'S—
SHE...
...HAS NOTHING TO DO WITH THIS.

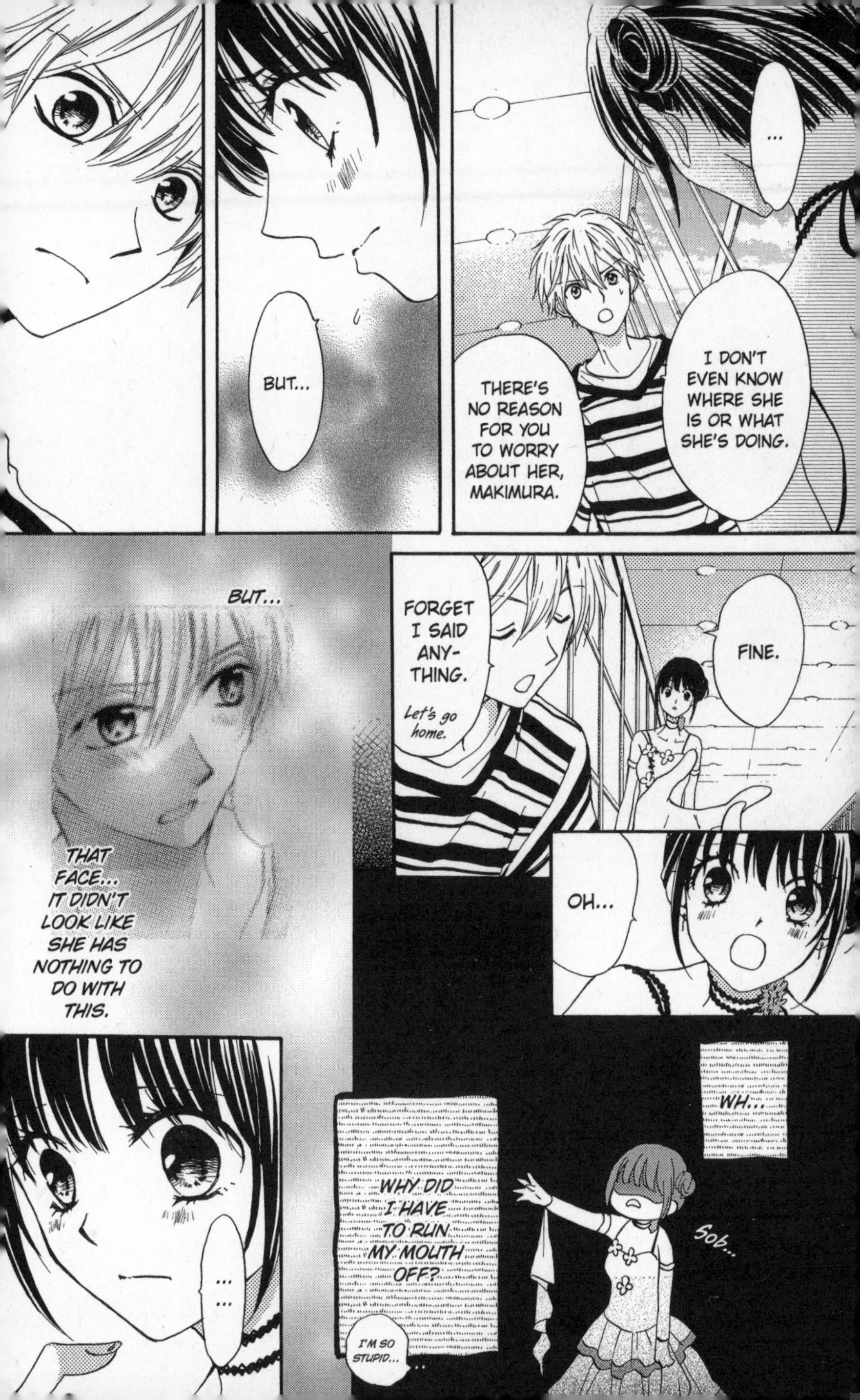
...
I DON'T EVEN KNOW WHERE SHE IS OR WHAT SHE'S DOING.
THERE'S NO REASON FOR YOU TO WORRY ABOUT HER, MAKIMURA.
BUT...
FINE.
FORGET I SAID ANYTHING.
Let's go home.
OH...
BUT...
THAT FACE... IT DIDN'T LOOK LIKE SHE HAS NOTHING TO DO WITH THIS.
WH...
WHY DID I HAVE TO RUN MY MOUTH OFF?
Sob...
I'M SO STUPID...
... ...

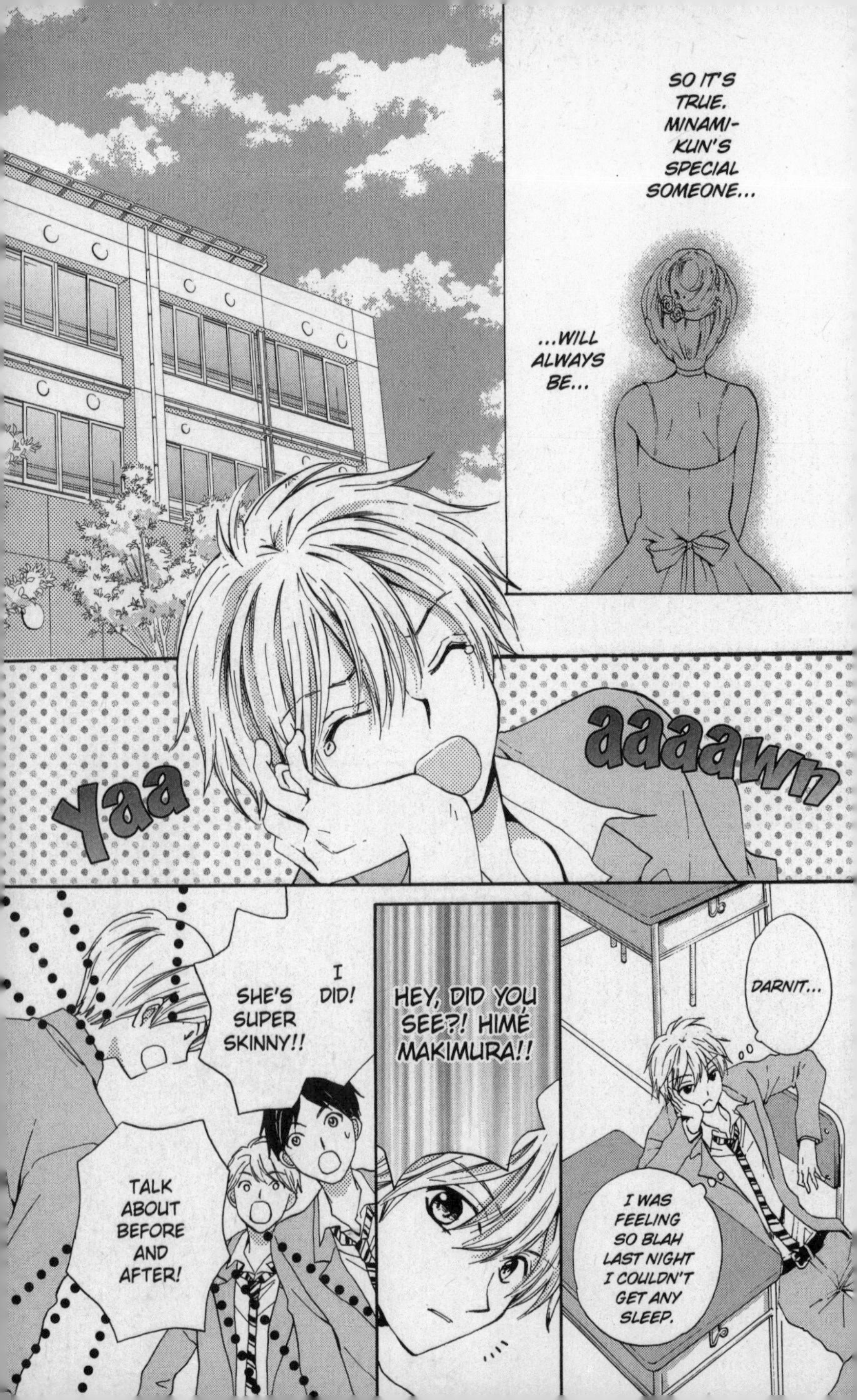
SO IT'S TRUE. MINAMI-KUN'S SPECIAL SOMEONE...
...WILL ALWAYS BE...
Yaa
aaaawn
DARNIT...
I WAS FEELING SO BLAH LAST NIGHT I COULDN'T GET ANY SLEEP.
HEY, DID YOU SEE?! HIMÉ MAKIMURA!!
I DID!
SHE'S SUPER SKINNY!!
TALK ABOUT BEFORE AND AFTER!

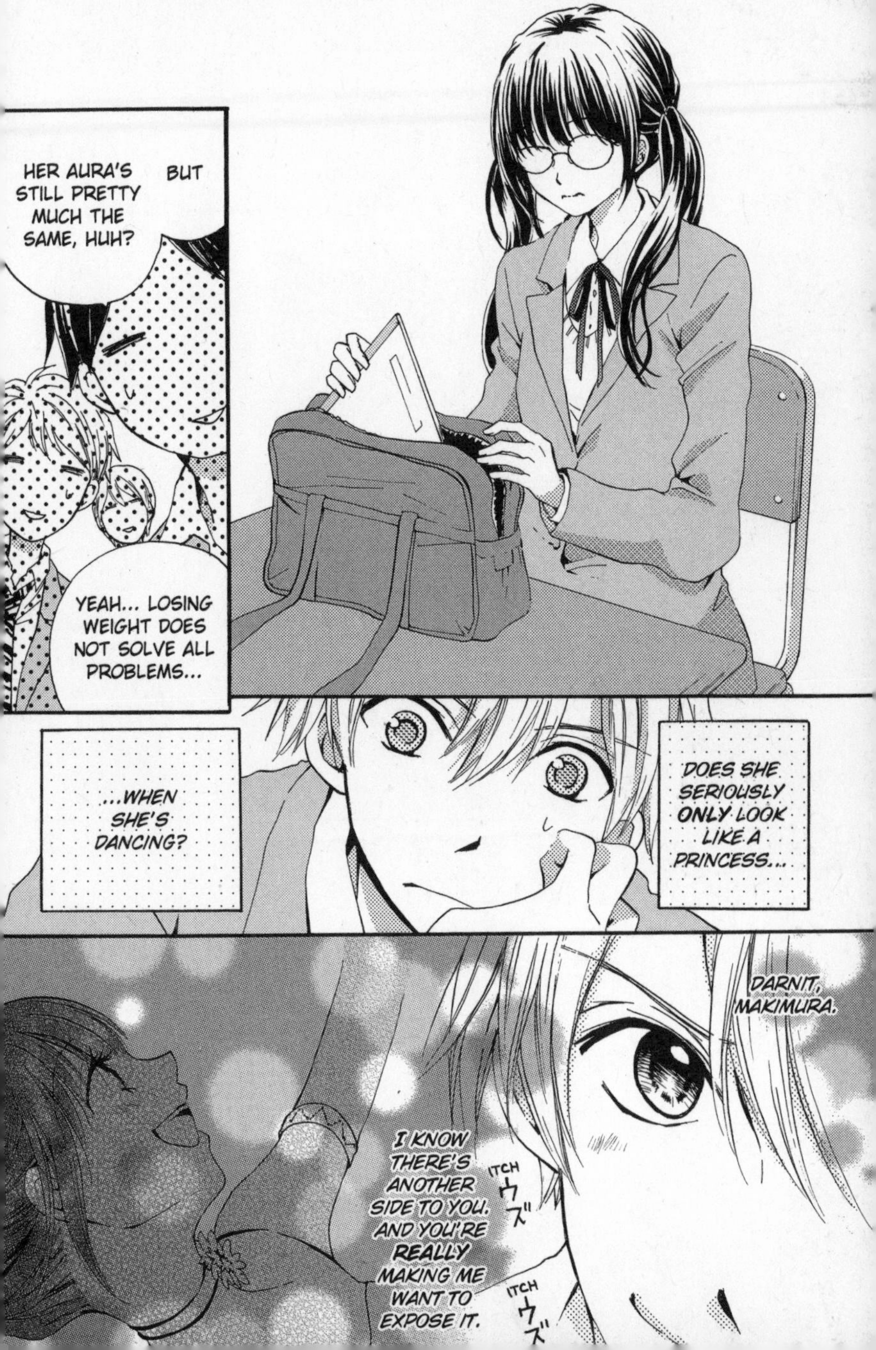
BUT
HER AURA'S STILL PRETTY MUCH THE SAME, HUH?
YEAH... LOSING WEIGHT DOES NOT SOLVE ALL PROBLEMS...
DOES SHE SERIOUSLY ONLY LOOK LIKE A PRINCESS...
...WHEN SHE'S DANCING?
DARNIT, MAKIMURA.
ITCH ウズ
I KNOW THERE'S ANOTHER SIDE TO YOU. AND YOU'RE REALLY MAKING ME WANT TO EXPOSE IT.
ITCH ウズ

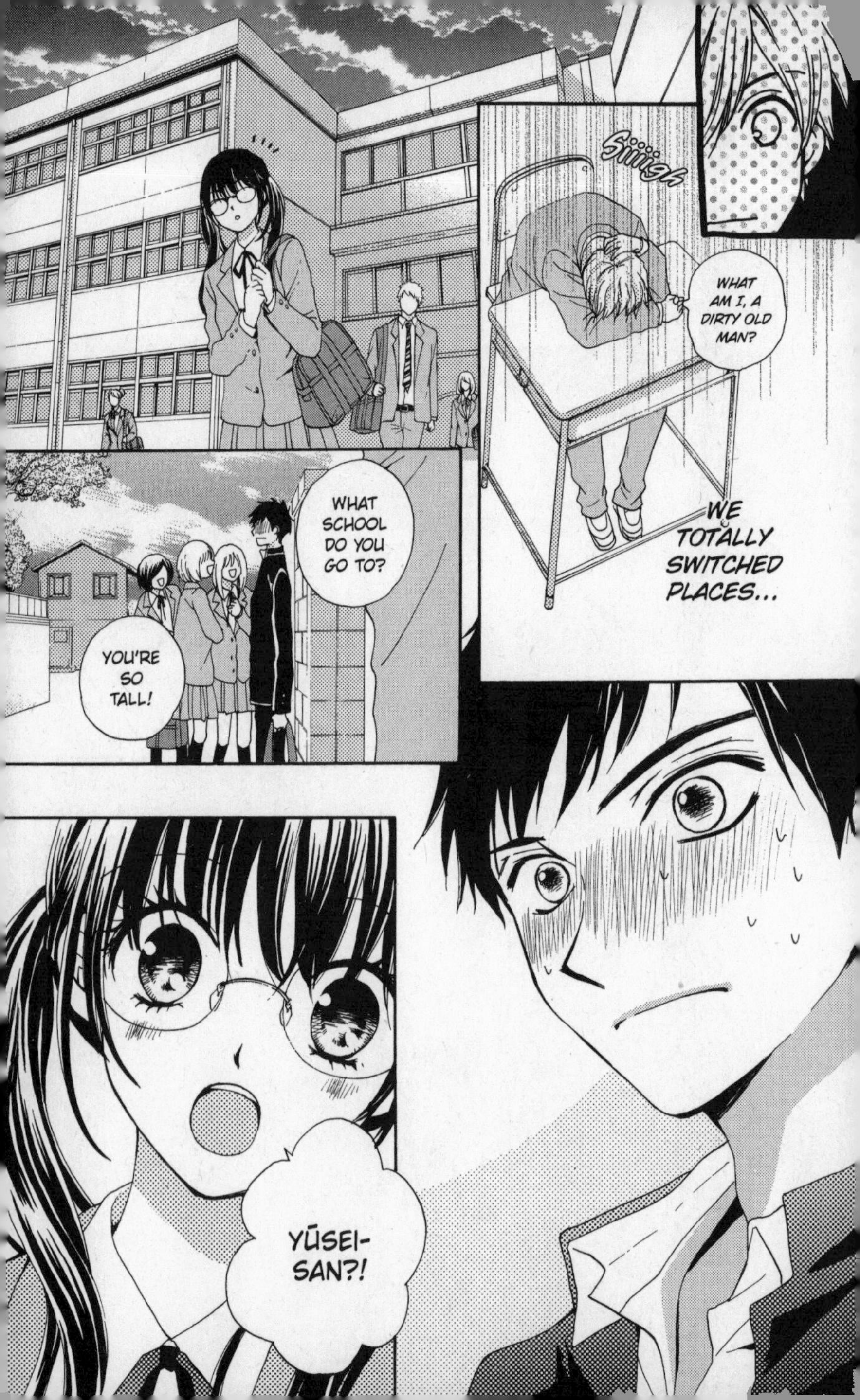

Siiiigh
WHAT AM I, A DIRTY OLD MAN?
WE TOTALLY SWITCHED PLACES...
WHAT SCHOOL DO YOU GO TO?
YOU'RE SO TALL!
YŪSEI-SAN?!

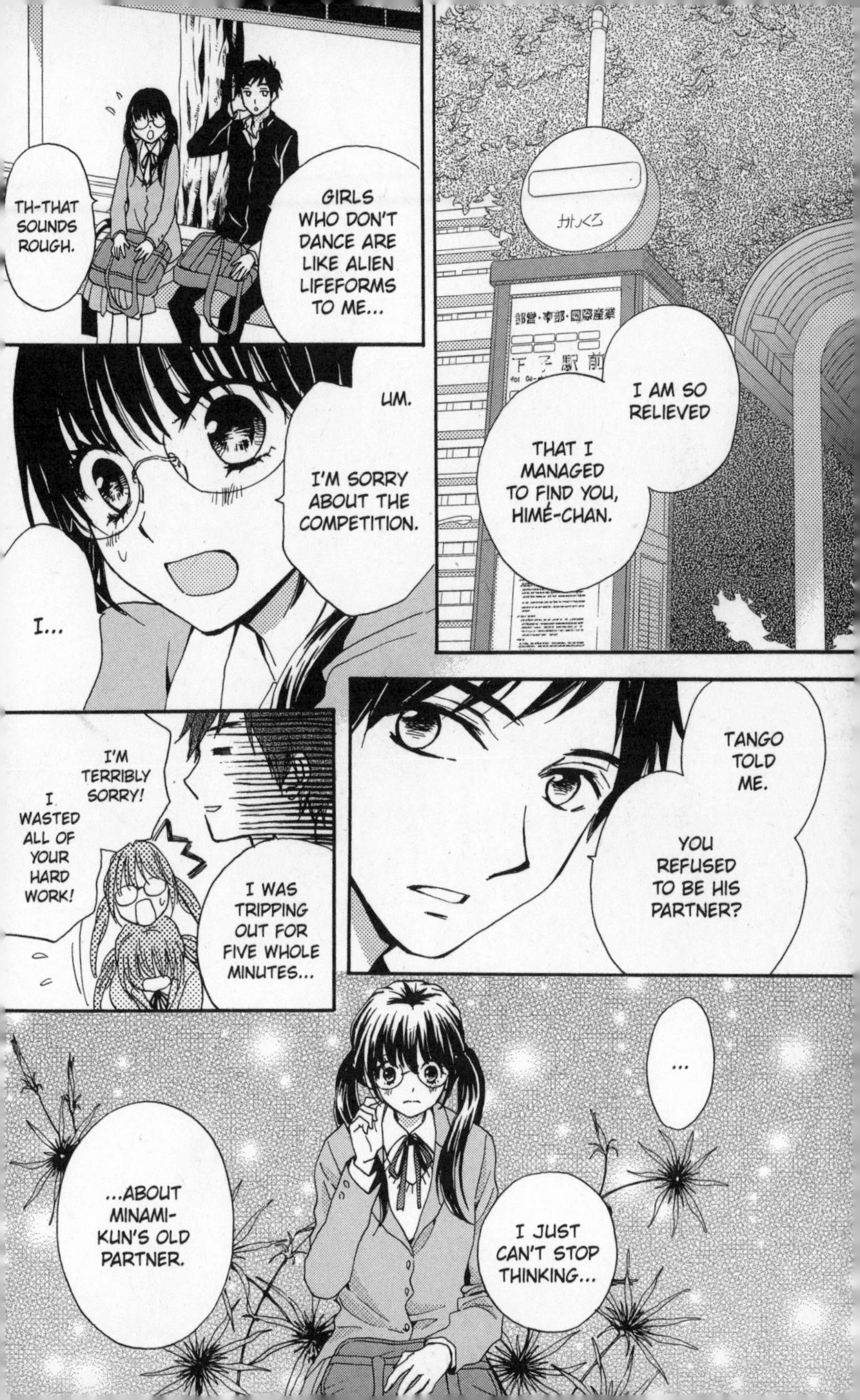
I AM SO RELIEVED
THAT I MANAGED TO FIND YOU, HIMÉ-CHAN.
GIRLS WHO DON'T DANCE ARE LIKE ALIEN LIFEFORMS TO ME...
TH-THAT SOUNDS ROUGH.
UM.
I'M SORRY ABOUT THE COMPETITION.
I...
TANGO TOLD ME.
YOU REFUSED TO BE HIS PARTNER?
I'M TERRIBLY SORRY!
I WASTED ALL OF YOUR HARD WORK!
I WAS TRIPPING OUT FOR FIVE WHOLE MINUTES...
...
I JUST CAN'T STOP THINKING...
...ABOUT MINAMI-KUN'S OLD PARTNER.

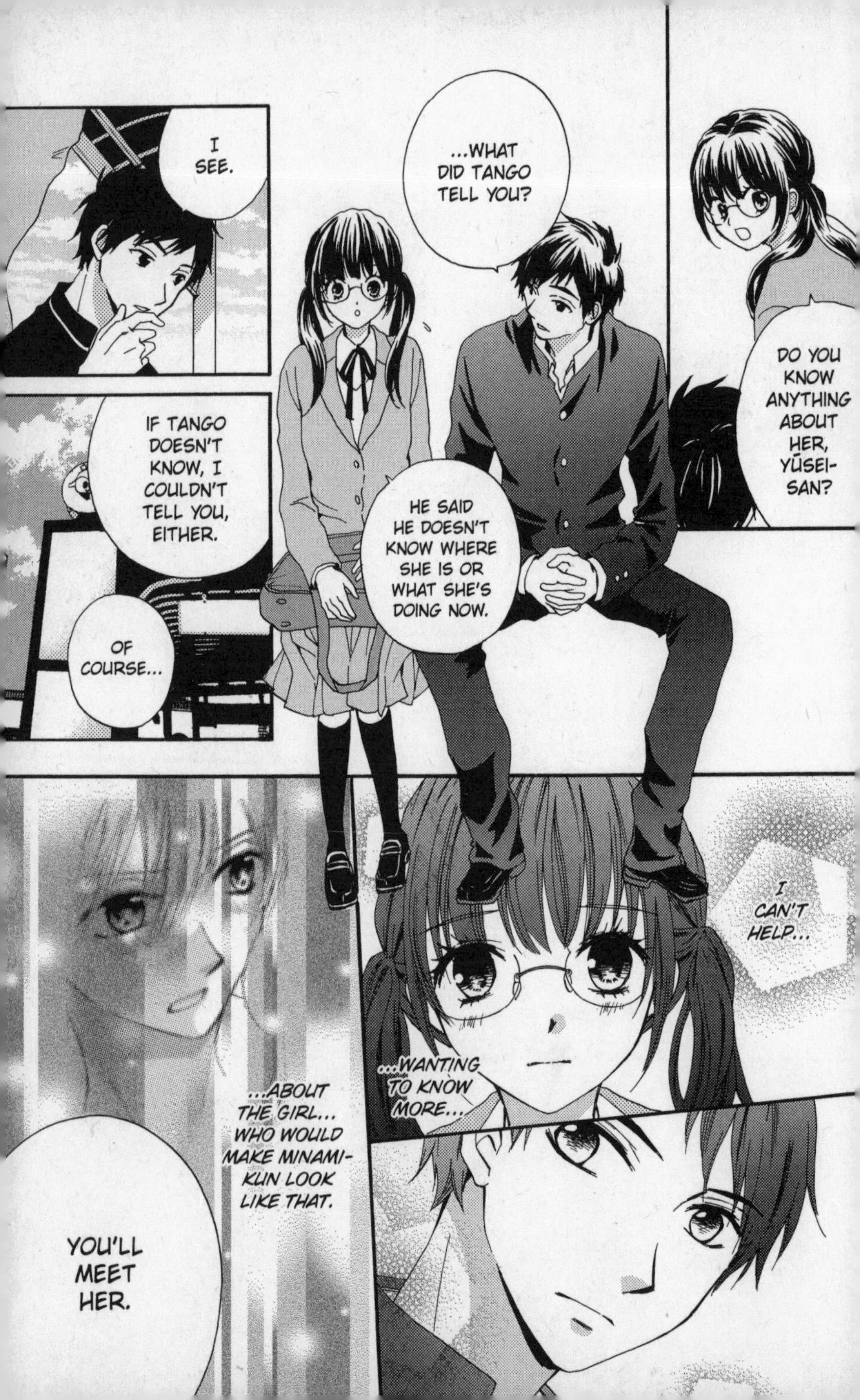
DO YOU KNOW ANYTHING ABOUT HER, YŪSEI-SAN?
...WHAT DID TANGO TELL YOU?
HE SAID HE DOESN'T KNOW WHERE SHE IS OR WHAT SHE'S DOING NOW.
I SEE.
IF TANGO DOESN'T KNOW, I COULDN'T TELL YOU, EITHER.
OF COURSE...
I CAN'T HELP...
...WANTING TO KNOW MORE...
...ABOUT THE GIRL... WHO WOULD MAKE MINAMI-KUN LOOK LIKE THAT.
YOU'LL MEET HER.

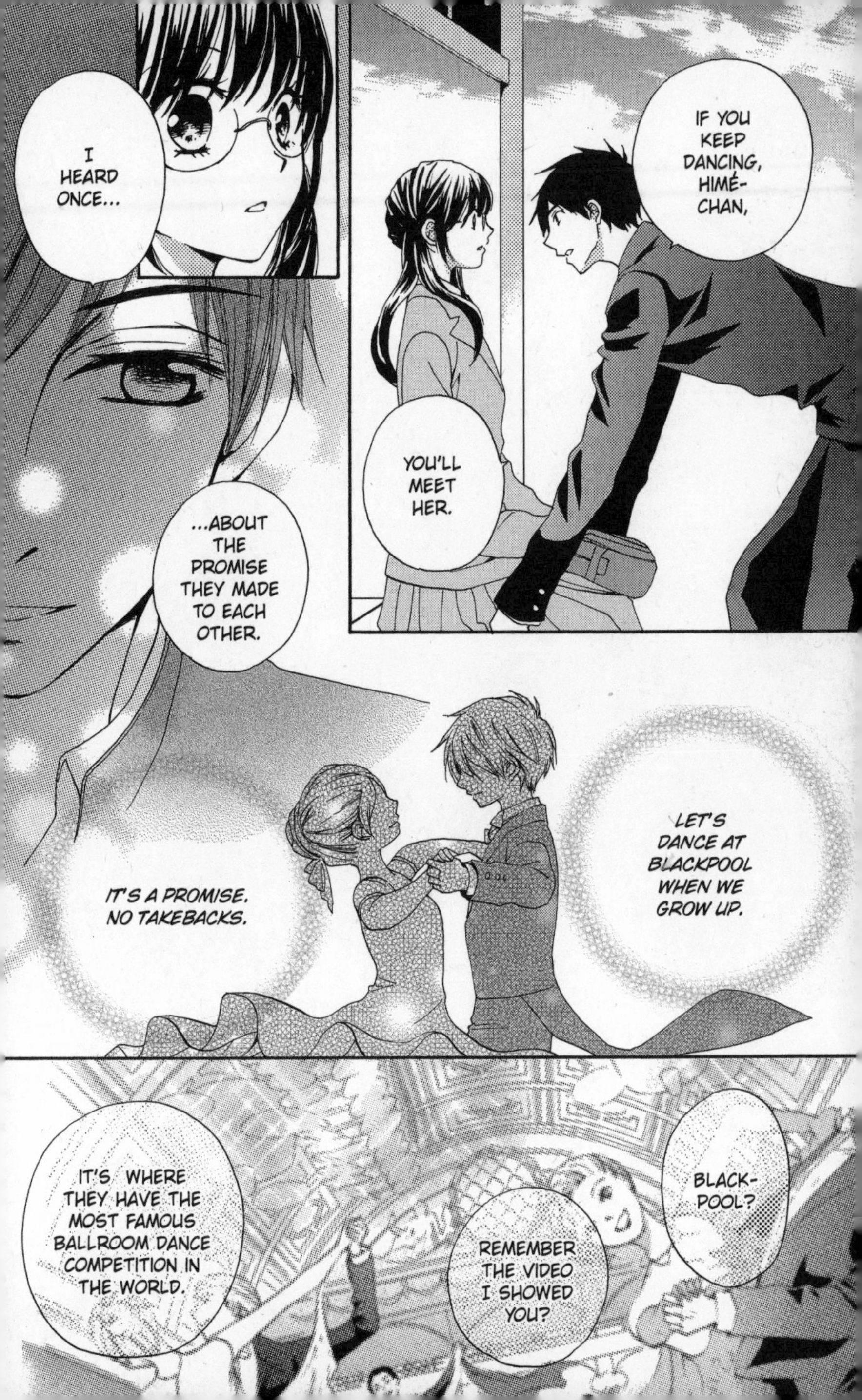
IF YOU KEEP DANCING, HIMÉ-CHAN,
YOU'LL MEET HER.
I HEARD ONCE...
...ABOUT THE PROMISE THEY MADE TO EACH OTHER.
LET'S DANCE AT BLACKPOOL WHEN WE GROW UP.
IT'S A PROMISE. NO TAKEBACKS.
BLACK-POOL?
REMEMBER THE VIDEO I SHOWED YOU?
IT'S WHERE THEY HAVE THE MOST FAMOUS BALLROOM DANCE COMPETITION IN THE WORLD.

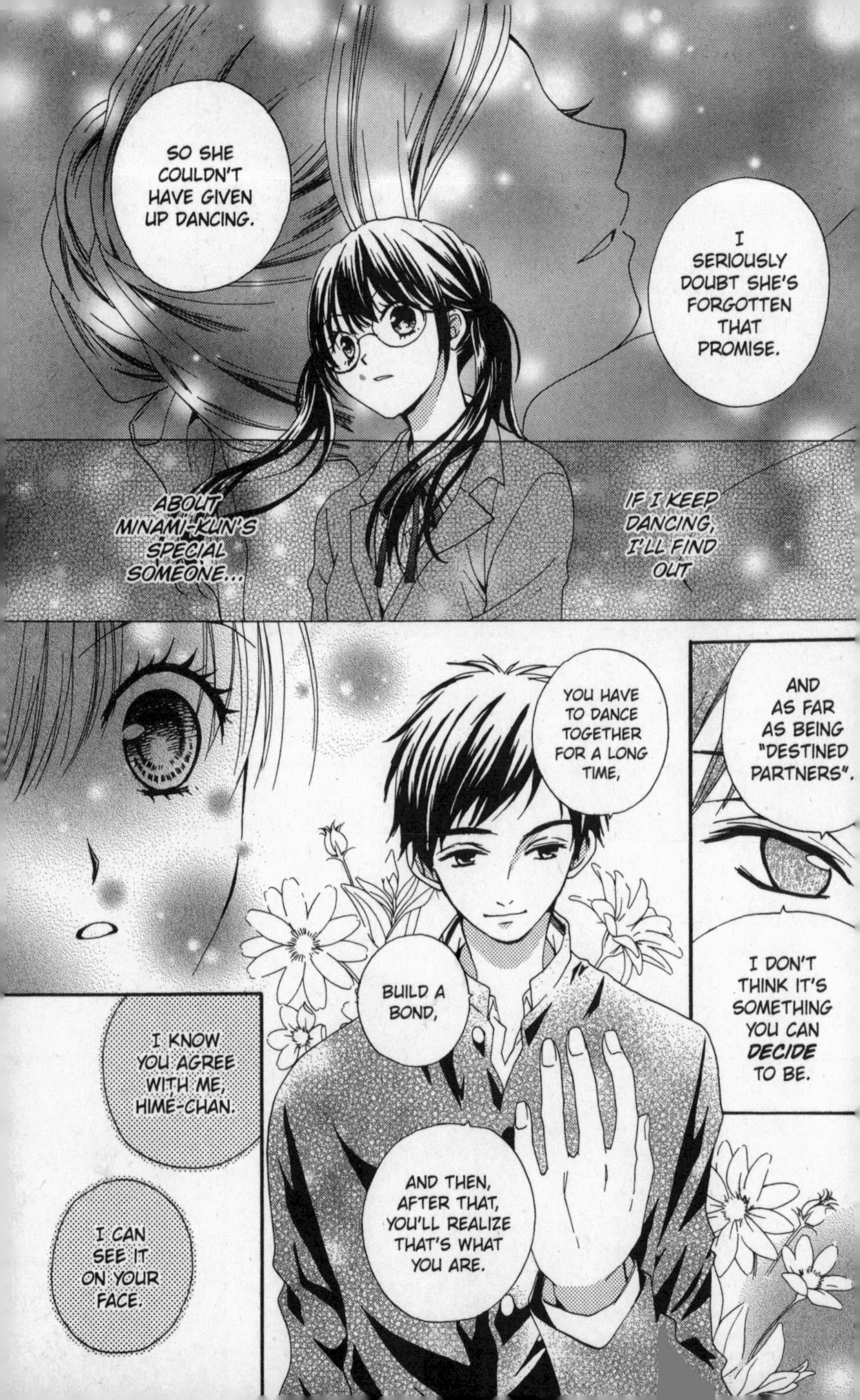
I SERIOUSLY DOUBT SHE'S FORGOTTEN THAT PROMISE.
SO SHE COULDN'T HAVE GIVEN UP DANCING.
IF I KEEP DANCING, I'LL FIND OUT
ABOUT MINAMI-KUN'S SPECIAL SOMEONE...
AND AS FAR AS BEING "DESTINED PARTNERS".
I DON'T THINK IT'S SOMETHING YOU CAN *DECIDE* TO BE.
YOU HAVE TO DANCE TOGETHER FOR A LONG TIME,
BUILD A BOND,
AND THEN, AFTER THAT, YOU'LL REALIZE THAT'S WHAT YOU ARE.
I KNOW YOU AGREE WITH ME, HIME-CHAN.
I CAN SEE IT ON YOUR FACE.

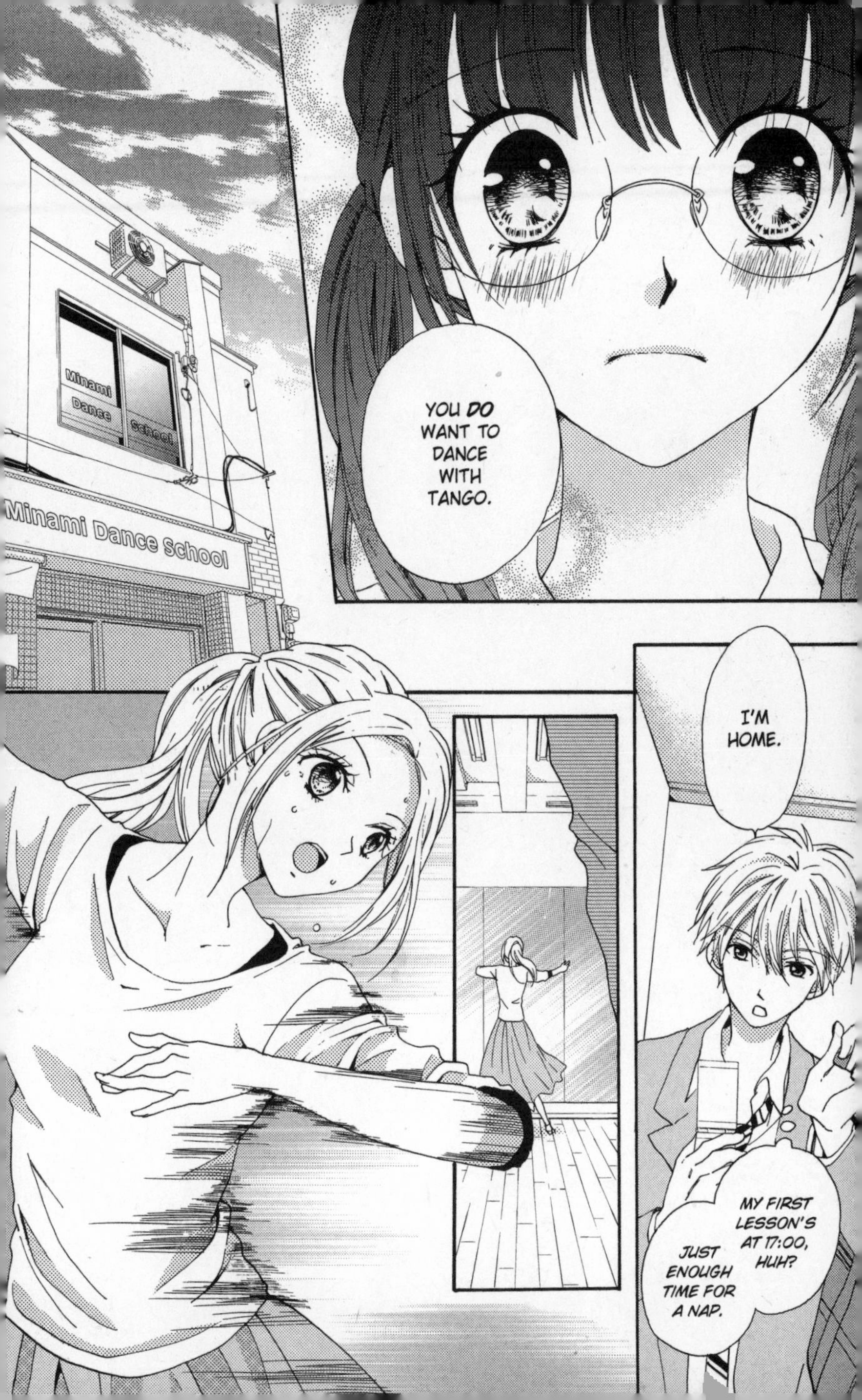
YOU DO WANT TO DANCE WITH TANGO.
Minami Dance School
Minami Dance School
I'M HOME.
MY FIRST LESSON'S AT 17:00, HUH?
JUST ENOUGH TIME FOR A NAP.

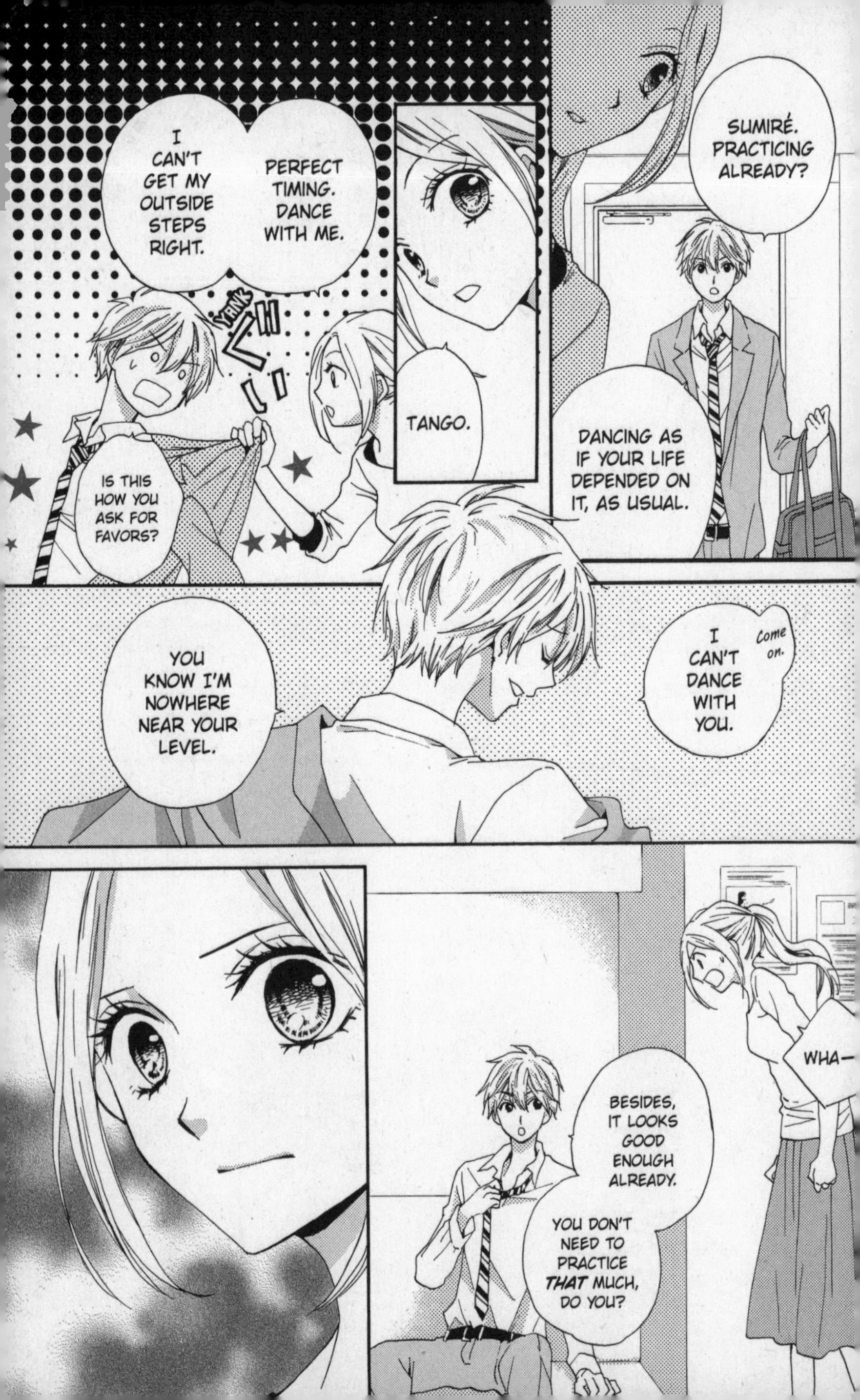
SUMIRÉ. PRACTICING ALREADY?
DANCING AS IF YOUR LIFE DEPENDED ON IT, AS USUAL.
TANGO.
PERFECT TIMING. DANCE WITH ME.
I CAN'T GET MY OUTSIDE STEPS RIGHT.
YANK
IS THIS HOW YOU ASK FOR FAVORS?
Come on.
I CAN'T DANCE WITH YOU.
YOU KNOW I'M NOWHERE NEAR YOUR LEVEL.
WHA—
BESIDES, IT LOOKS GOOD ENOUGH ALREADY.
YOU DON'T NEED TO PRACTICE *THAT* MUCH, DO YOU?

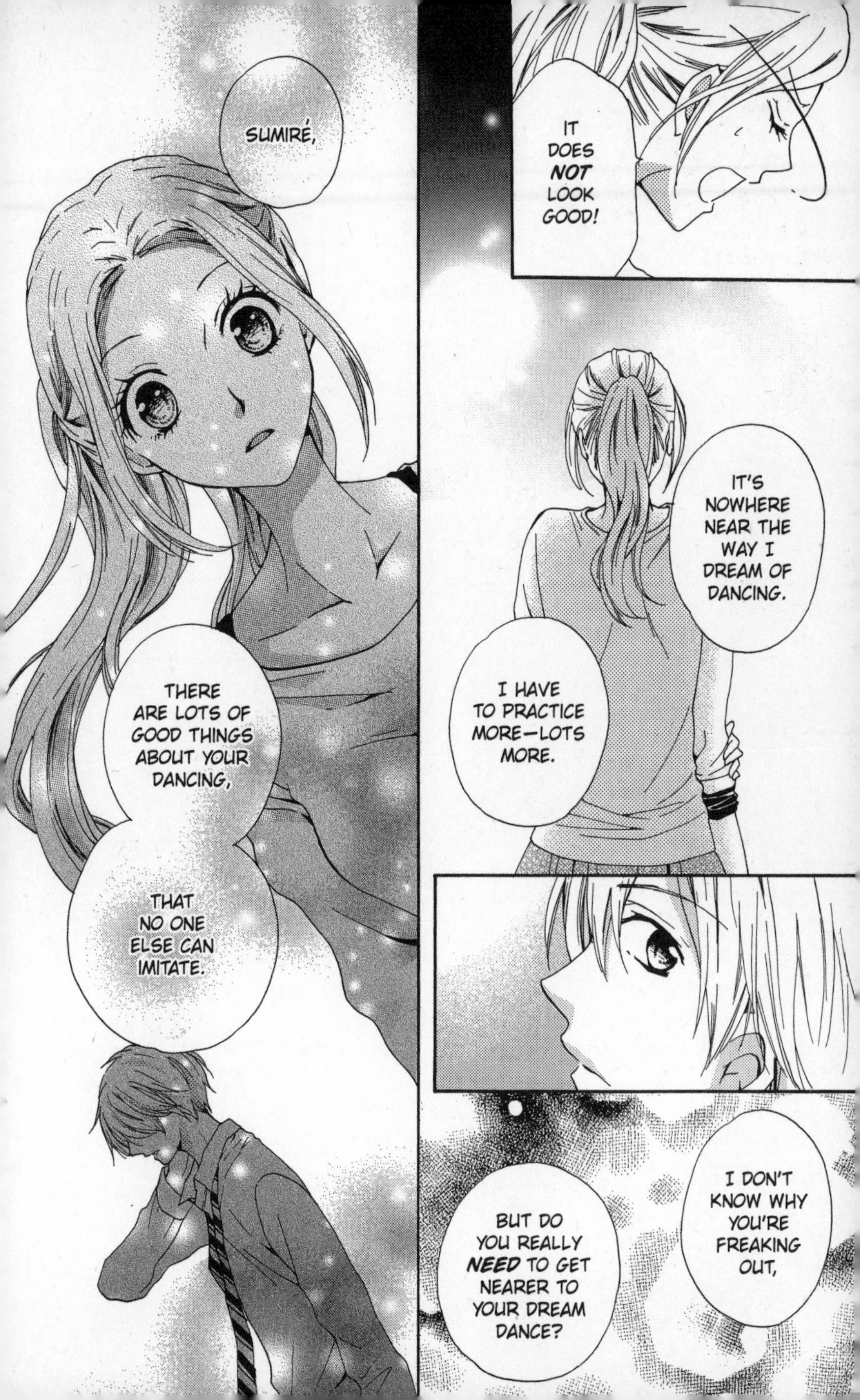
IT DOES **NOT** LOOK GOOD!
IT'S NOWHERE NEAR THE WAY I DREAM OF DANCING.
I HAVE TO PRACTICE MORE—LOTS MORE.
I DON'T KNOW WHY YOU'RE FREAKING OUT,
BUT DO YOU REALLY **NEED** TO GET NEARER TO YOUR DREAM DANCE?
SUMIRÉ,
THERE ARE LOTS OF GOOD THINGS ABOUT YOUR DANCING,
THAT NO ONE ELSE CAN IMITATE.

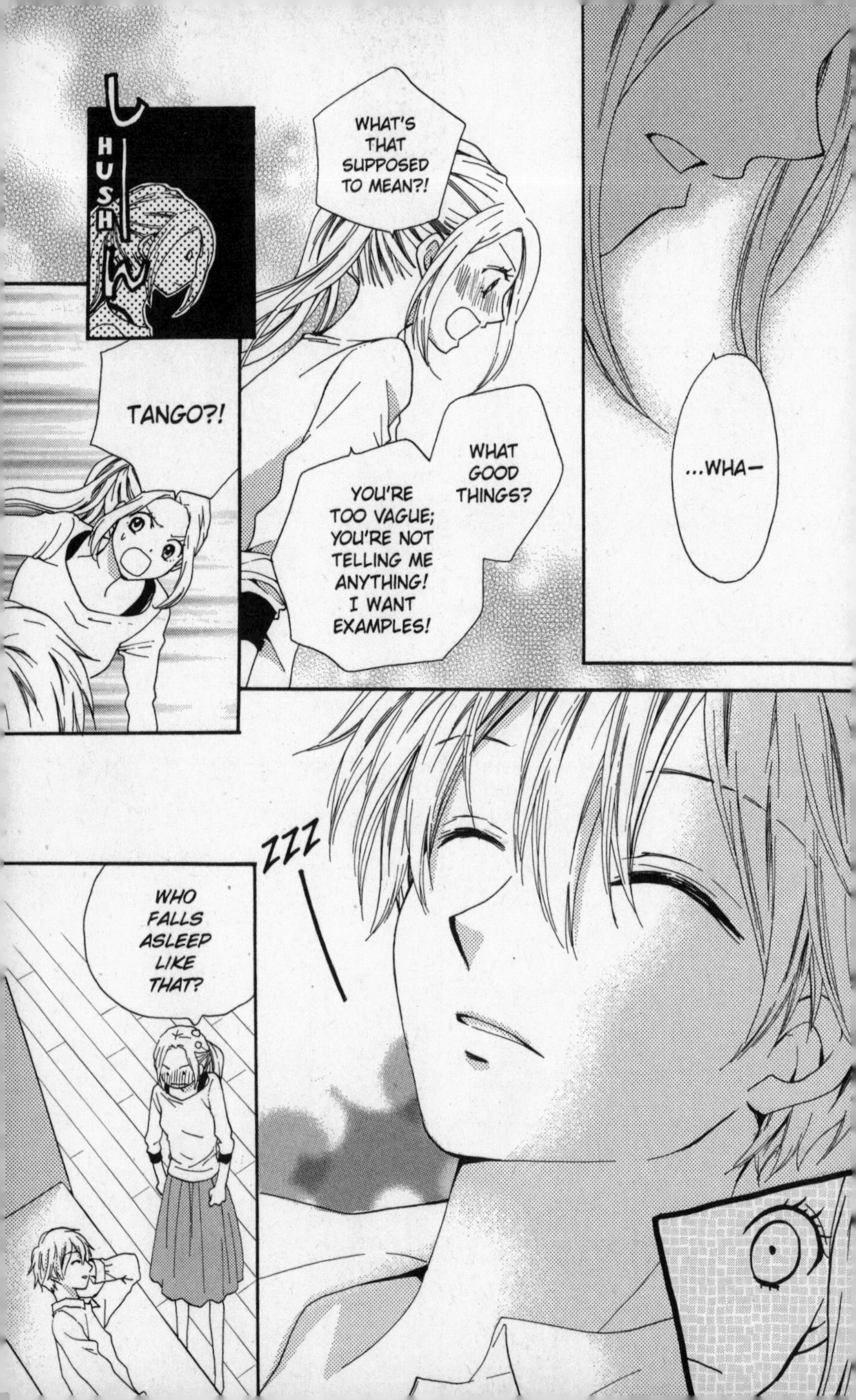
...WHA-
WHAT'S THAT SUPPOSED TO MEAN?!
WHAT GOOD THINGS?
YOU'RE TOO VAGUE; YOU'RE NOT TELLING ME ANYTHING! I WANT EXAMPLES!
し HUSH ん
TANGO?!
ZZZ
WHO FALLS ASLEEP LIKE THAT?

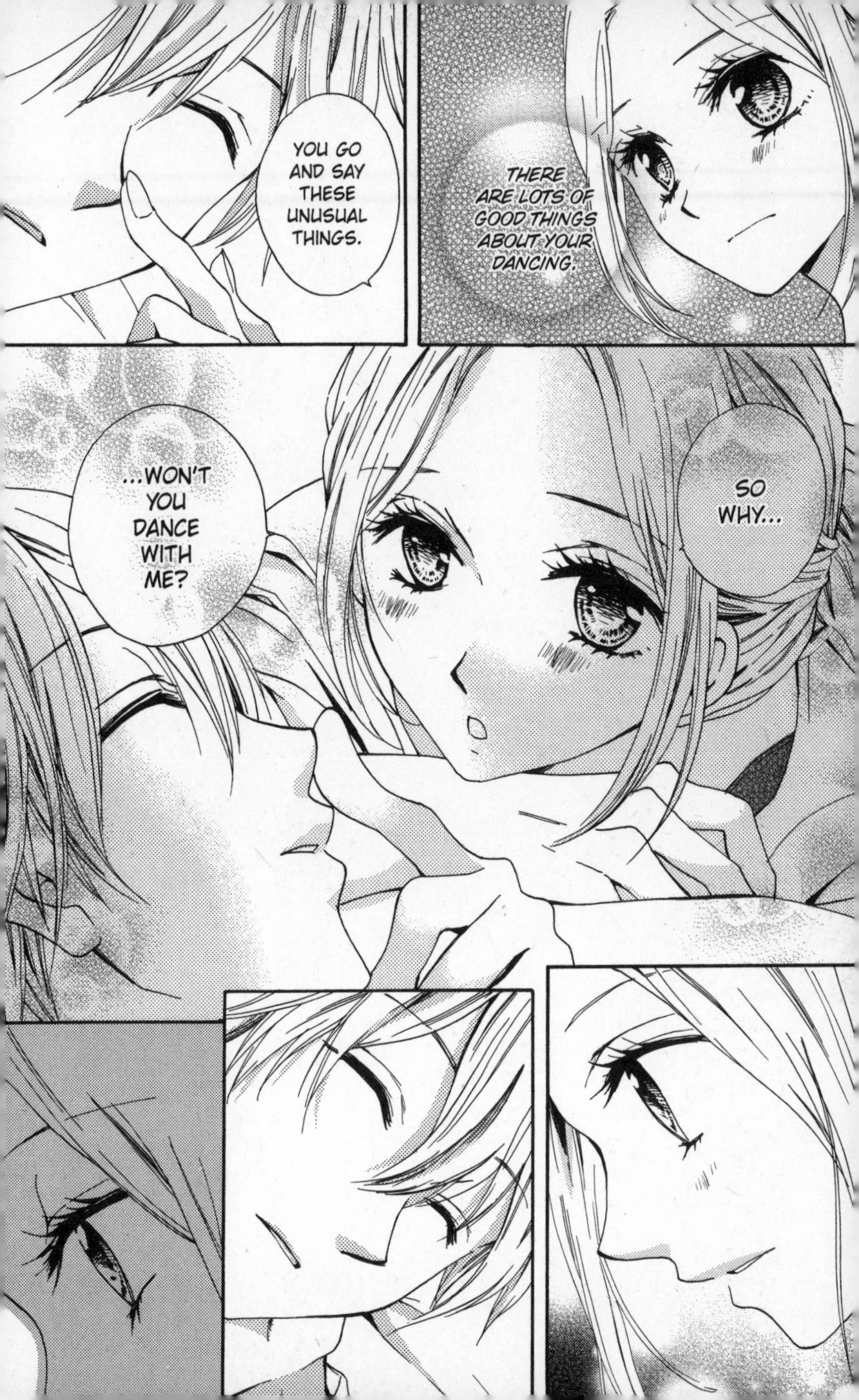
THERE ARE LOTS OF GOOD THINGS ABOUT YOUR DANCING.
YOU GO AND SAY THESE UNUSUAL THINGS.
SO WHY...
...WON'T YOU DANCE WITH ME?

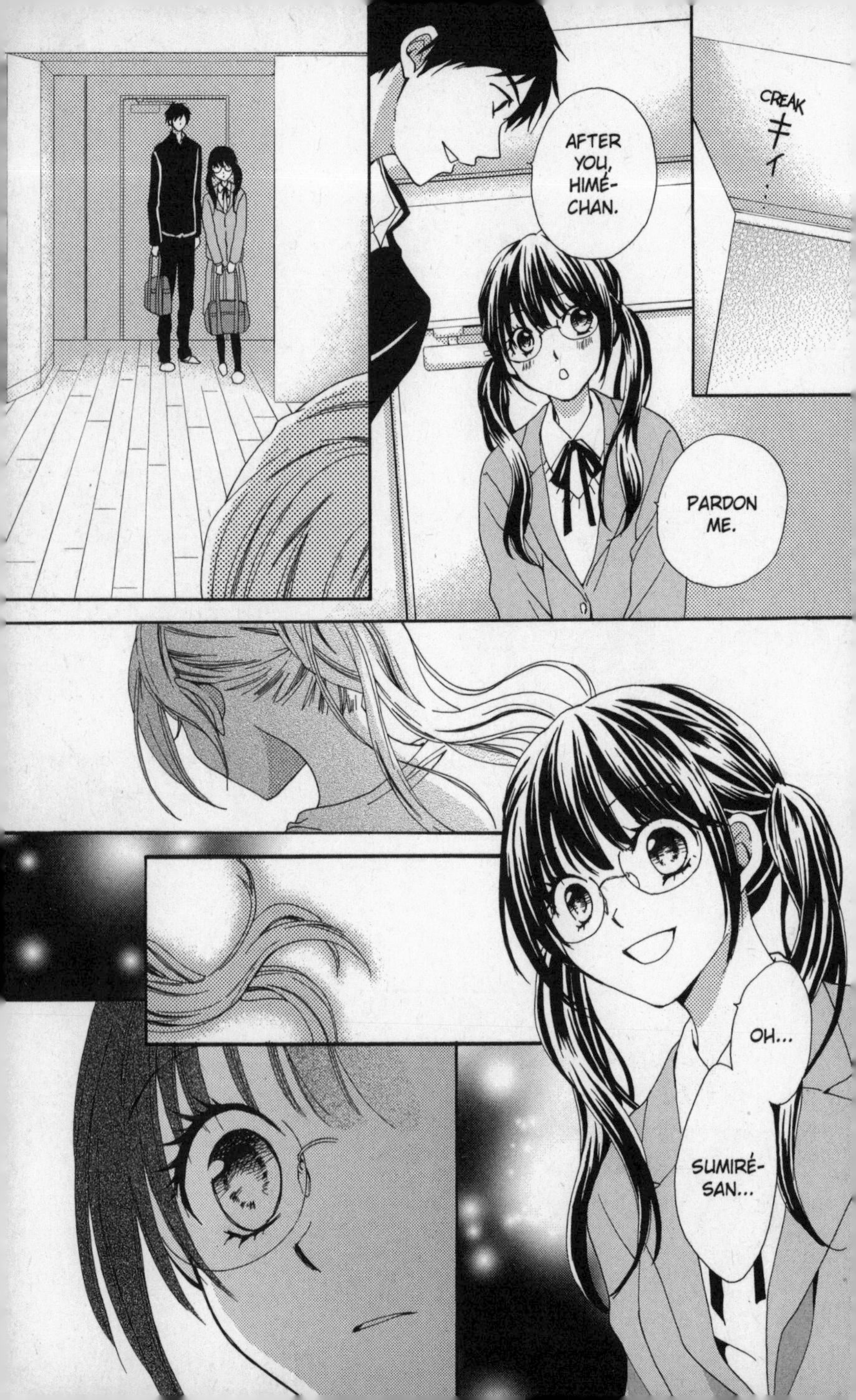
CREAK
キィ…
AFTER YOU, HIMÉ-CHAN.
PARDON ME.
OH...
SUMIRÉ-SAN...

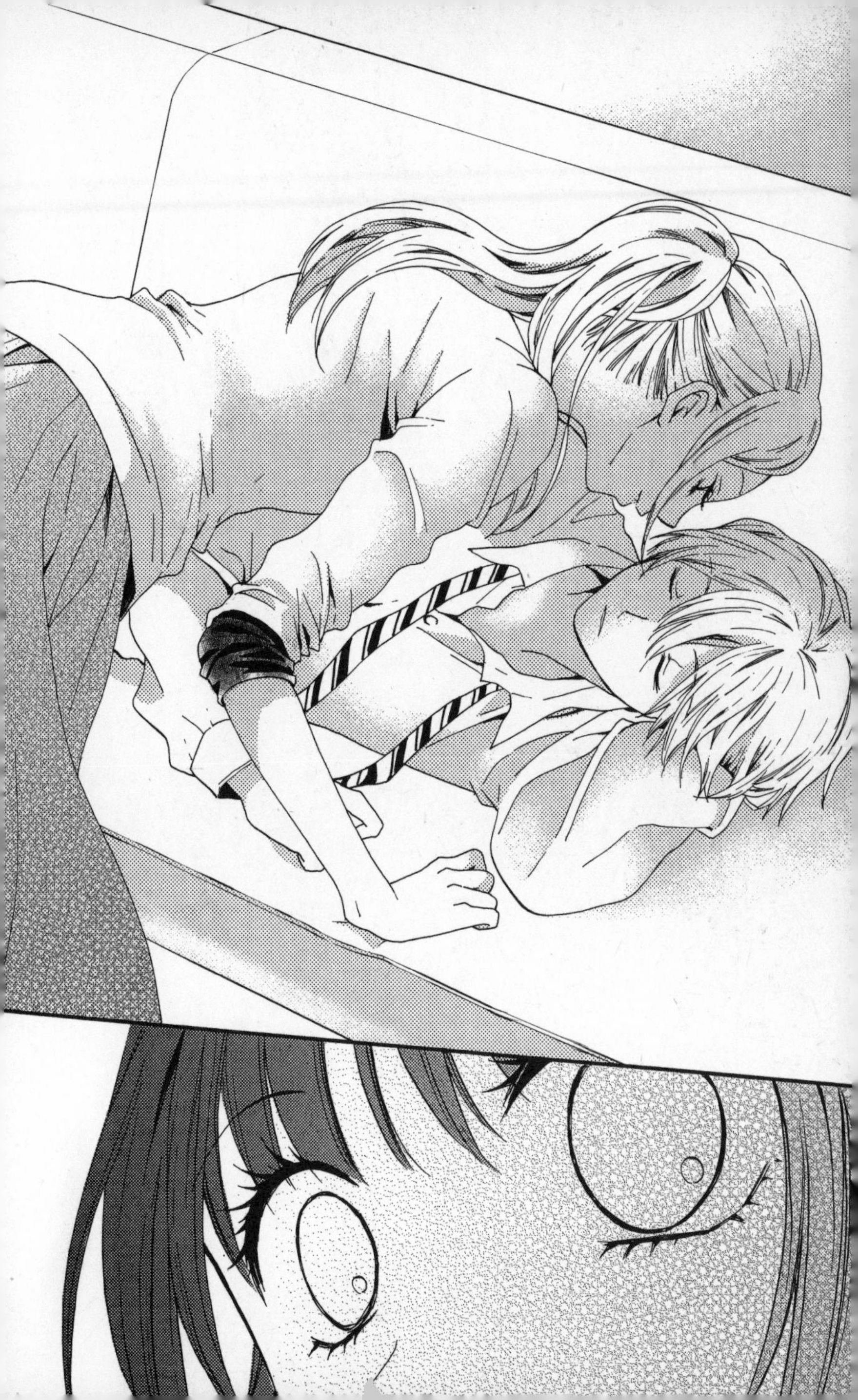

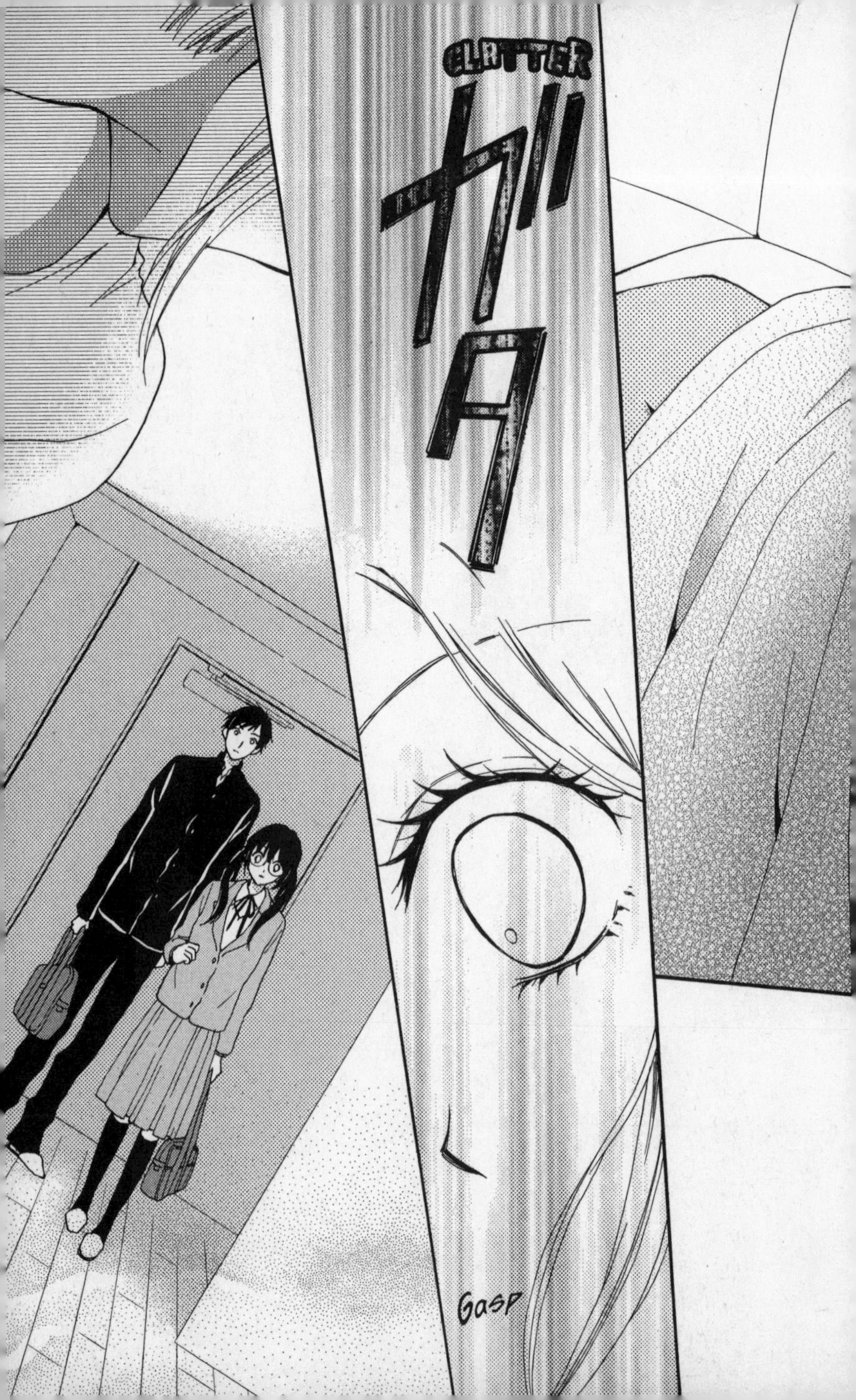
CLATTER
ガタ
Gasp

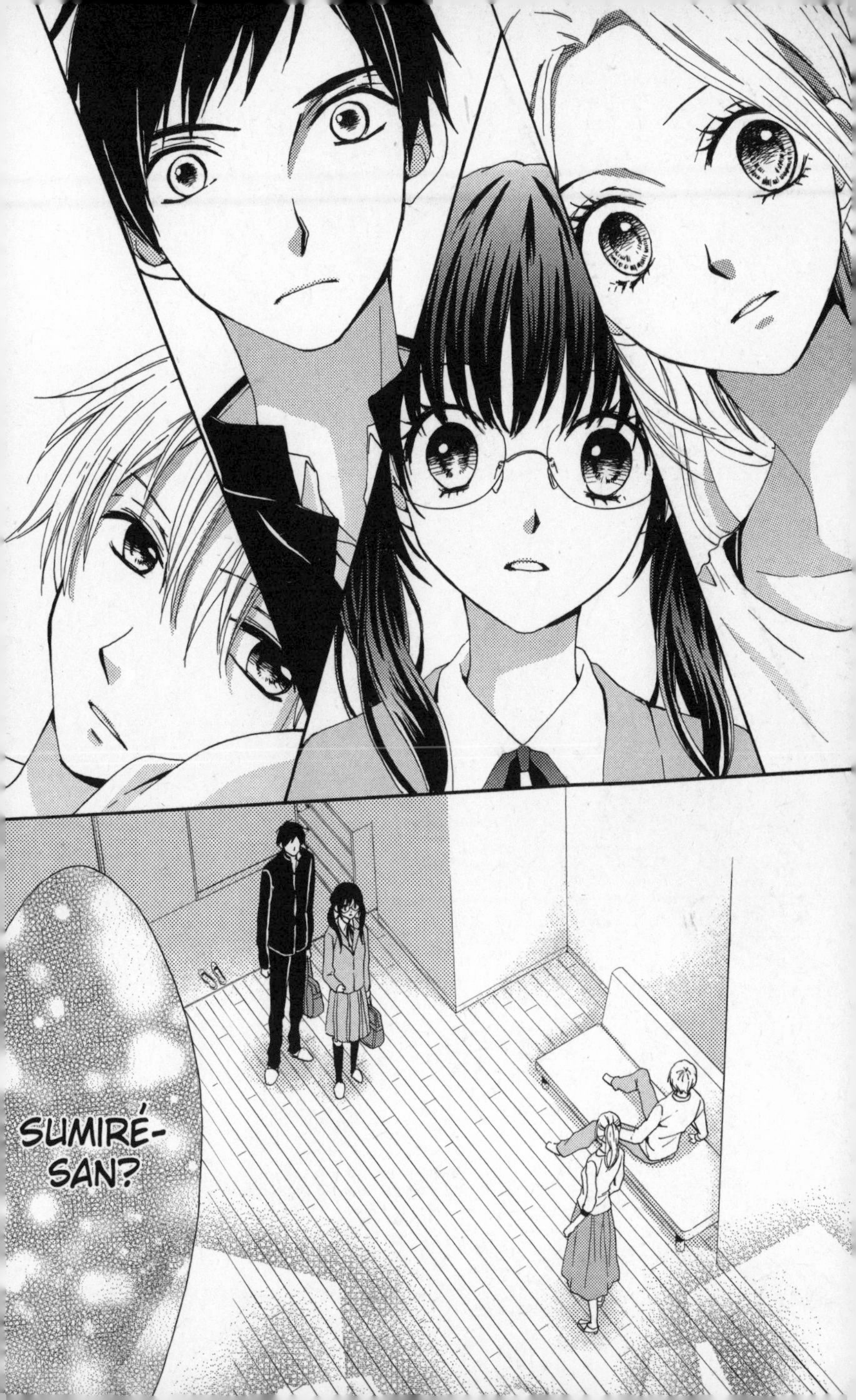
SUMIRÉ-SAN?

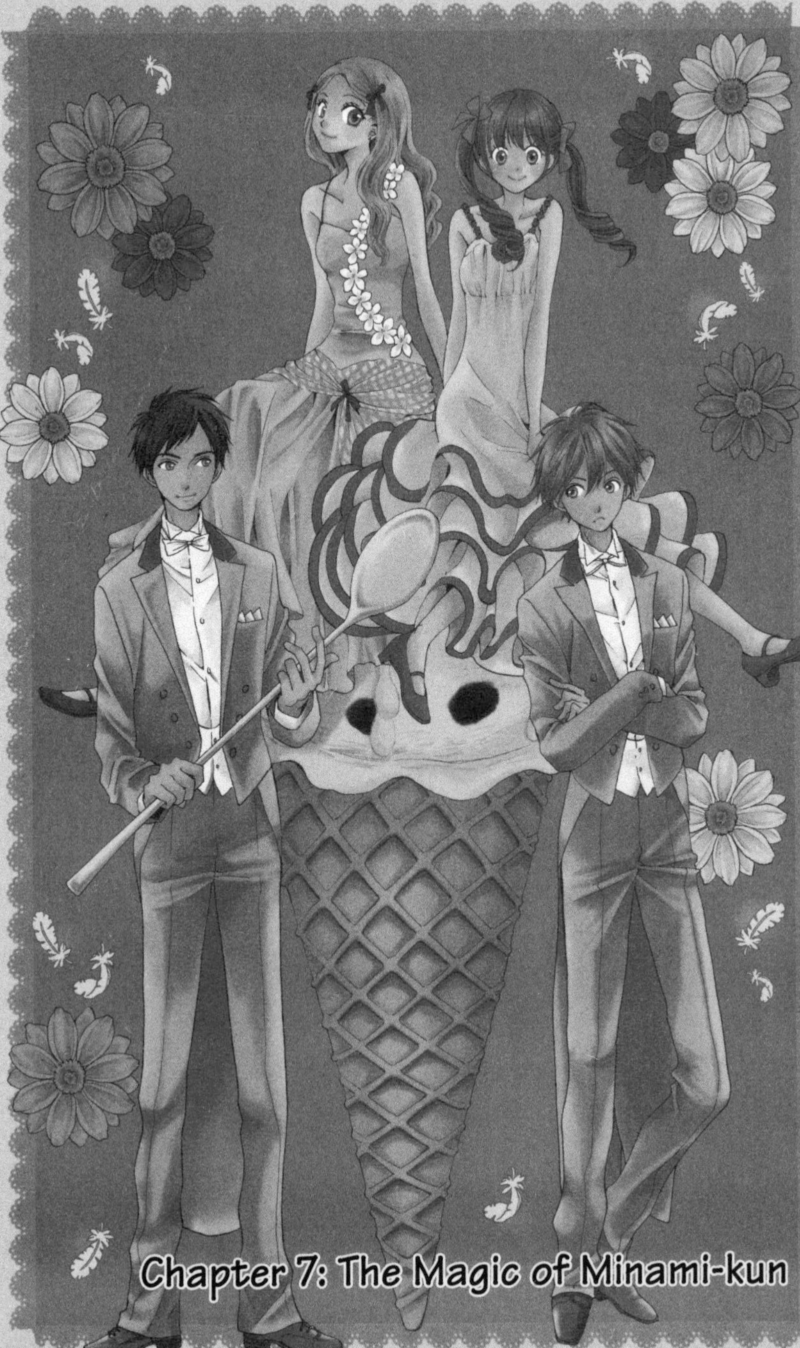

Chapter 7: The Magic of Minami-kun

LET'S READ A FOUR-PANEL COMIC

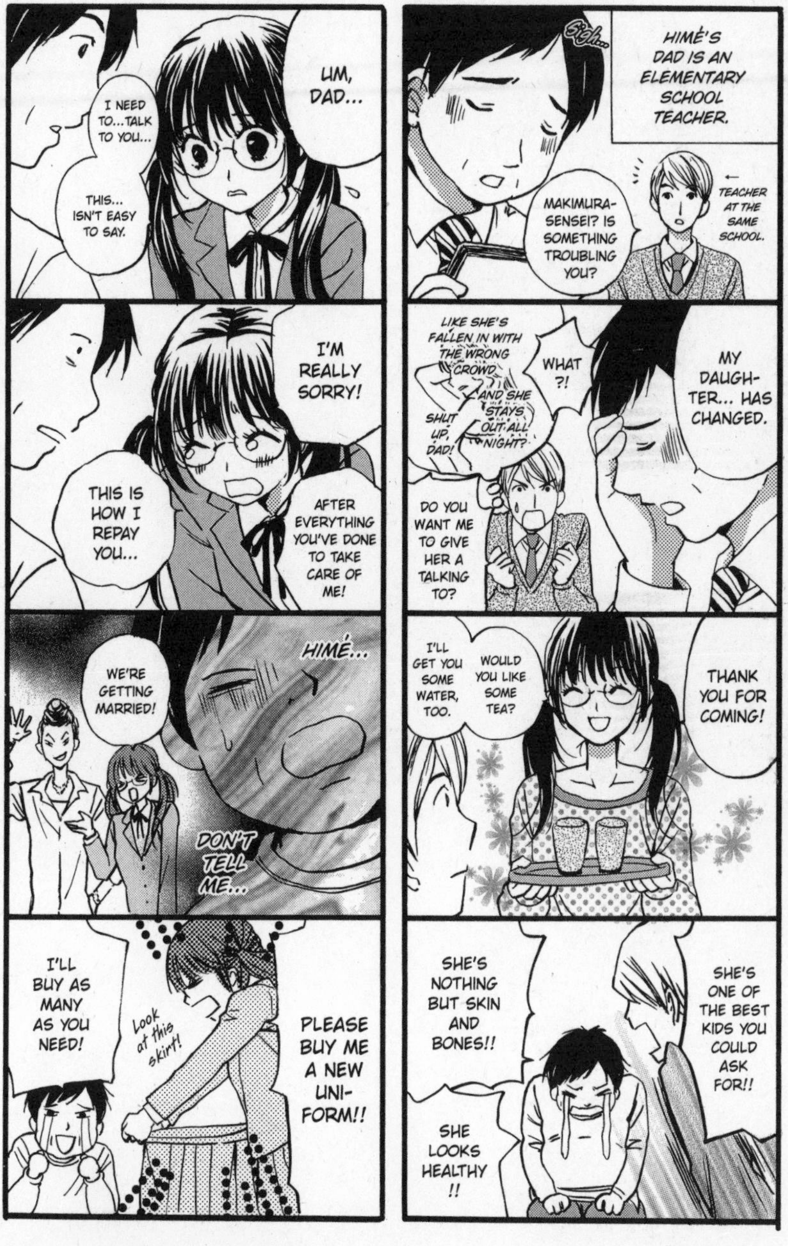

Sigh...
HIMÉ'S DAD IS AN ELEMENTARY SCHOOL TEACHER.
← TEACHER AT THE SAME SCHOOL.
MAKIMURA-SENSEI? IS SOMETHING TROUBLING YOU?
MY DAUGHTER... HAS CHANGED.
WHAT?!
LIKE SHE'S FALLEN IN WITH THE WRONG CROWD
AND SHE STAYS OUT ALL NIGHT?
SHUT UP, DAD!
DO YOU WANT ME TO GIVE HER A TALKING TO?
THANK YOU FOR COMING!
WOULD YOU LIKE SOME TEA?
I'LL GET YOU SOME WATER, TOO.
SHE'S ONE OF THE BEST KIDS YOU COULD ASK FOR!!
SHE'S NOTHING BUT SKIN AND BONES!!
SHE LOOKS HEALTHY!!
UM, DAD...
I NEED TO...TALK TO YOU...
THIS... ISN'T EASY TO SAY.
I'M REALLY SORRY!
AFTER EVERYTHING YOU'VE DONE TO TAKE CARE OF ME!
THIS IS HOW I REPAY YOU...
HIMÉ...
WE'RE GETTING MARRIED!
DON'T TELL ME...
PLEASE BUY ME A NEW UNIFORM!!
Look at this skirt!
I'LL BUY AS MANY AS YOU NEED!

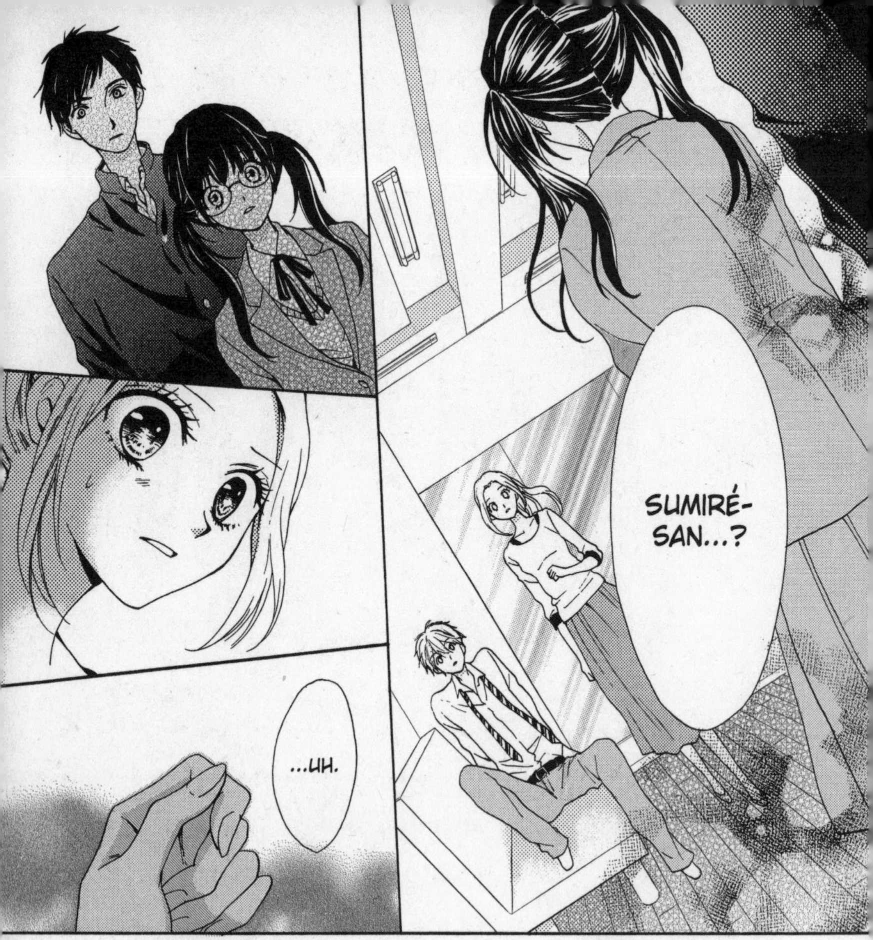
SUMIRÉ-SAN...?
...UH.

The Slow Foxtrot

A dance characterized by its flowing movement. Rumor has it that it got its name because it resembles the movement of a sneaky fox. Its dancers look very elegant as they glide across the floor!

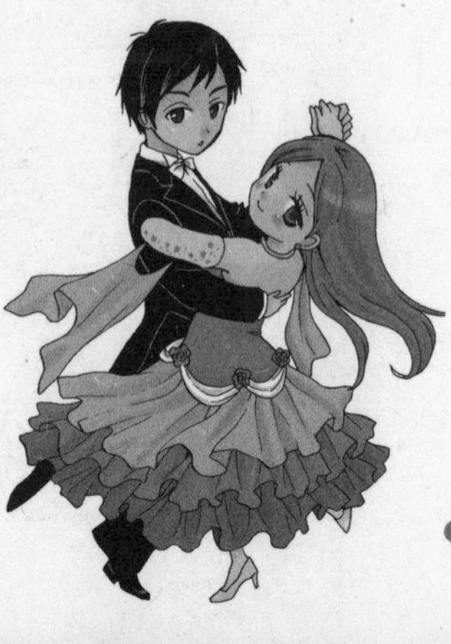

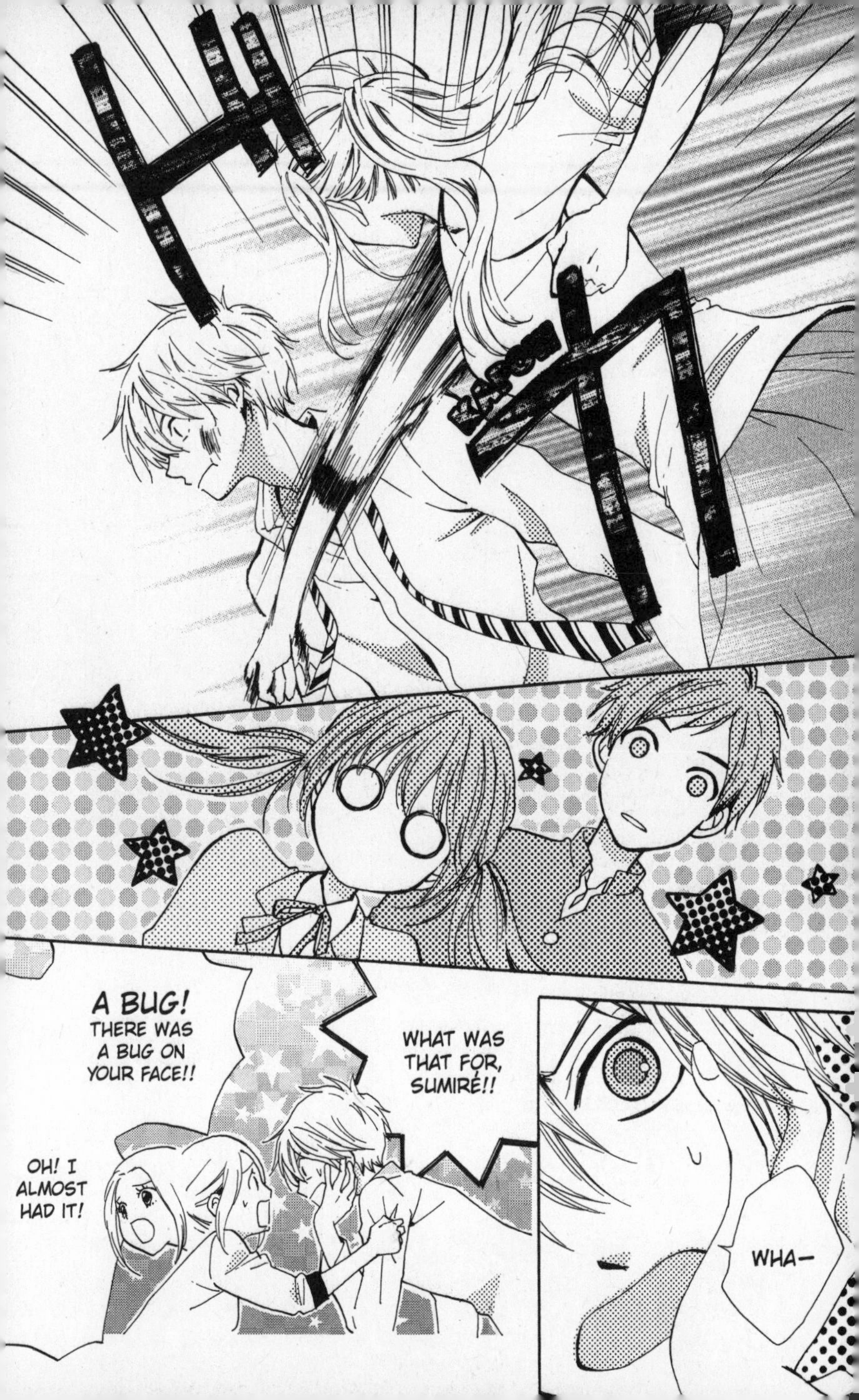
WHA—
WHAT WAS THAT FOR, SUMIRÉ!!
A BUG! THERE WAS A BUG ON YOUR FACE!!
OH! I ALMOST HAD IT!

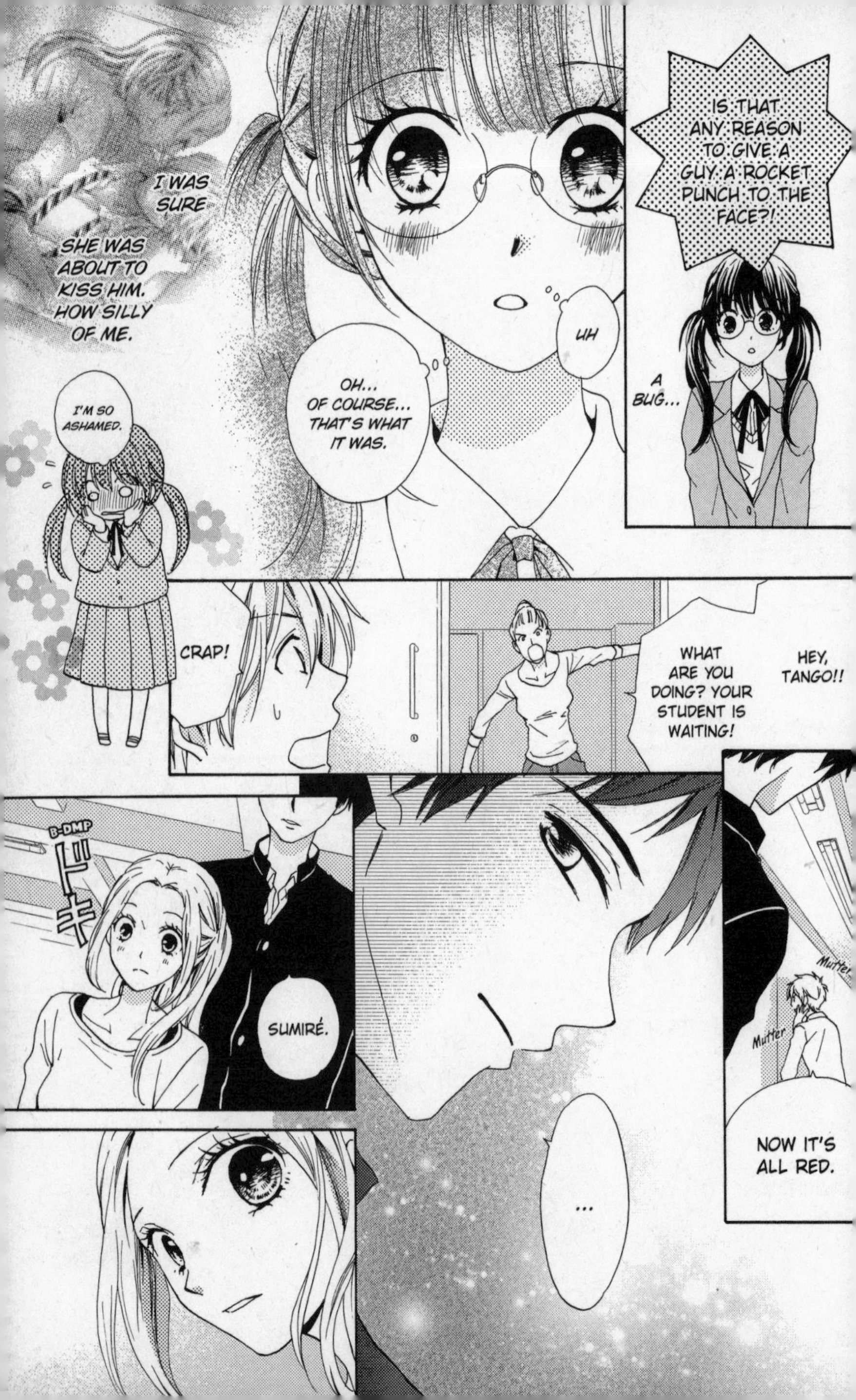
IS THAT ANY REASON TO GIVE A GUY A ROCKET PUNCH TO THE FACE?!
A BUG...
UH
OH... OF COURSE... THAT'S WHAT IT WAS.
I WAS SURE
SHE WAS ABOUT TO KISS HIM. HOW SILLY OF ME.
I'M SO ASHAMED.
HEY, TANGO!!
WHAT ARE YOU DOING? YOUR STUDENT IS WAITING!
CRAP!
Mutter
Mutter
NOW IT'S ALL RED.
...
SUMIRÉ.
B-DMP
ドキ

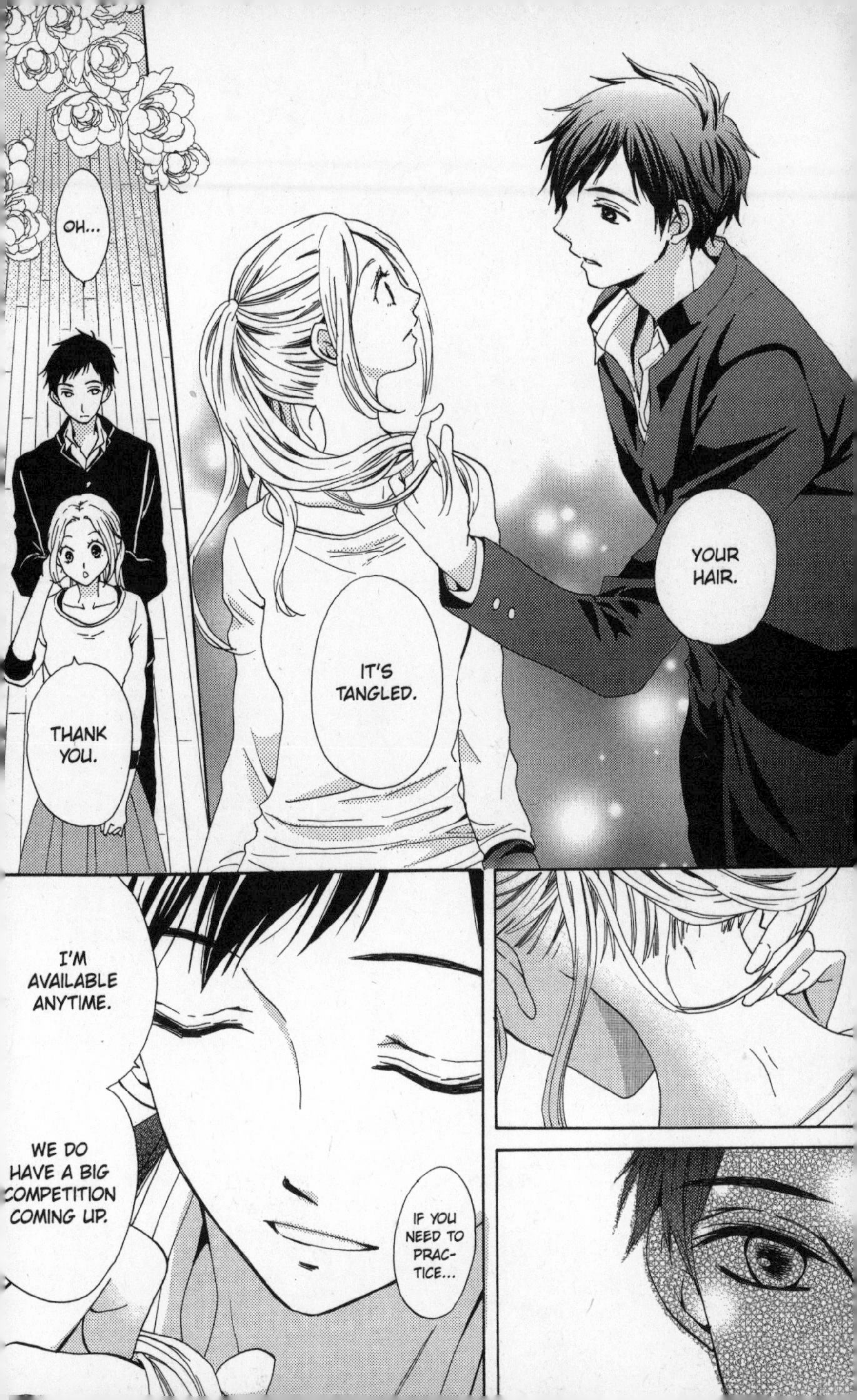
YOUR HAIR.
IT'S TANGLED.
OH...
THANK YOU.
I'M AVAILABLE ANYTIME.
IF YOU NEED TO PRAC- TICE...
WE DO HAVE A BIG COMPETITION COMING UP.

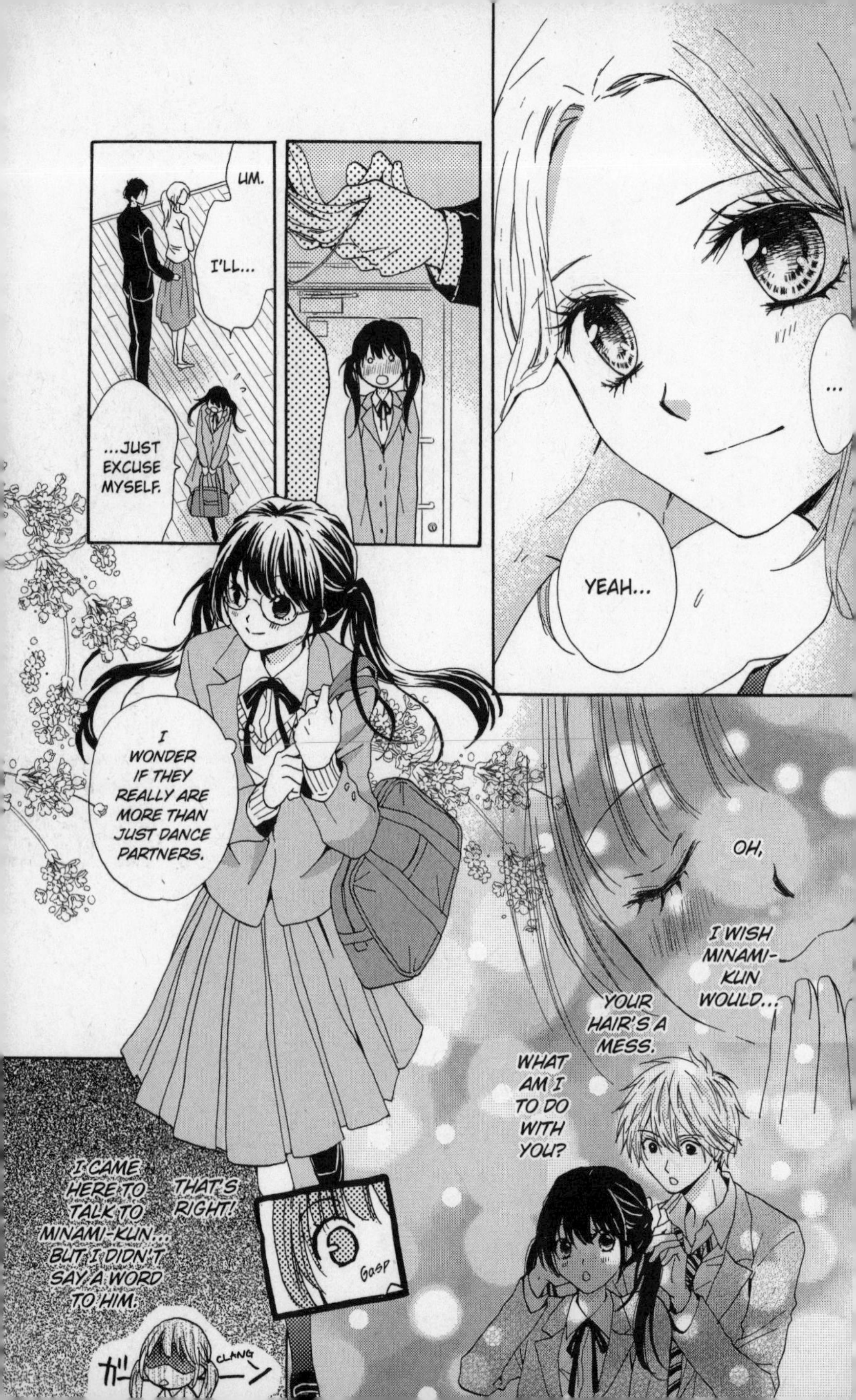
...
YEAH...
UM.
I'LL...
...JUST EXCUSE MYSELF.
OH,
I WISH MINAMI-KUN WOULD...
YOUR HAIR'S A MESS.
WHAT AM I TO DO WITH YOU?
I WONDER IF THEY REALLY ARE MORE THAN JUST DANCE PARTNERS.
THAT'S RIGHT!
Gasp
I CAME HERE TO TALK TO MINAMI-KUN... BUT I DIDN'T SAY A WORD TO HIM.
ガーン
CLANG

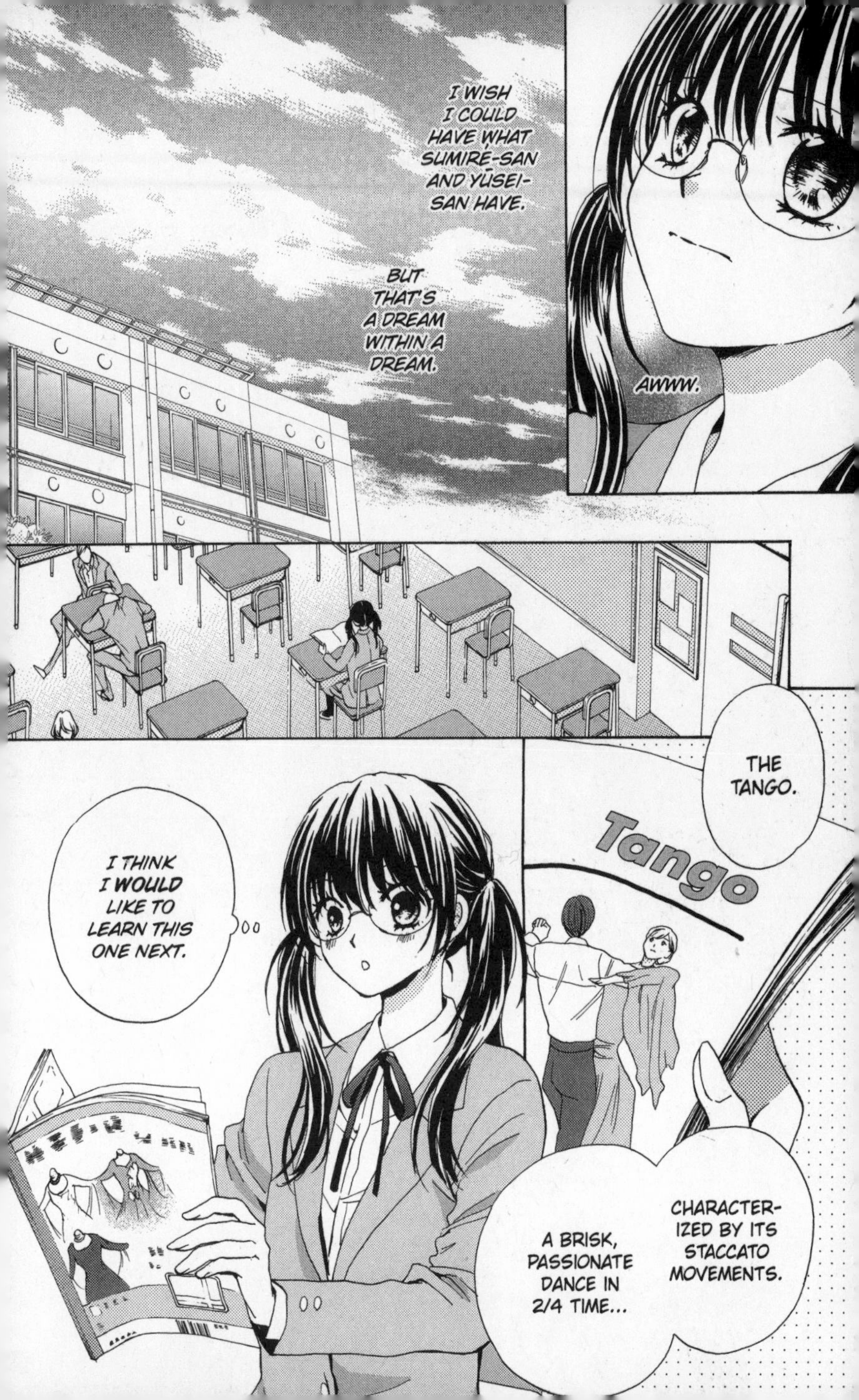
AWWW.
I WISH I COULD HAVE WHAT SUMIRE-SAN AND YŪSEI-SAN HAVE.
BUT THAT'S A DREAM WITHIN A DREAM.
THE TANGO.
Tango
CHARACTER-IZED BY ITS STACCATO MOVEMENTS.
A BRISK, PASSIONATE DANCE IN 2/4 TIME...
I THINK I WOULD LIKE TO LEARN THIS ONE NEXT.

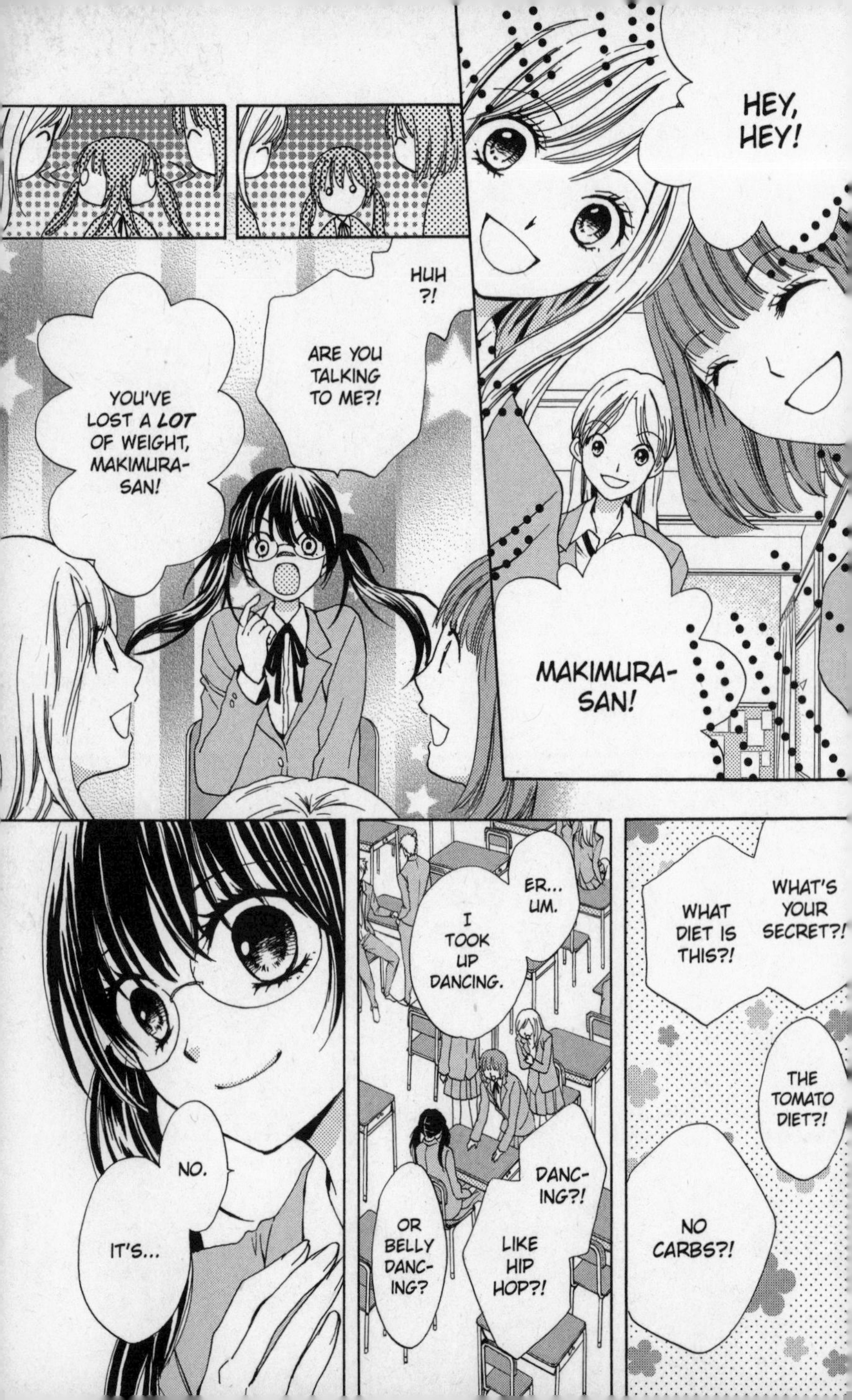
HEY, HEY!
MAKIMURA-SAN!
HUH?!
ARE YOU TALKING TO ME?!
YOU'VE LOST A *LOT* OF WEIGHT, MAKIMURA-SAN!
WHAT'S YOUR SECRET?!
WHAT DIET IS THIS?!
THE TOMATO DIET?!
NO CARBS?!
ER... UM.
I TOOK UP DANCING.
DANC-ING?!
LIKE HIP HOP?!
OR BELLY DANC-ING?
NO.
IT'S...

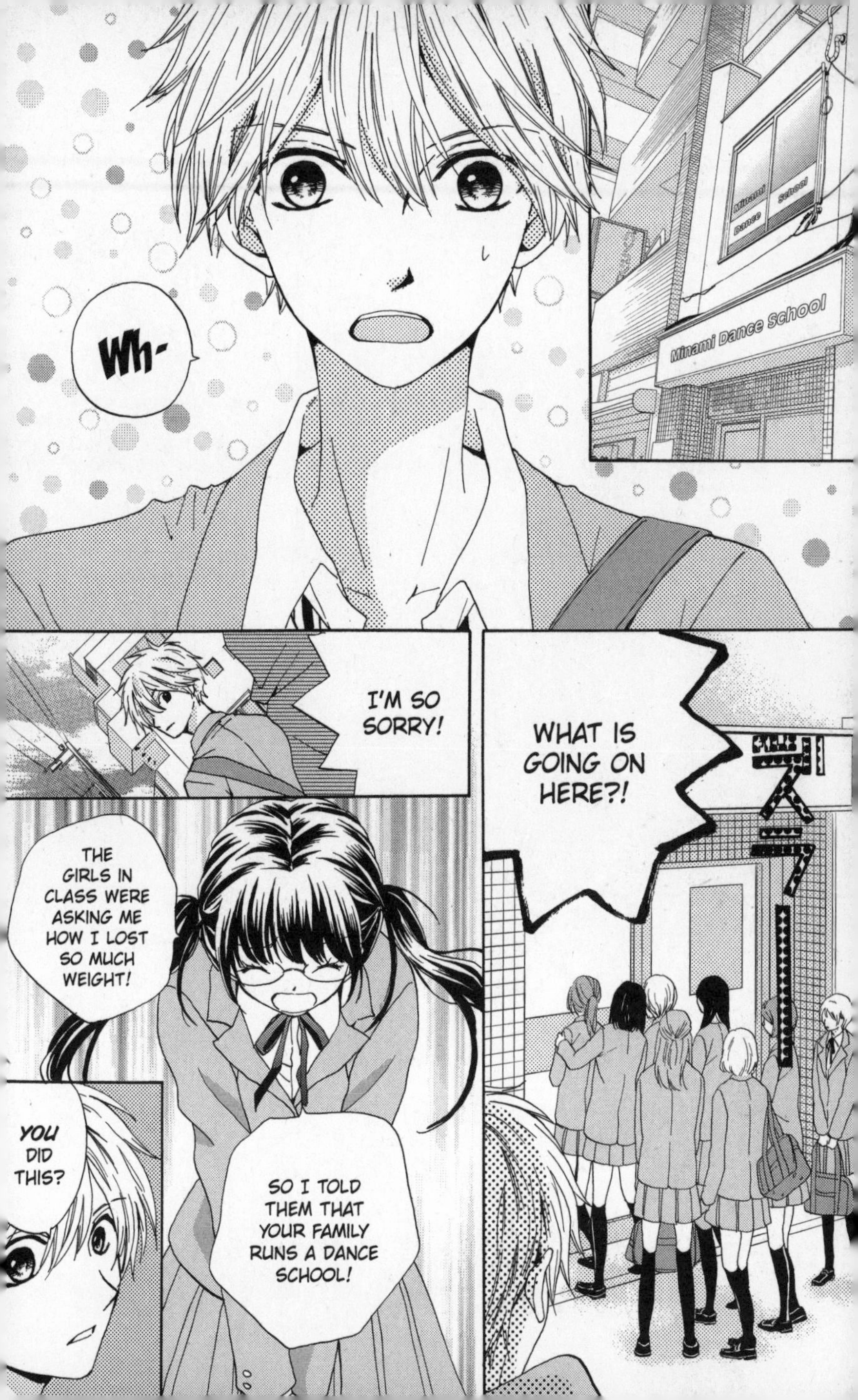

Minami Dance School
Minami Dance School
Wh-
WHAT IS GOING ON HERE?!
I'M SO SORRY!
THE GIRLS IN CLASS WERE ASKING ME HOW I LOST SO MUCH WEIGHT!
SO I TOLD THEM THAT YOUR FAMILY RUNS A DANCE SCHOOL!
YOU DID THIS?

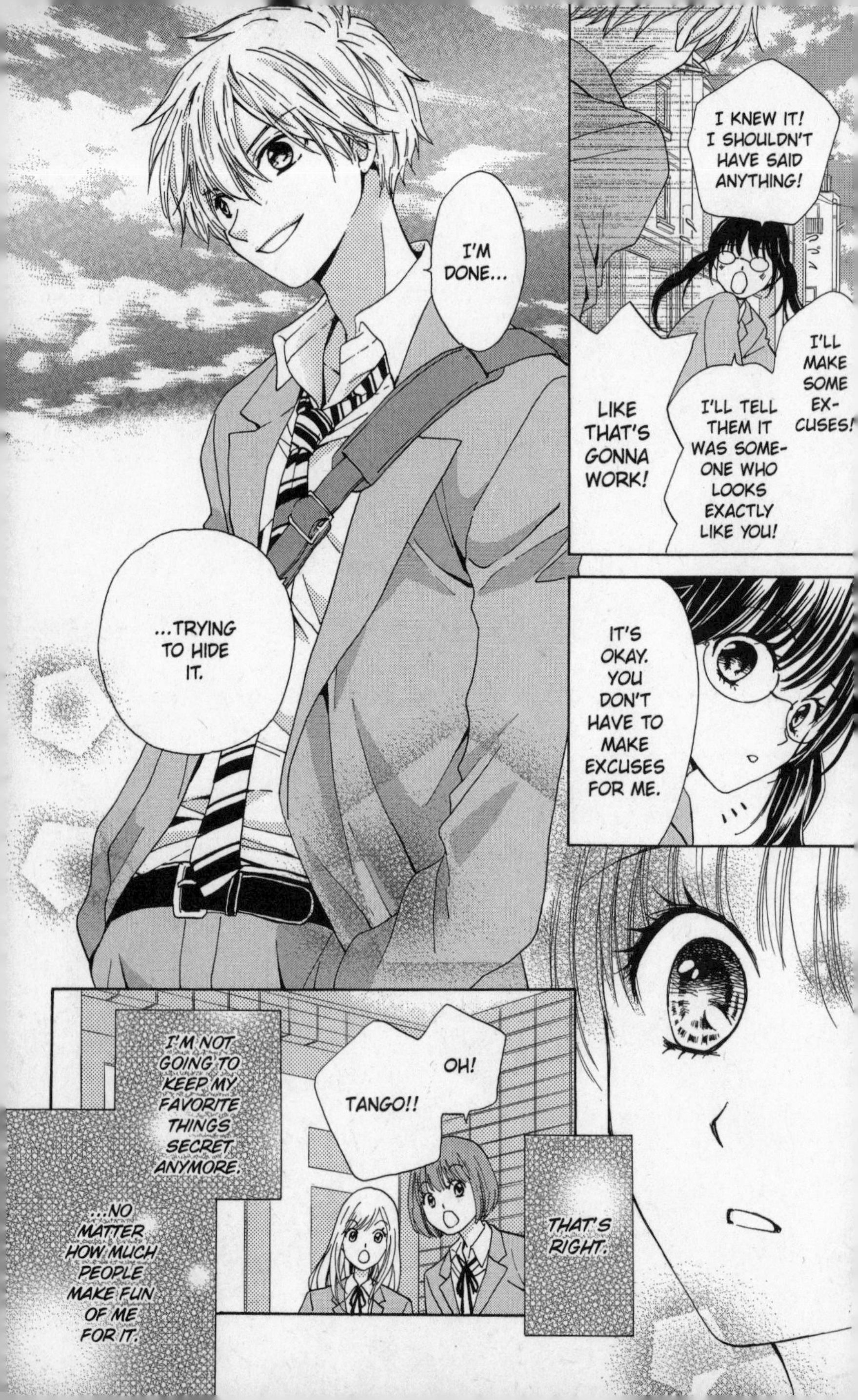
I KNEW IT! I SHOULDN'T HAVE SAID ANYTHING!
I'LL MAKE SOME EX-CUSES!
I'LL TELL THEM IT WAS SOME-ONE WHO LOOKS EXACTLY LIKE YOU!
LIKE THAT'S GONNA WORK!
IT'S OKAY. YOU DON'T HAVE TO MAKE EXCUSES FOR ME.
I'M DONE...
...TRYING TO HIDE IT.
THAT'S RIGHT.
I'M NOT GOING TO KEEP MY FAVORITE THINGS SECRET ANYMORE.
...NO MATTER HOW MUCH PEOPLE MAKE FUN OF ME FOR IT.
OH! TANGO!!

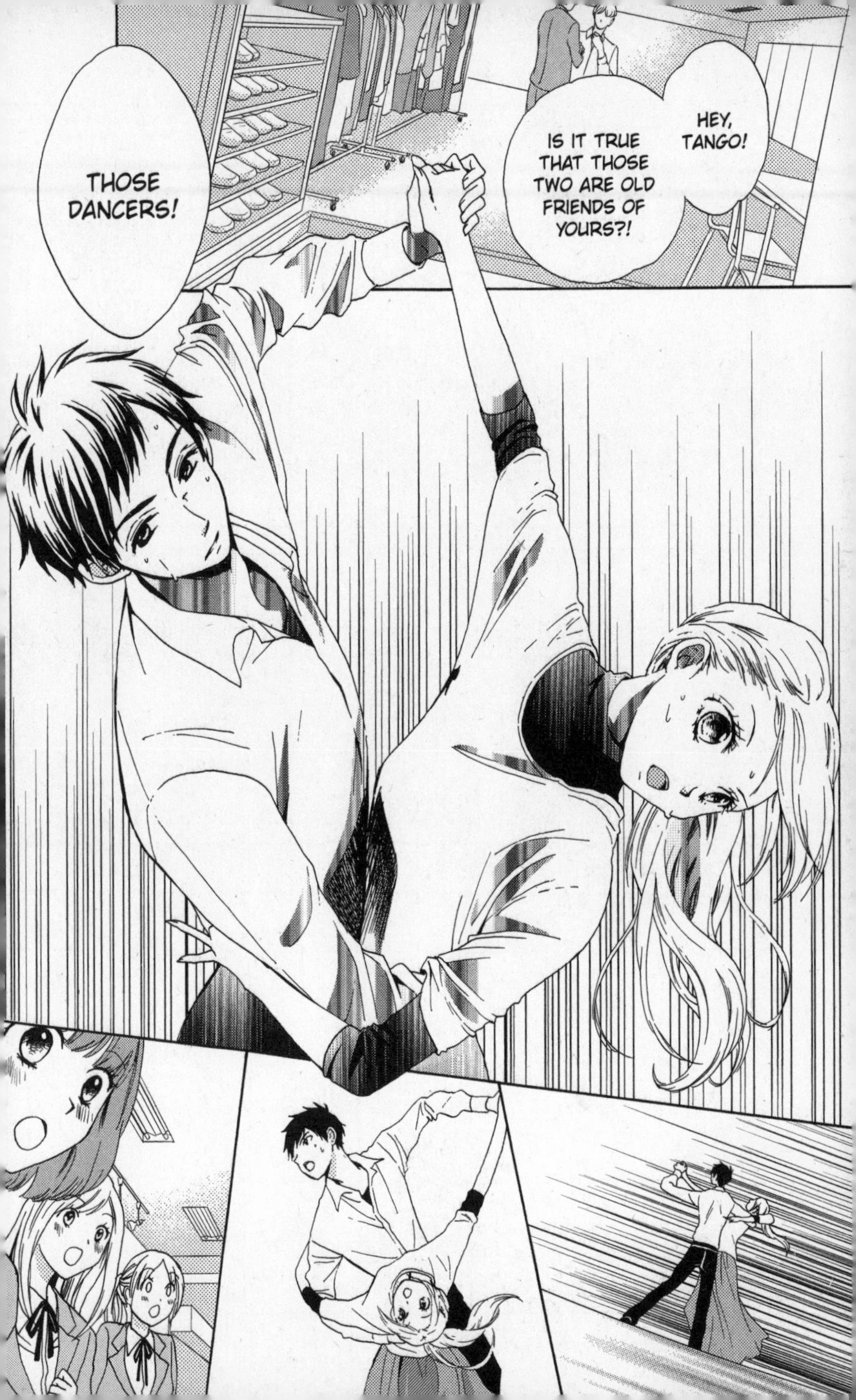
HEY, TANGO!
IS IT TRUE THAT THOSE TWO ARE OLD FRIENDS OF YOURS?!
THOSE DANCERS!

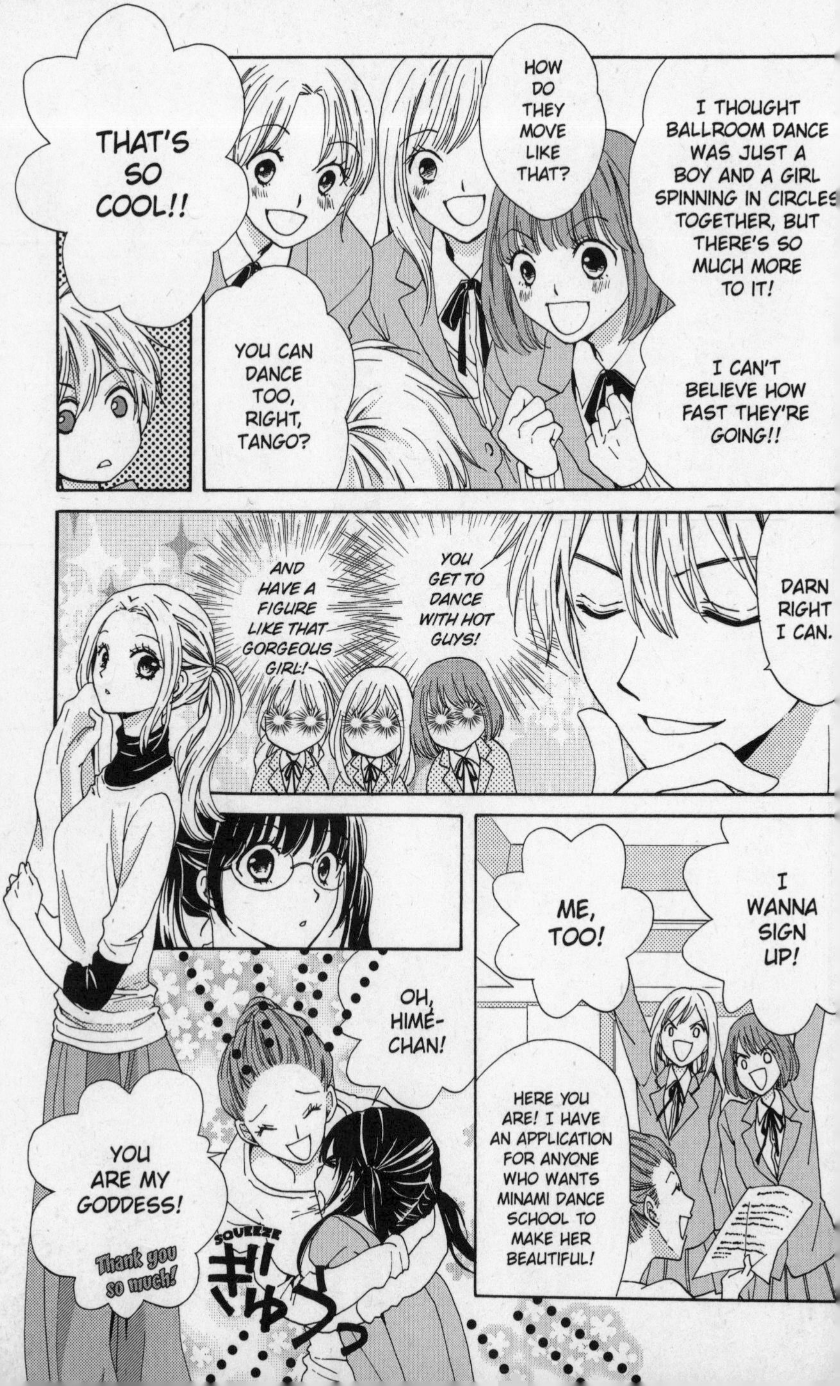
I THOUGHT BALLROOM DANCE WAS JUST A BOY AND A GIRL SPINNING IN CIRCLES TOGETHER, BUT THERE'S SO MUCH MORE TO IT!
I CAN'T BELIEVE HOW FAST THEY'RE GOING!!
HOW DO THEY MOVE LIKE THAT?
THAT'S SO COOL!!
YOU CAN DANCE TOO, RIGHT, TANGO?
DARN RIGHT I CAN.
YOU GET TO DANCE WITH HOT GUYS!
AND HAVE A FIGURE LIKE THAT GORGEOUS GIRL!
I WANNA SIGN UP!
ME, TOO!
HERE YOU ARE! I HAVE AN APPLICATION FOR ANYONE WHO WANTS MINAMI DANCE SCHOOL TO MAKE HER BEAUTIFUL!
OH, HIME-CHAN!
YOU ARE MY GODDESS!
Thank you so much!
SQUEEZE
ぎゅっ

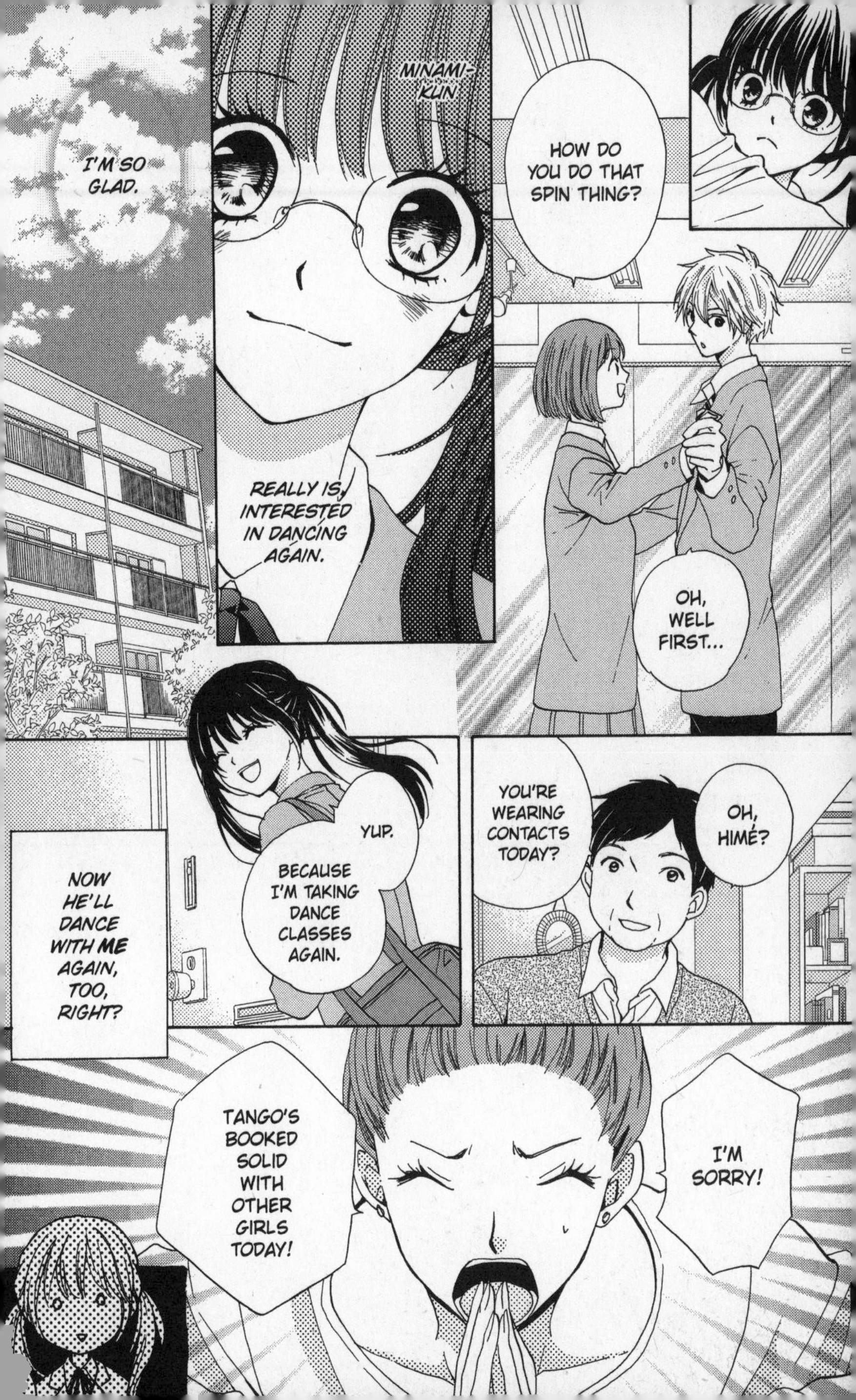

HOW DO YOU DO THAT SPIN THING?
OH, WELL FIRST...
MINAMI-KUN
REALLY IS, INTERESTED IN DANCING AGAIN.
I'M SO GLAD.
OH, HIMÉ?
YOU'RE WEARING CONTACTS TODAY?
YUP.
BECAUSE I'M TAKING DANCE CLASSES AGAIN.
NOW HE'LL DANCE WITH ME AGAIN, TOO, RIGHT?
I'M SORRY!
TANGO'S BOOKED SOLID WITH OTHER GIRLS TODAY!

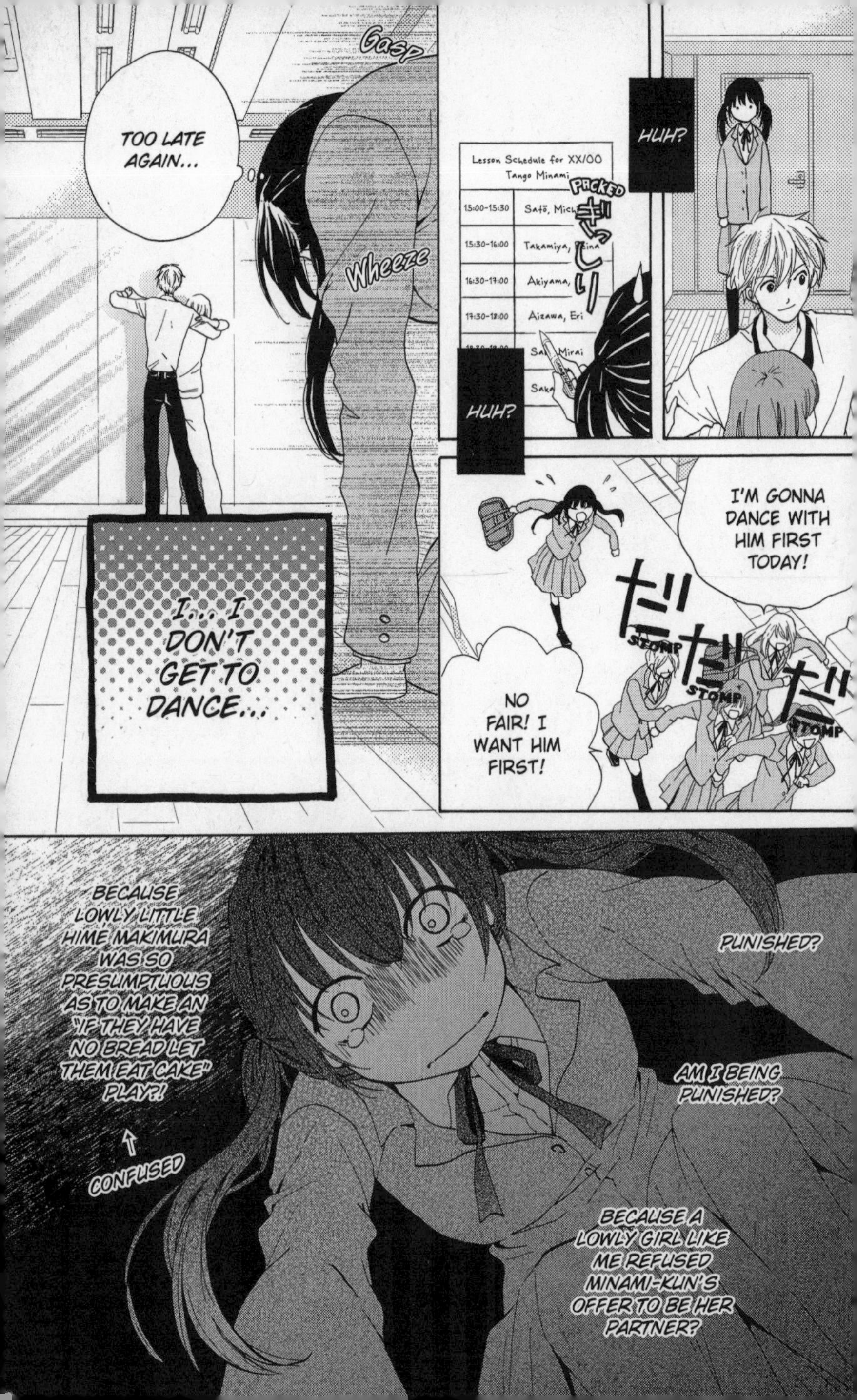
HUH?
Lesson Schedule for XX/OO
Tango Minami
15:00-15:30 Satō, Mich
15:30-16:00 Takamiya,
16:30-17:00 Akiyama,
17:30-18:00 Aizawa, Eri
Mirai
PACKED
HUH?
I'M GONNA DANCE WITH HIM FIRST TODAY!
STOMP
STOMP
STOMP
NO FAIR! I WANT HIM FIRST!
Gasp
Wheeze
TOO LATE AGAIN...
I... I DON'T GET TO DANCE...
PUNISHED?
AM I BEING PUNISHED?
BECAUSE A LOWLY GIRL LIKE ME REFUSED MINAMI-KUN'S OFFER TO BE HER PARTNER?
BECAUSE LOWLY LITTLE HIME MAKIMURA WAS SO PRESUMPTUOUS AS TO MAKE AN "IF THEY HAVE NO BREAD LET THEM EAT CAKE" PLAY?!
CONFUSED

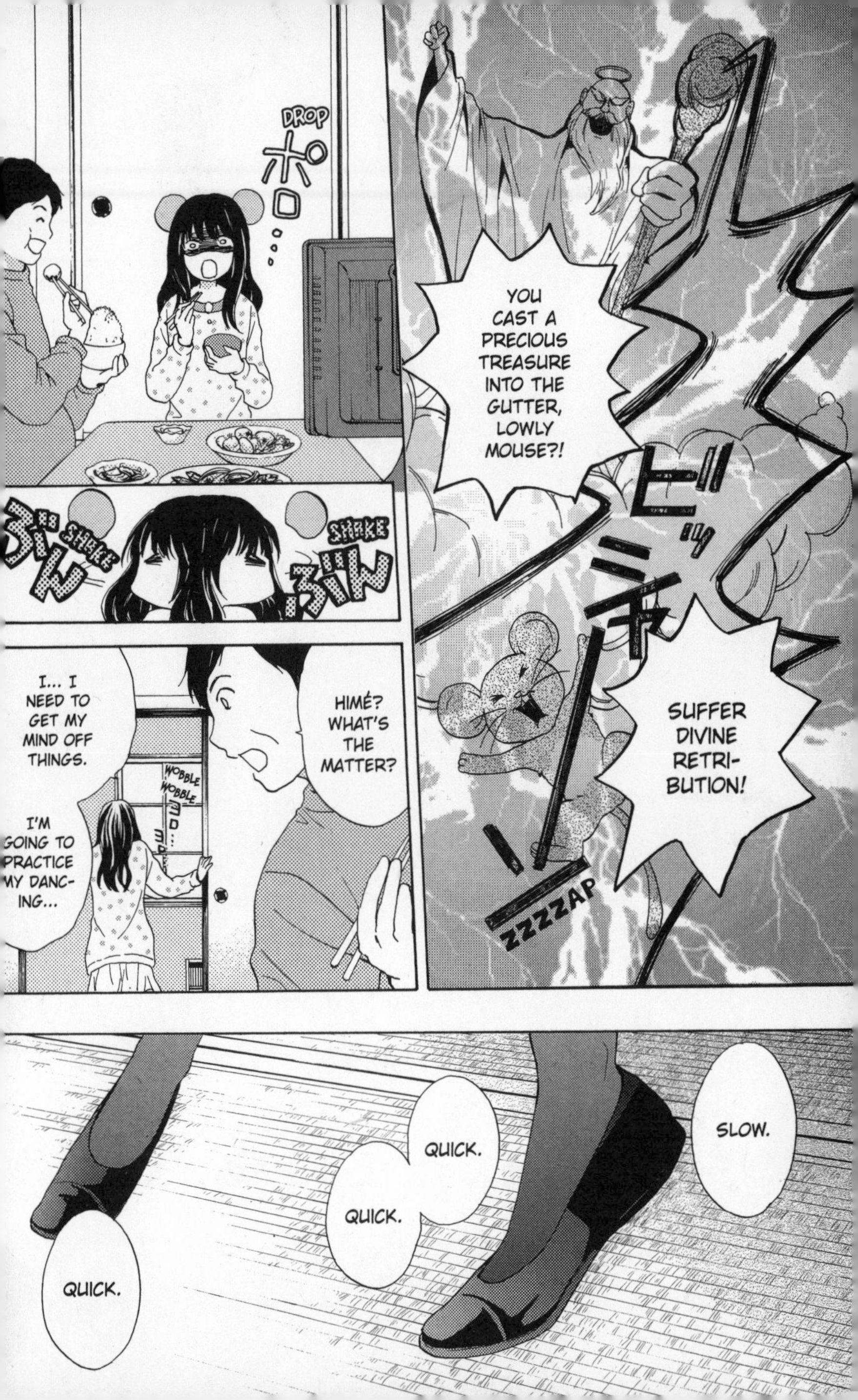
YOU CAST A PRECIOUS TREASURE INTO THE GUTTER, LOWLY MOUSE?!
ビッシャ
SUFFER DIVINE RETRI-BUTION!
ZZZZAP
DROP
ポロ
SHAKE
ぶん
SHAKE
ぶん
HIMÉ? WHAT'S THE MATTER?
I... I NEED TO GET MY MIND OFF THINGS.
I'M GOING TO PRACTICE MY DANC-ING...
WOBBLE WOBBLE
SLOW.
QUICK.
QUICK.
QUICK.

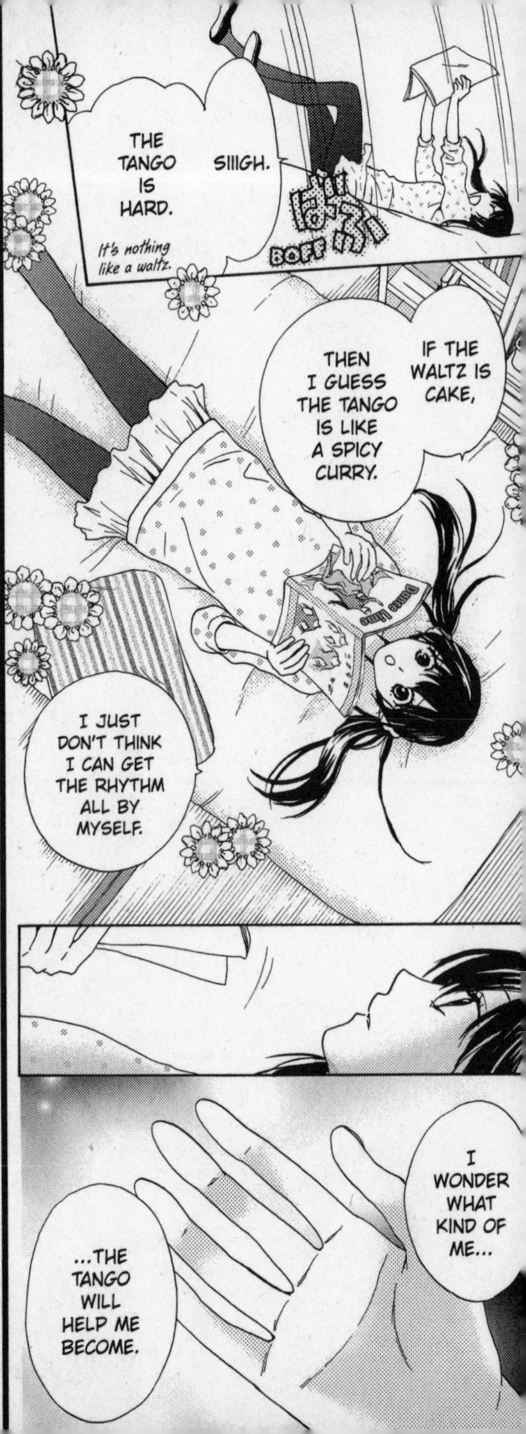
SIIIGH.
THE TANGO IS HARD.
It's nothing like a waltz.
BOFF
IF THE WALTZ IS CAKE,
THEN I GUESS THE TANGO IS LIKE A SPICY CURRY.
I JUST DON'T THINK I CAN GET THE RHYTHM ALL BY MYSELF.
I WONDER WHAT KIND OF ME...
...THE TANGO WILL HELP ME BECOME.

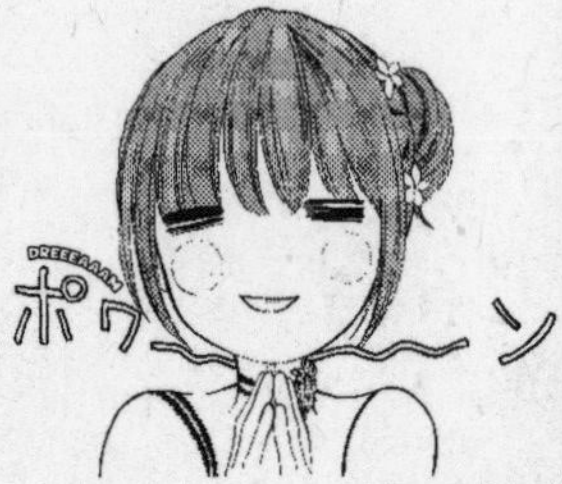
DREEEAAAM
ポワーン

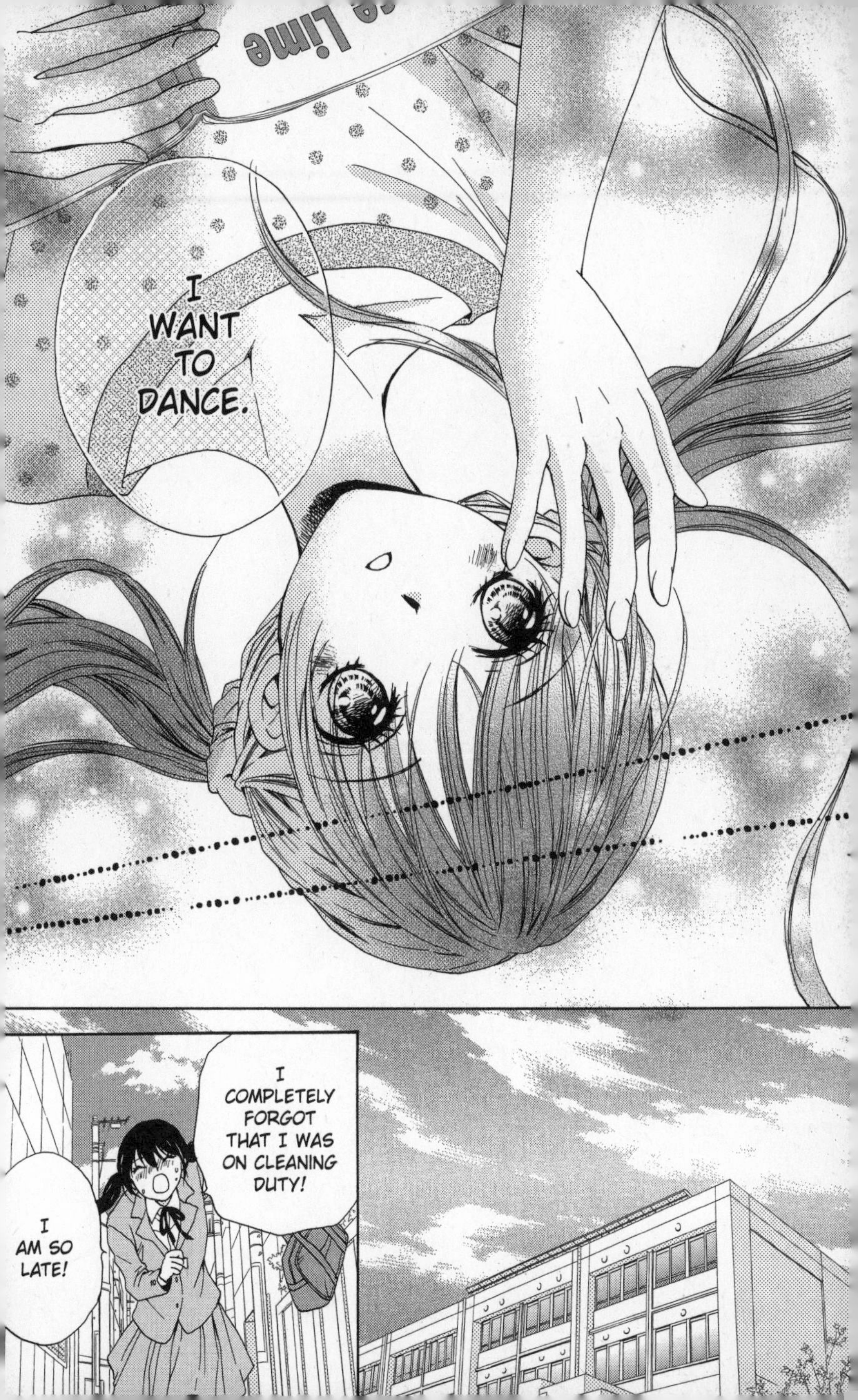
I WANT TO DANCE.
I COMPLETELY FORGOT THAT I WAS ON CLEANING DUTY!
I AM SO LATE!

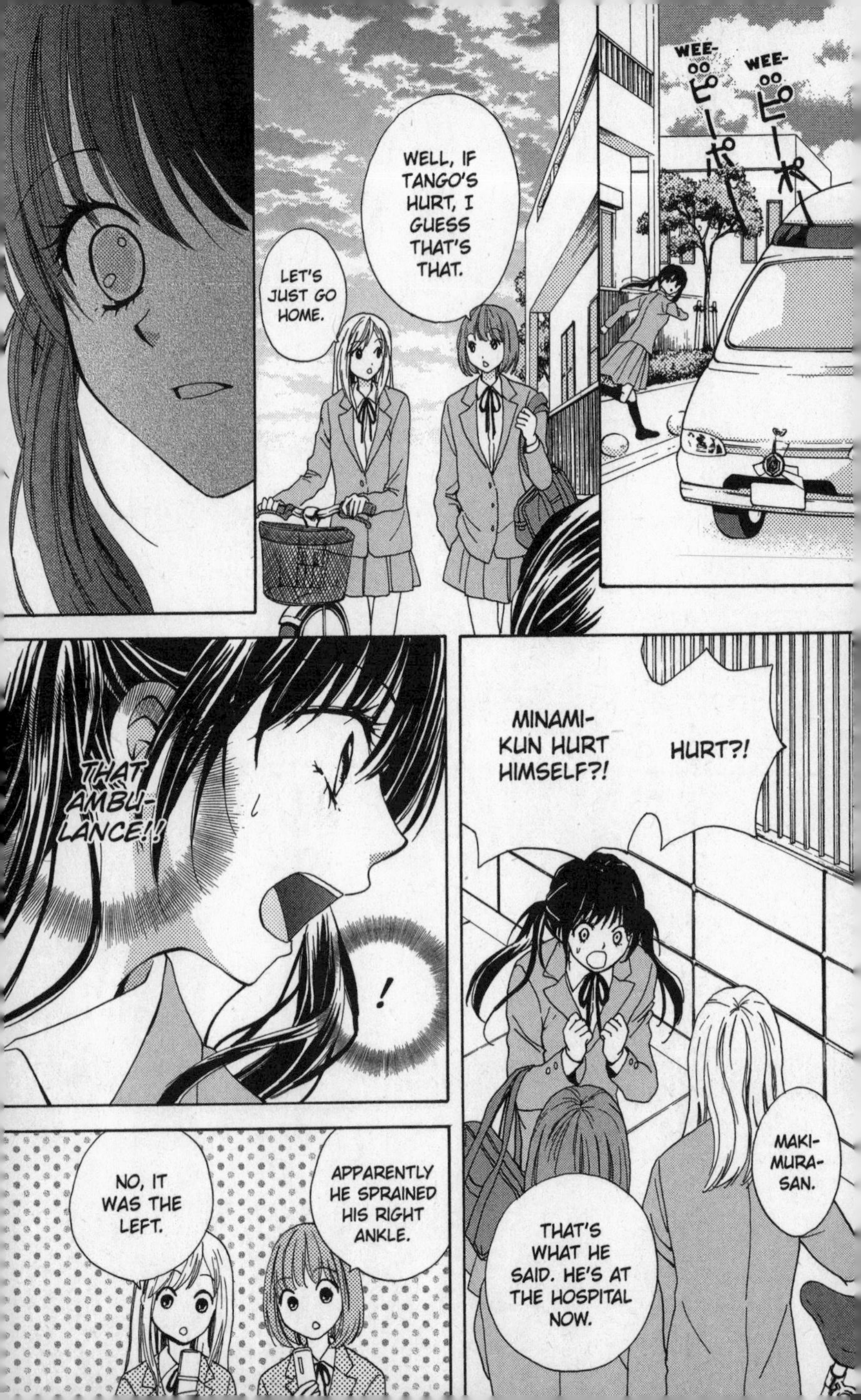
WEE-OO ピーポー
WEE-OO ピーポー
WELL, IF TANGO'S HURT, I GUESS THAT'S THAT.
LET'S JUST GO HOME.
HURT?!
MINAMI-KUN HURT HIMSELF?!
MAKIMURA-SAN.
THAT'S WHAT HE SAID. HE'S AT THE HOSPITAL NOW.
THAT AMBULANCE!!
!
APPARENTLY HE SPRAINED HIS RIGHT ANKLE.
NO, IT WAS THE LEFT.

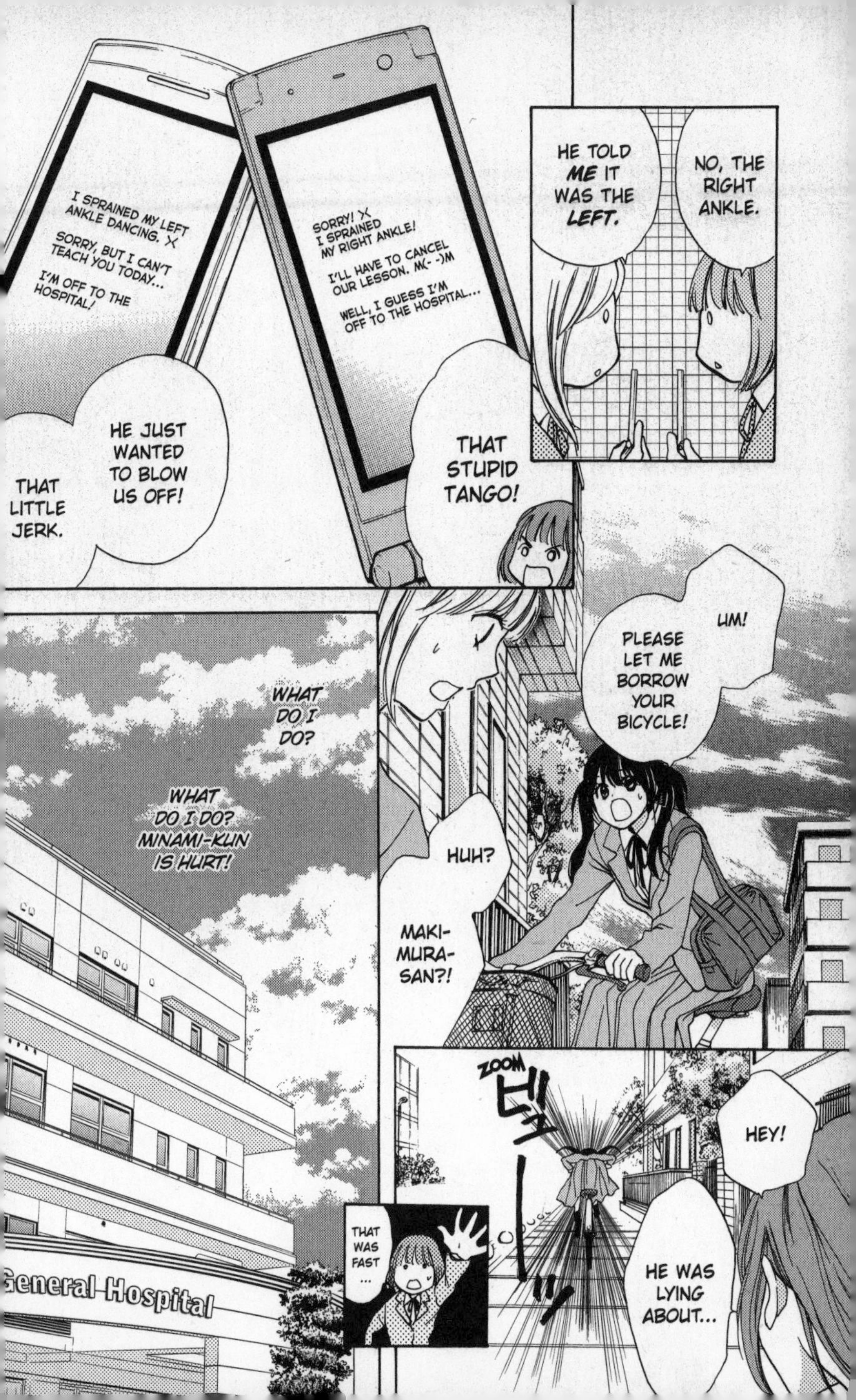
SORRY! ><
I SPRAINED MY RIGHT ANKLE!
I'LL HAVE TO CANCEL OUR LESSON. M(- -)M
WELL, I GUESS I'M OFF TO THE HOSPITAL...
I SPRAINED MY LEFT ANKLE DANCING. ><
SORRY, BUT I CAN'T TEACH YOU TODAY...
I'M OFF TO THE HOSPITAL!
NO, THE RIGHT ANKLE.
HE TOLD ME IT WAS THE LEFT.
THAT STUPID TANGO!
HE JUST WANTED TO BLOW US OFF!
THAT LITTLE JERK.
UM!
PLEASE LET ME BORROW YOUR BICYCLE!
HUH?
MAKI-MURA-SAN?!
HEY!
HE WAS LYING ABOUT...
ZOOM
THAT WAS FAST ...
WHAT DO I DO?
WHAT DO I DO? MINAMI-KUN IS HURT!
General Hospital

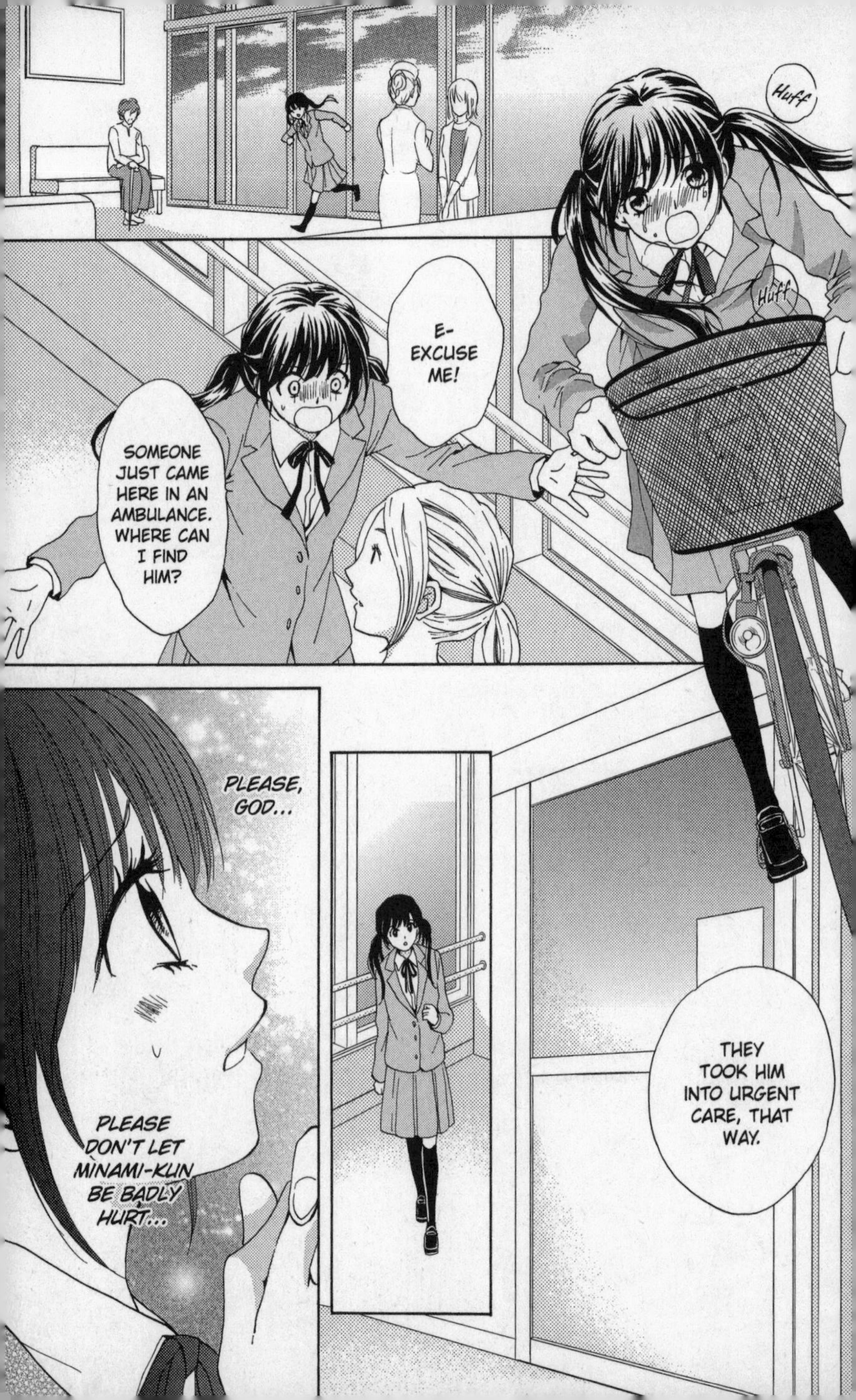
Huff
Huff
E- EXCUSE ME!
SOMEONE JUST CAME HERE IN AN AMBULANCE. WHERE CAN I FIND HIM?
THEY TOOK HIM INTO URGENT CARE, THAT WAY.
PLEASE, GOD...
PLEASE DON'T LET MINAMI-KUN BE BADLY HURT...

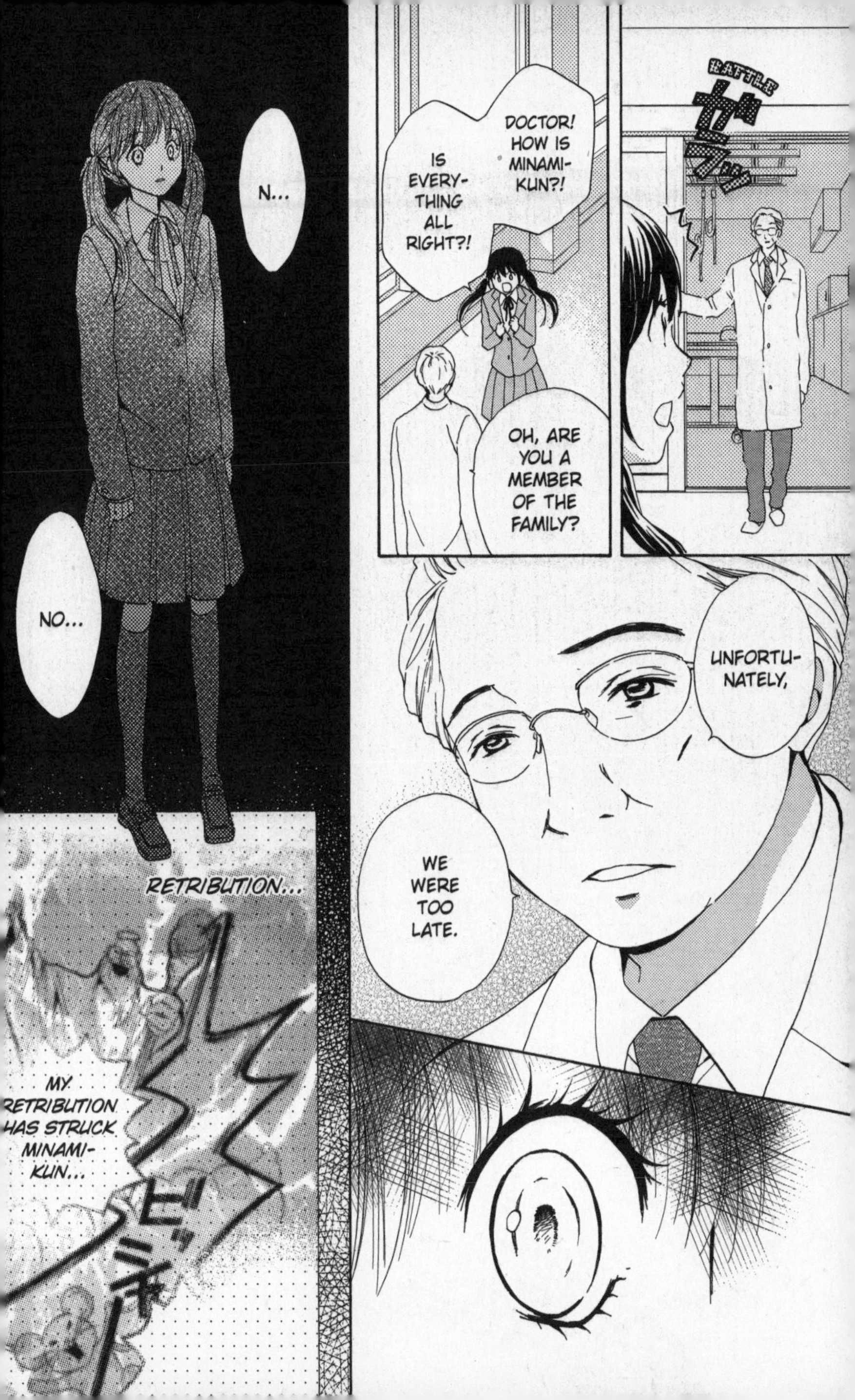
RATTLE
DOCTOR! HOW IS MINAMI-KUN?!
IS EVERY-THING ALL RIGHT?!
OH, ARE YOU A MEMBER OF THE FAMILY?
UNFORTU-NATELY,
WE WERE TOO LATE.
N...
NO...
RETRIBUTION...
MY RETRIBUTION HAS STRUCK MINAMI-KUN...

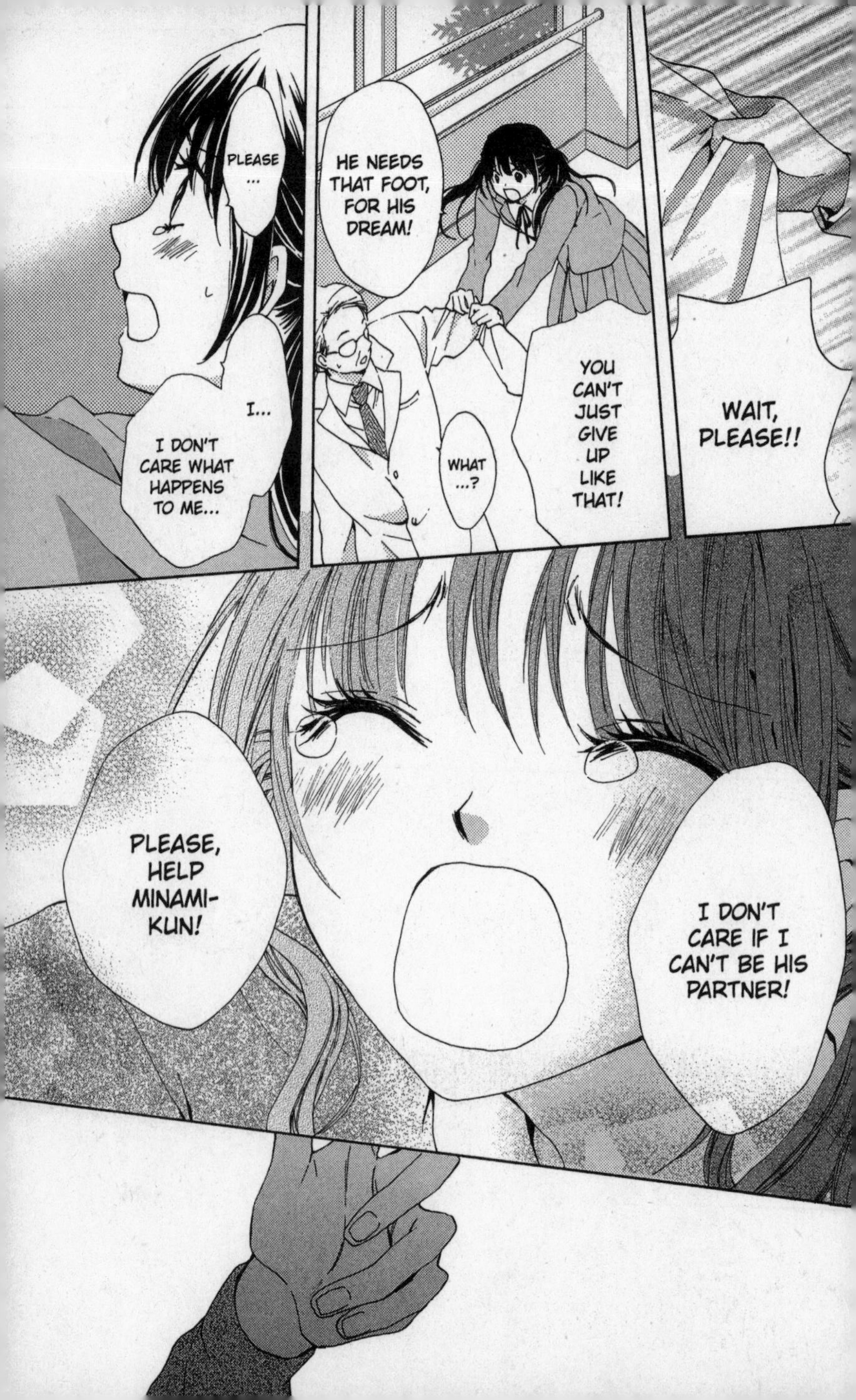
WAIT, PLEASE!!
YOU CAN'T JUST GIVE UP LIKE THAT!
HE NEEDS THAT FOOT, FOR HIS DREAM!
WHAT ...?
PLEASE ...
I...
I DON'T CARE WHAT HAPPENS TO ME...
I DON'T CARE IF I CAN'T BE HIS PARTNER!
PLEASE, HELP MINAMI-KUN!

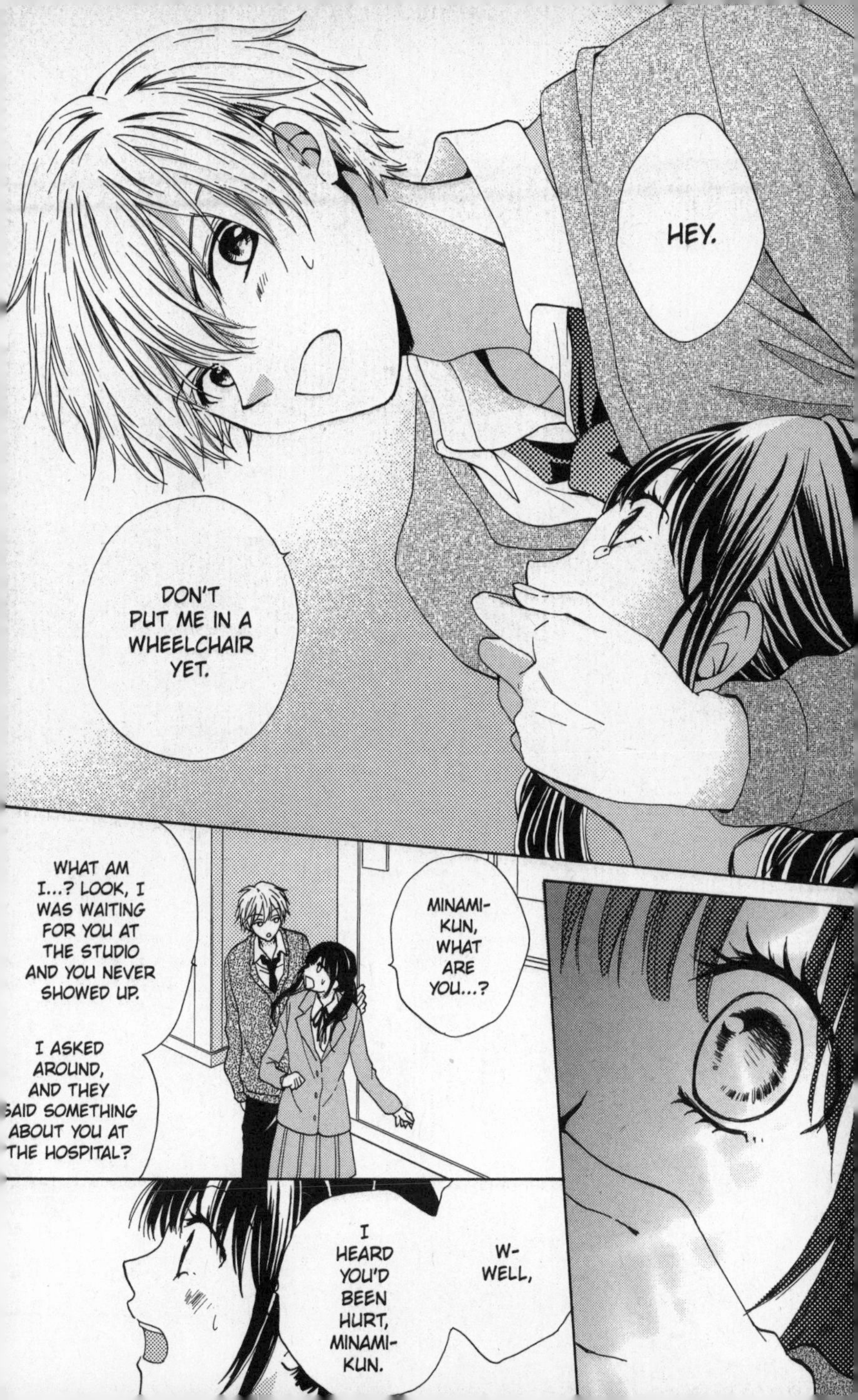
HEY.
DON'T PUT ME IN A WHEELCHAIR YET.
MINAMI-KUN, WHAT ARE YOU...?
WHAT AM I...? LOOK, I WAS WAITING FOR YOU AT THE STUDIO AND YOU NEVER SHOWED UP.
I ASKED AROUND, AND THEY SAID SOMETHING ABOUT YOU AT THE HOSPITAL?
W-WELL,
I HEARD YOU'D BEEN HURT, MINAMI-KUN.

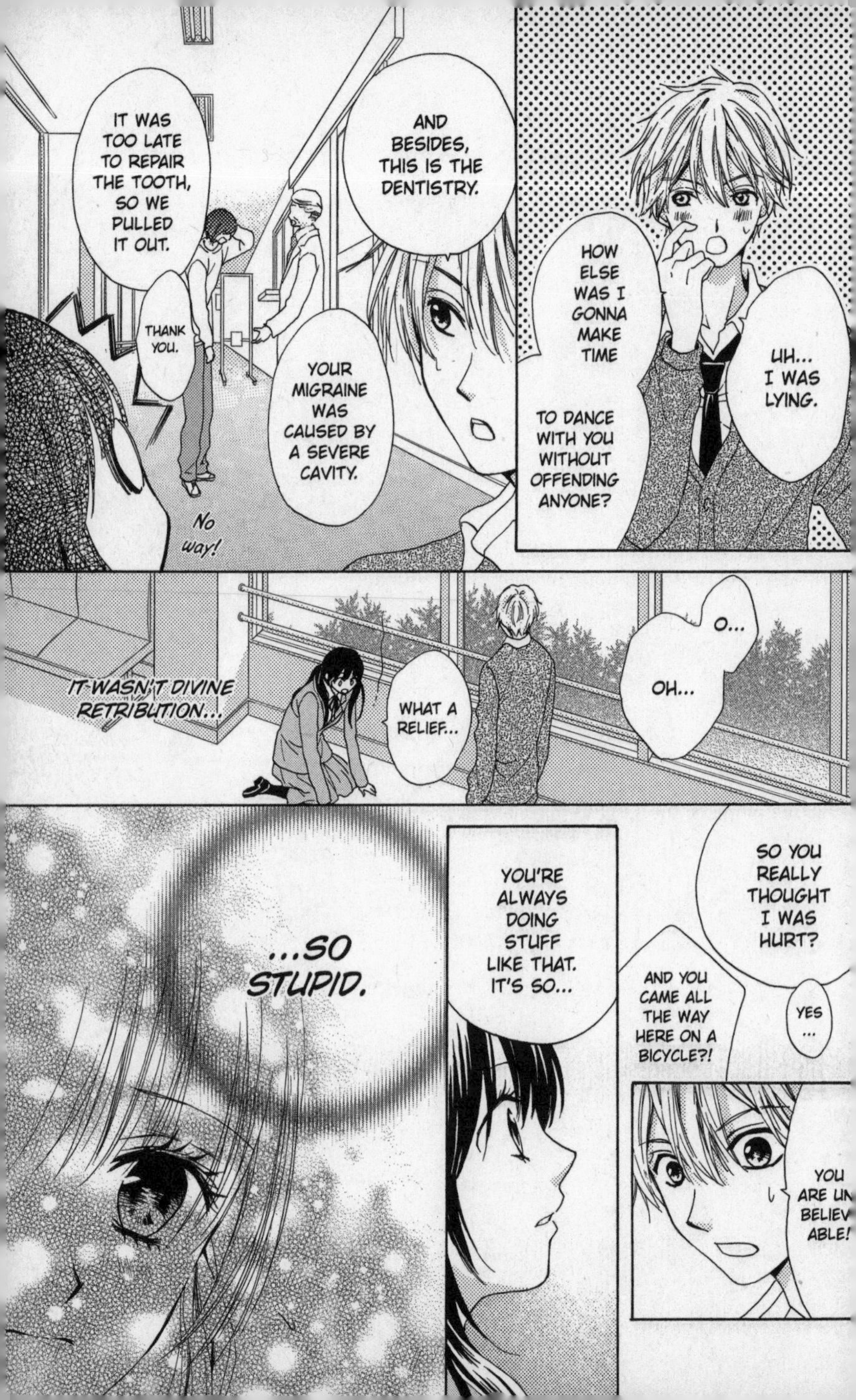
UH... I WAS LYING.
HOW ELSE WAS I GONNA MAKE TIME
TO DANCE WITH YOU WITHOUT OFFENDING ANYONE?
AND BESIDES, THIS IS THE DENTISTRY.
YOUR MIGRAINE WAS CAUSED BY A SEVERE CAVITY.
IT WAS TOO LATE TO REPAIR THE TOOTH, SO WE PULLED IT OUT.
THANK YOU.
No way!
O...
OH...
WHAT A RELIEF...
IT WASN'T DIVINE RETRIBUTION...
SO YOU REALLY THOUGHT I WAS HURT?
YES...
AND YOU CAME ALL THE WAY HERE ON A BICYCLE?!
YOU ARE UN BELIEV ABLE!
YOU'RE ALWAYS DOING STUFF LIKE THAT. IT'S SO...
...SO STUPID.

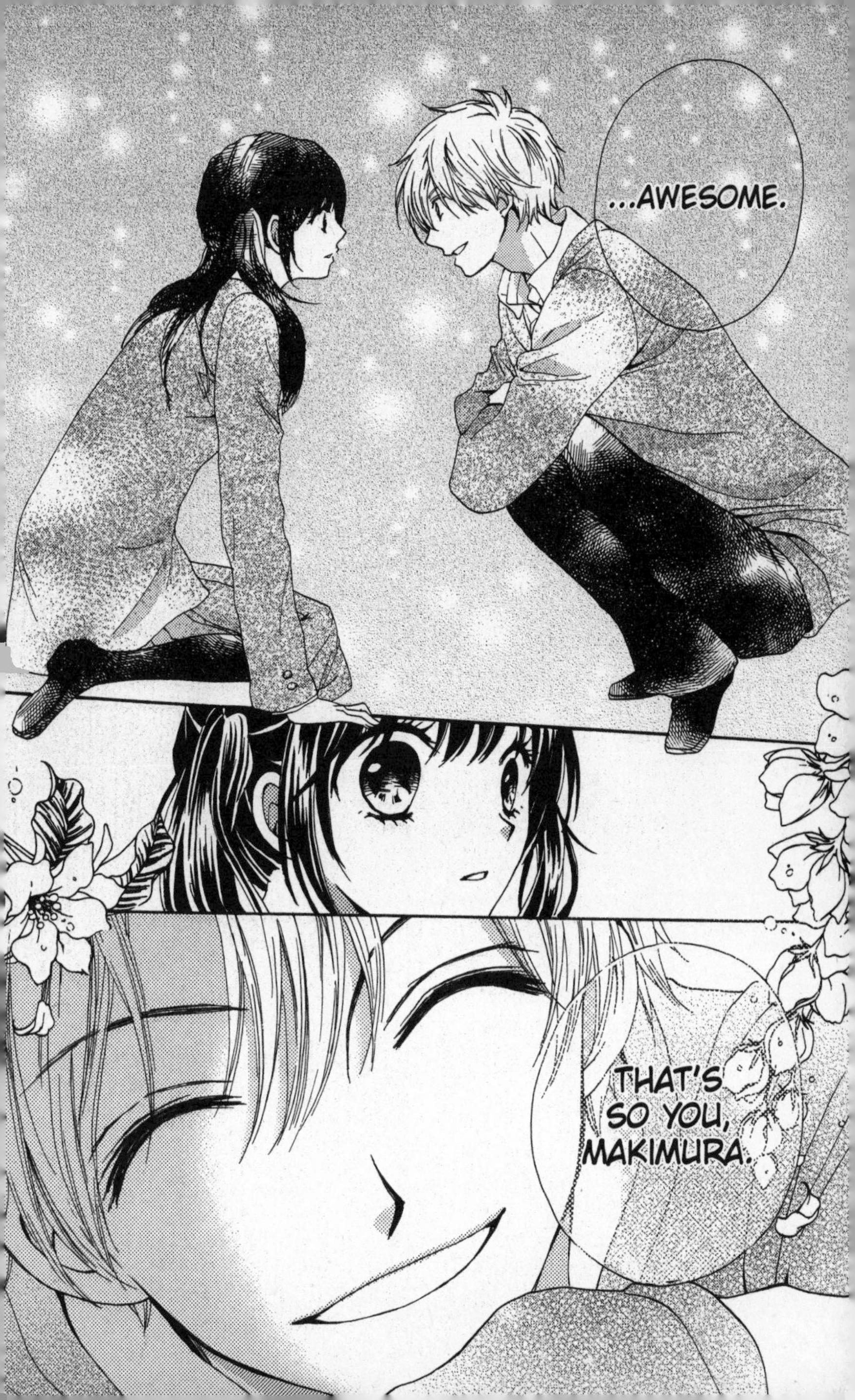
...AWESOME.
THAT'S SO YOU, MAKIMURA.

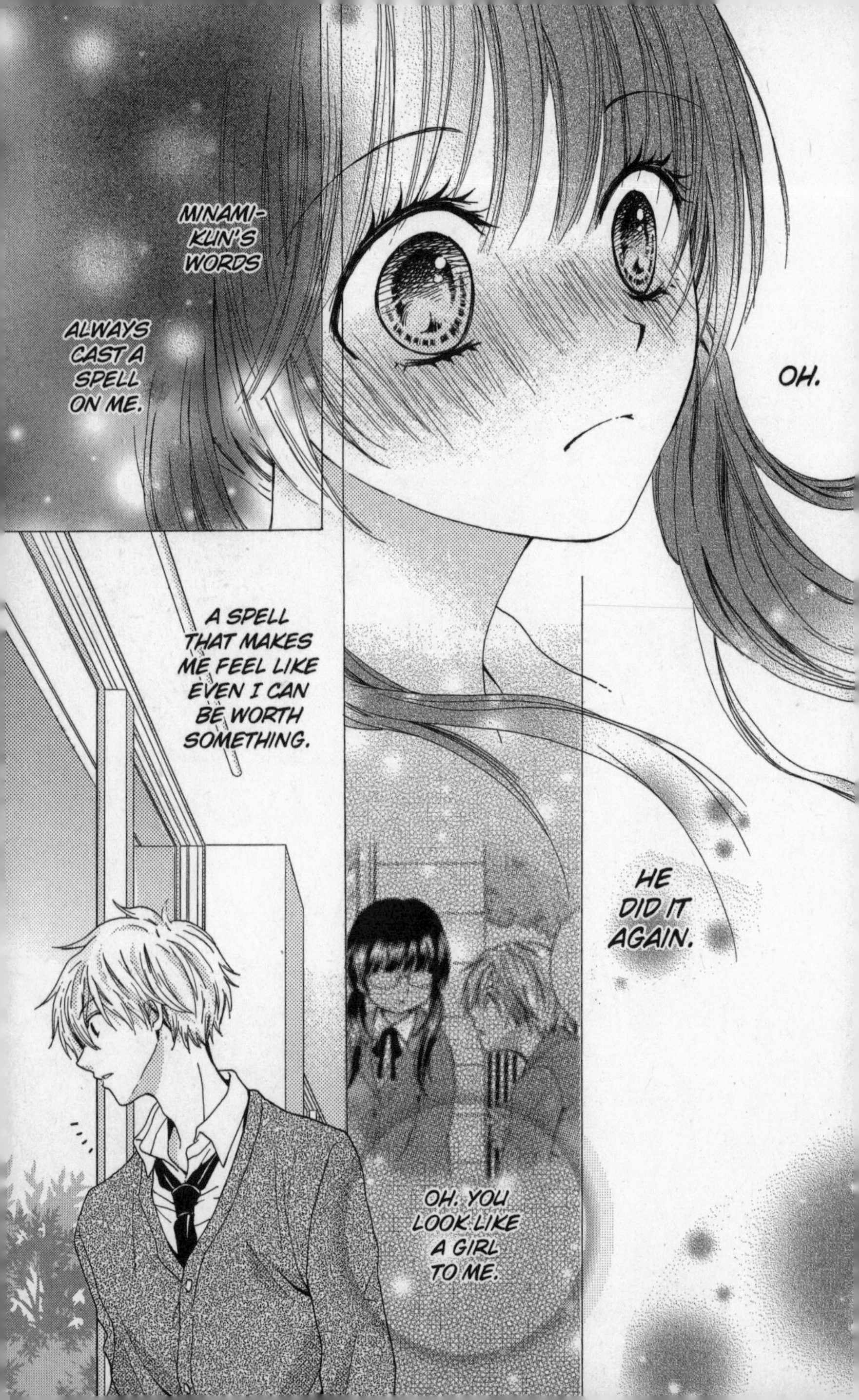
OH.
HE DID IT AGAIN.
OH. YOU LOOK LIKE A GIRL TO ME.
MINAMI-KUN'S WORDS
ALWAYS CAST A SPELL ON ME.
A SPELL THAT MAKES ME FEEL LIKE EVEN I CAN BE WORTH SOMETHING.

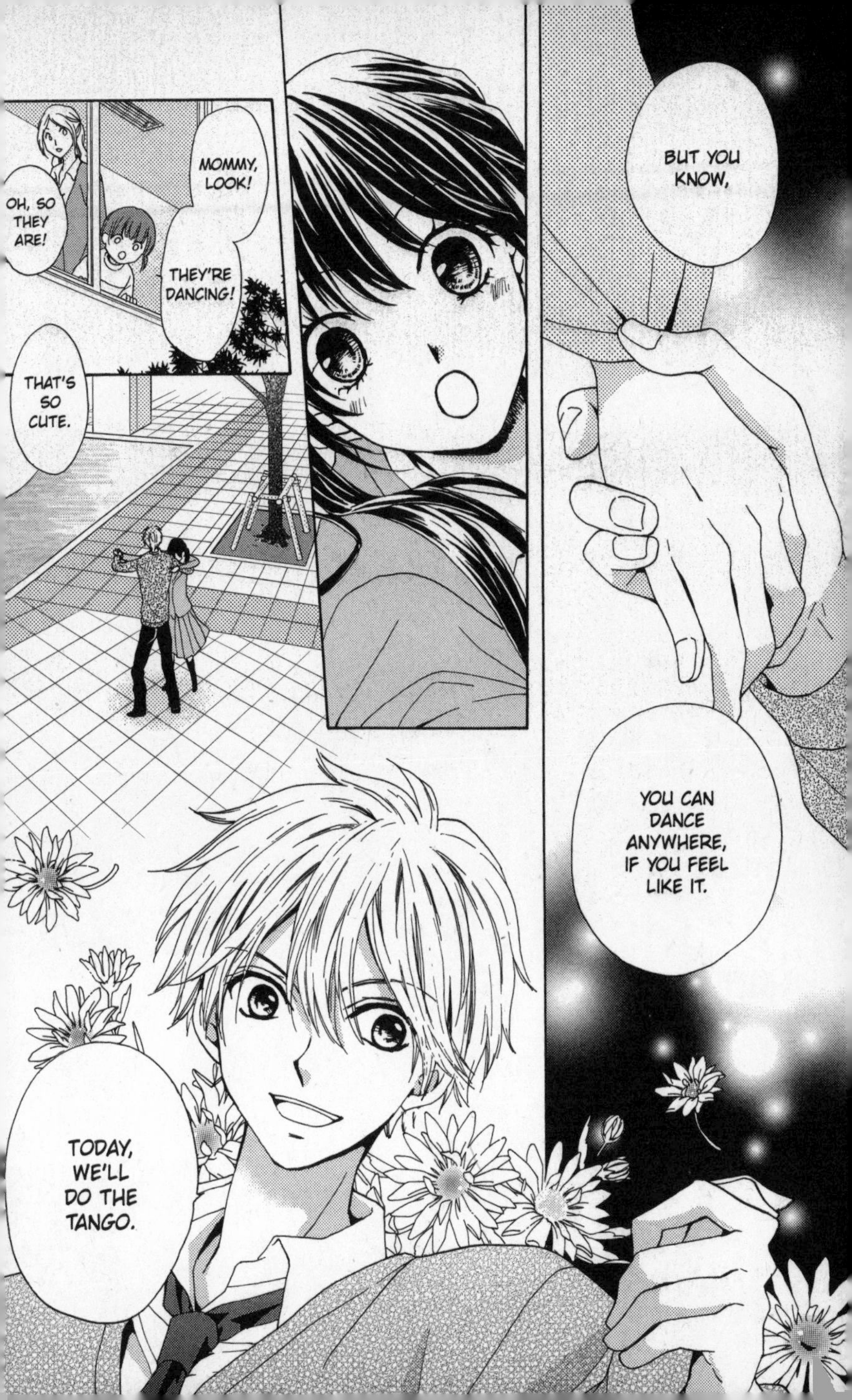
BUT YOU KNOW,
YOU CAN DANCE ANYWHERE, IF YOU FEEL LIKE IT.
MOMMY, LOOK!
THEY'RE DANCING!
OH, SO THEY ARE!
THAT'S SO CUTE.
TODAY, WE'LL DO THE TANGO.

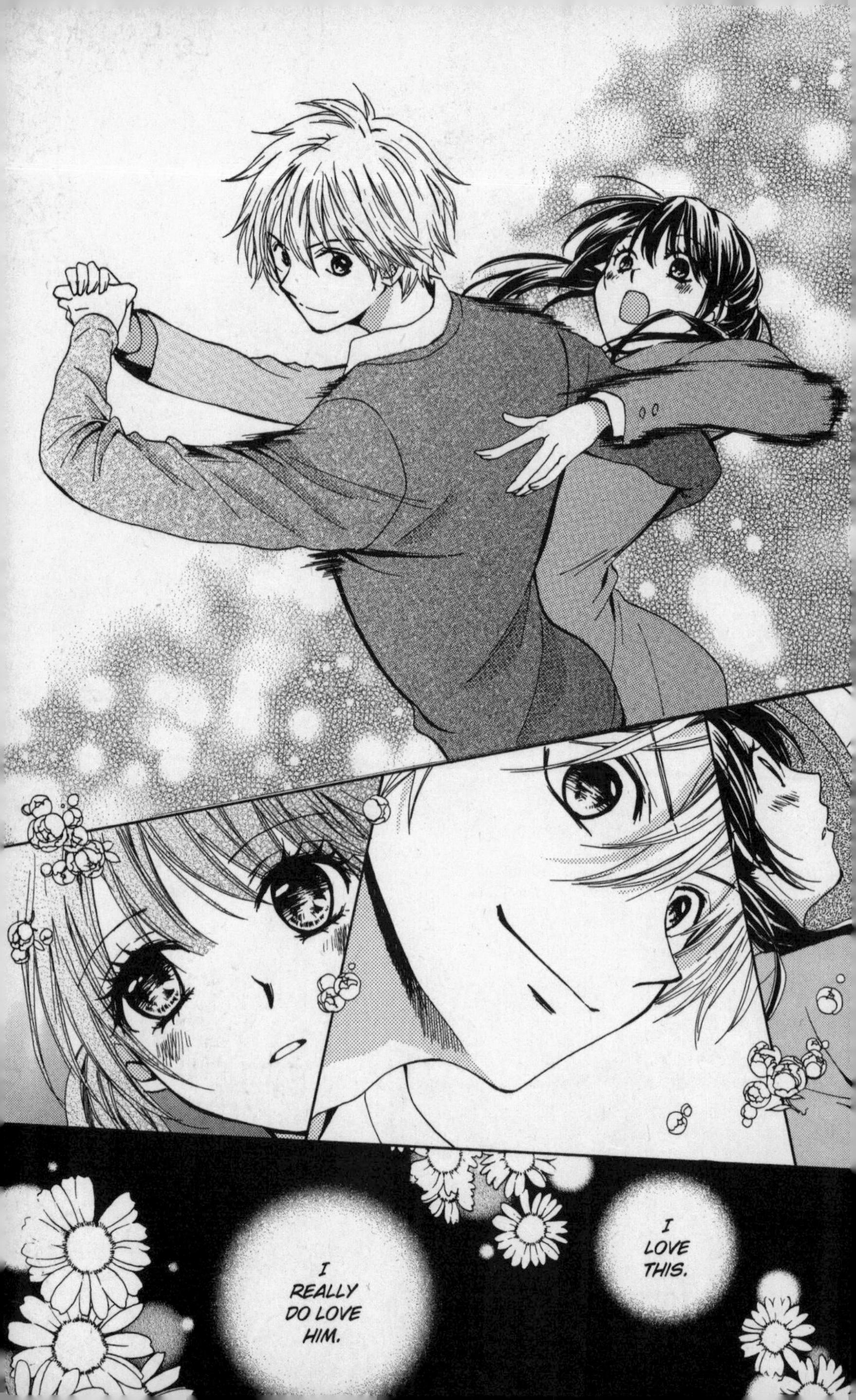
I LOVE THIS.
I REALLY DO LOVE HIM.

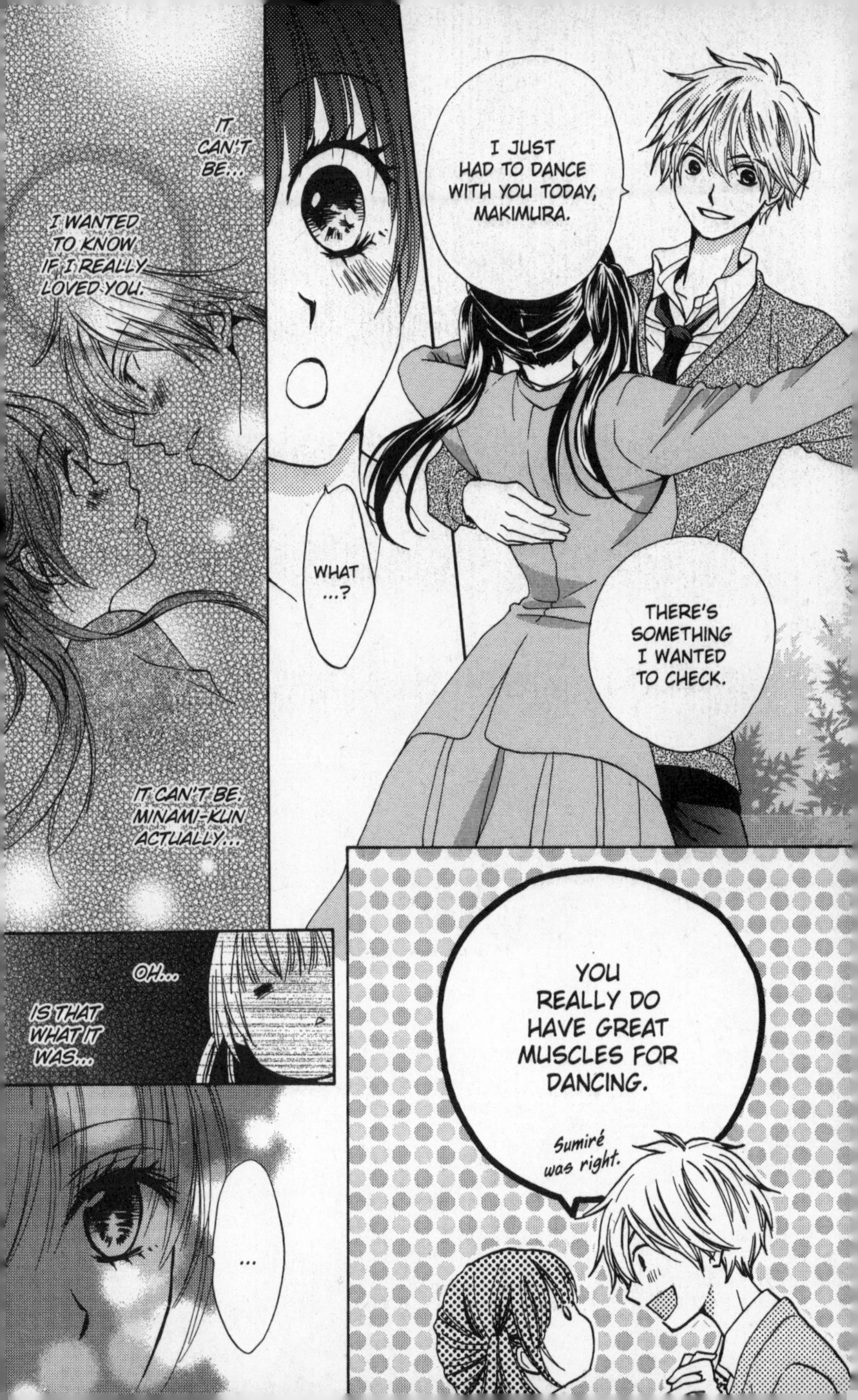

I JUST HAD TO DANCE WITH YOU TODAY, MAKIMURA.
WHAT ...?
THERE'S SOMETHING I WANTED TO CHECK.
IT CAN'T BE...
I WANTED TO KNOW IF I REALLY LOVED YOU.
IT CAN'T BE. MINAMI-KUN ACTUALLY...
YOU REALLY DO HAVE GREAT MUSCLES FOR DANCING.
Sumiré was right.
OH...
IS THAT WHAT IT WAS...
...

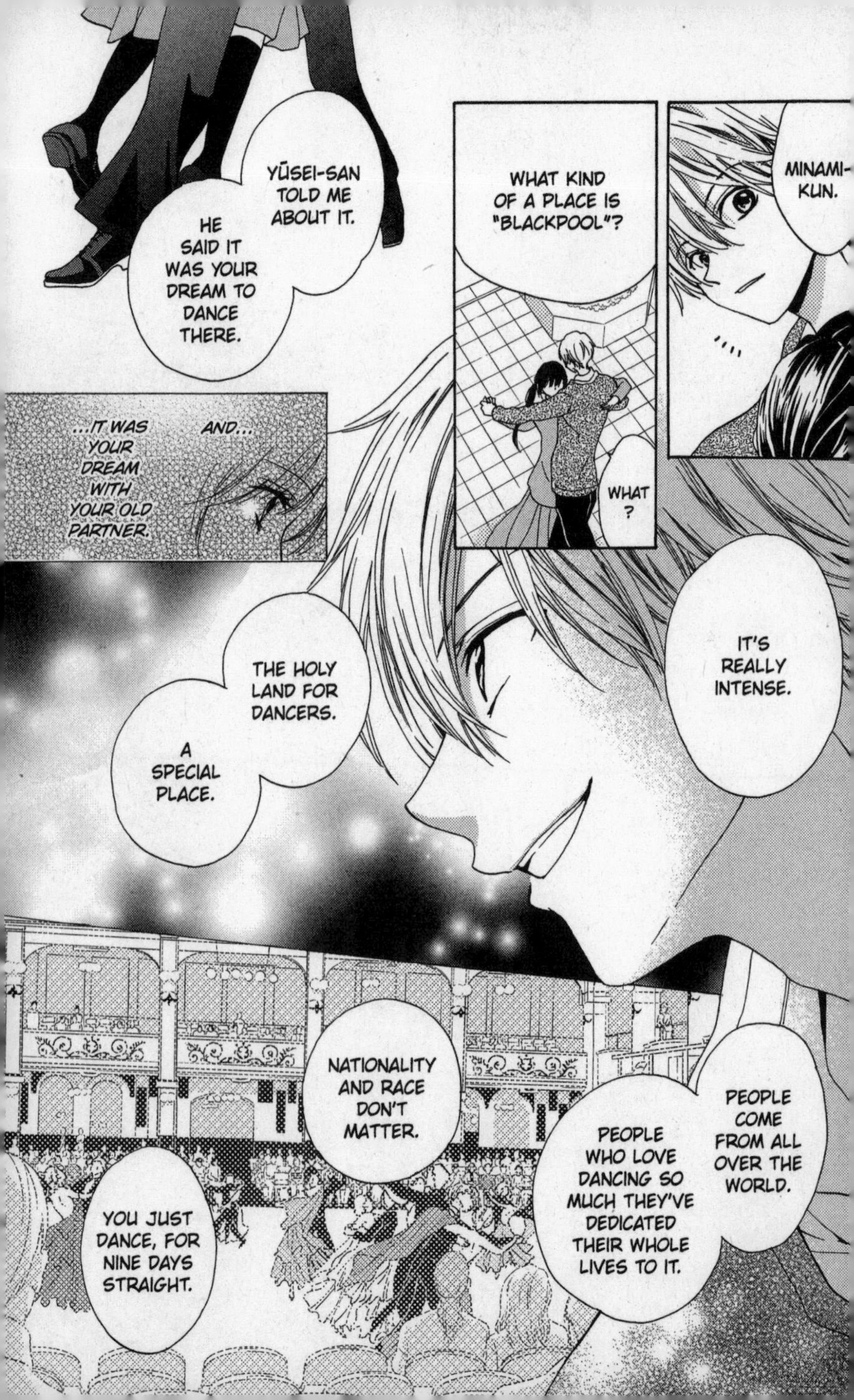
MINAMI-KUN.
...
WHAT KIND OF A PLACE IS "BLACKPOOL"?
WHAT?
YŪSEI-SAN TOLD ME ABOUT IT.
HE SAID IT WAS YOUR DREAM TO DANCE THERE.
AND...
...IT WAS YOUR DREAM WITH YOUR OLD PARTNER.
IT'S REALLY INTENSE.
THE HOLY LAND FOR DANCERS.
A SPECIAL PLACE.
PEOPLE COME FROM ALL OVER THE WORLD.
PEOPLE WHO LOVE DANCING SO MUCH THEY'VE DEDICATED THEIR WHOLE LIVES TO IT.
NATIONALITY AND RACE DON'T MATTER.
YOU JUST DANCE, FOR NINE DAYS STRAIGHT.

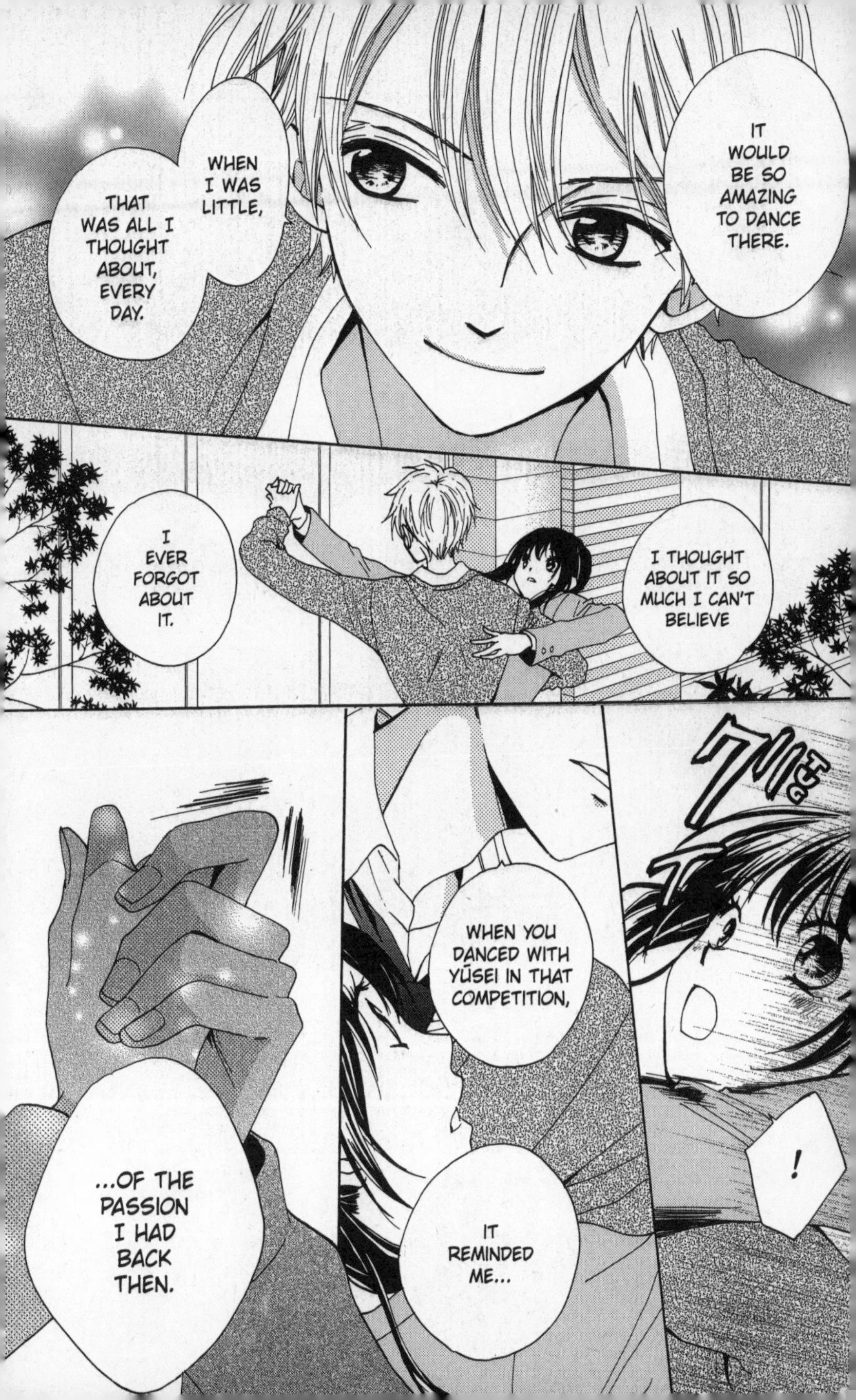
IT WOULD BE SO AMAZING TO DANCE THERE.
WHEN I WAS LITTLE,
THAT WAS ALL I THOUGHT ABOUT, EVERY DAY.
I THOUGHT ABOUT IT SO MUCH I CAN'T BELIEVE
I EVER FORGOT ABOUT IT.
!
WHEN YOU DANCED WITH YŪSEI IN THAT COMPETITION,
IT REMINDED ME...
...OF THE PASSION I HAD BACK THEN.

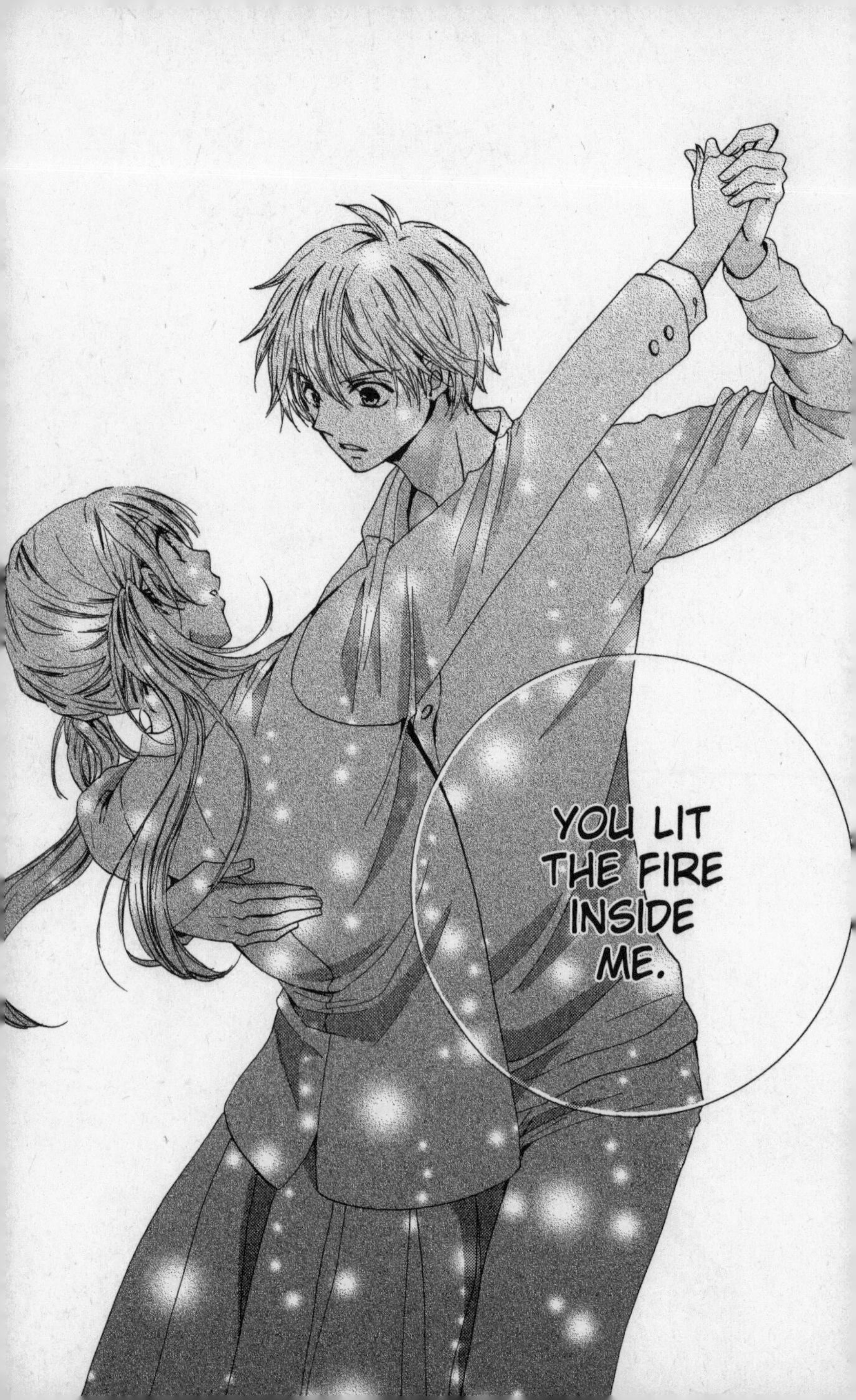
YOU LIT THE FIRE INSIDE ME.

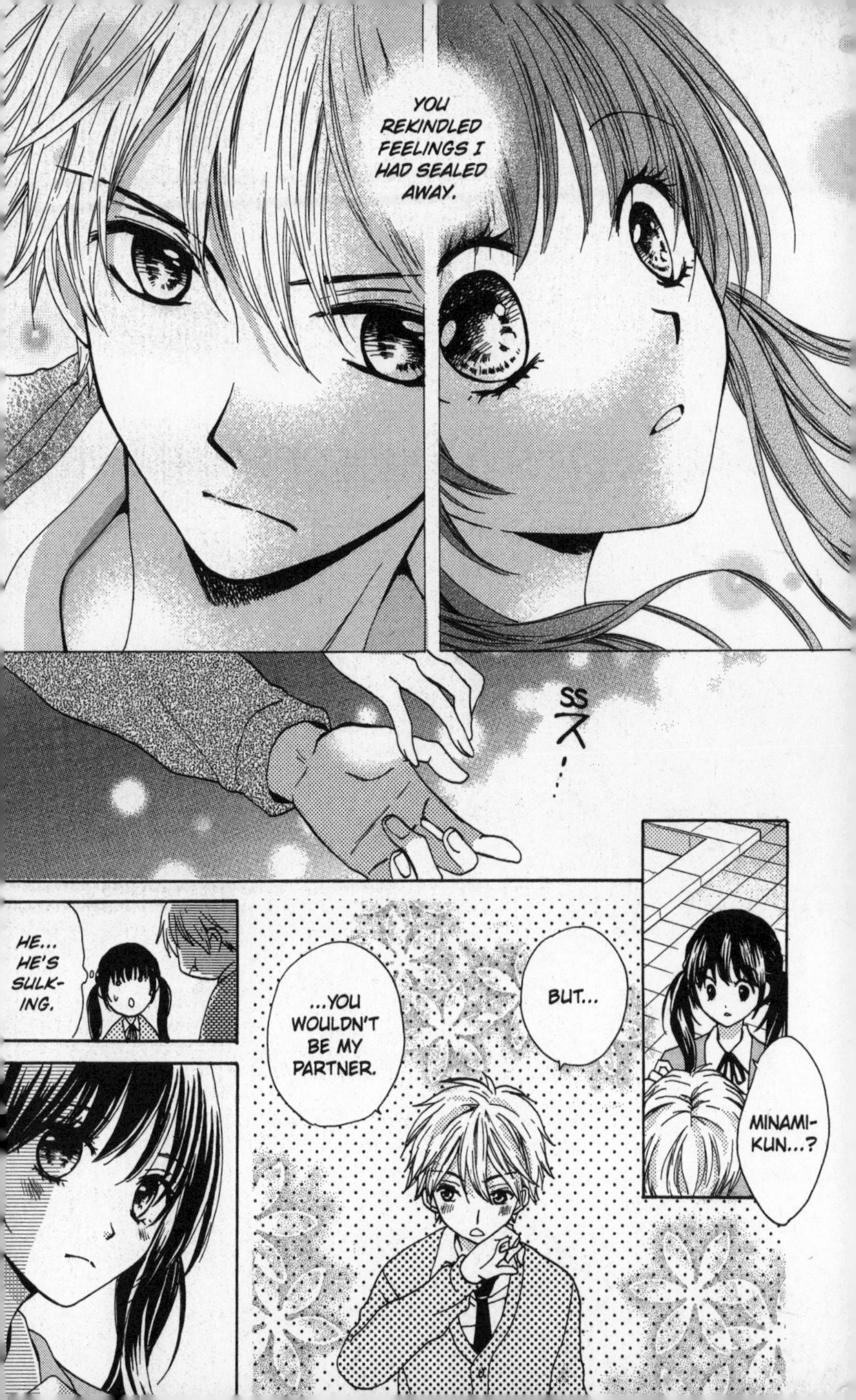
YOU REKINDLED FEELINGS I HAD SEALED AWAY.
SS
MINAMI-KUN...?
BUT...
...YOU WOULDN'T BE MY PARTNER.
HE... HE'S SULK-ING.

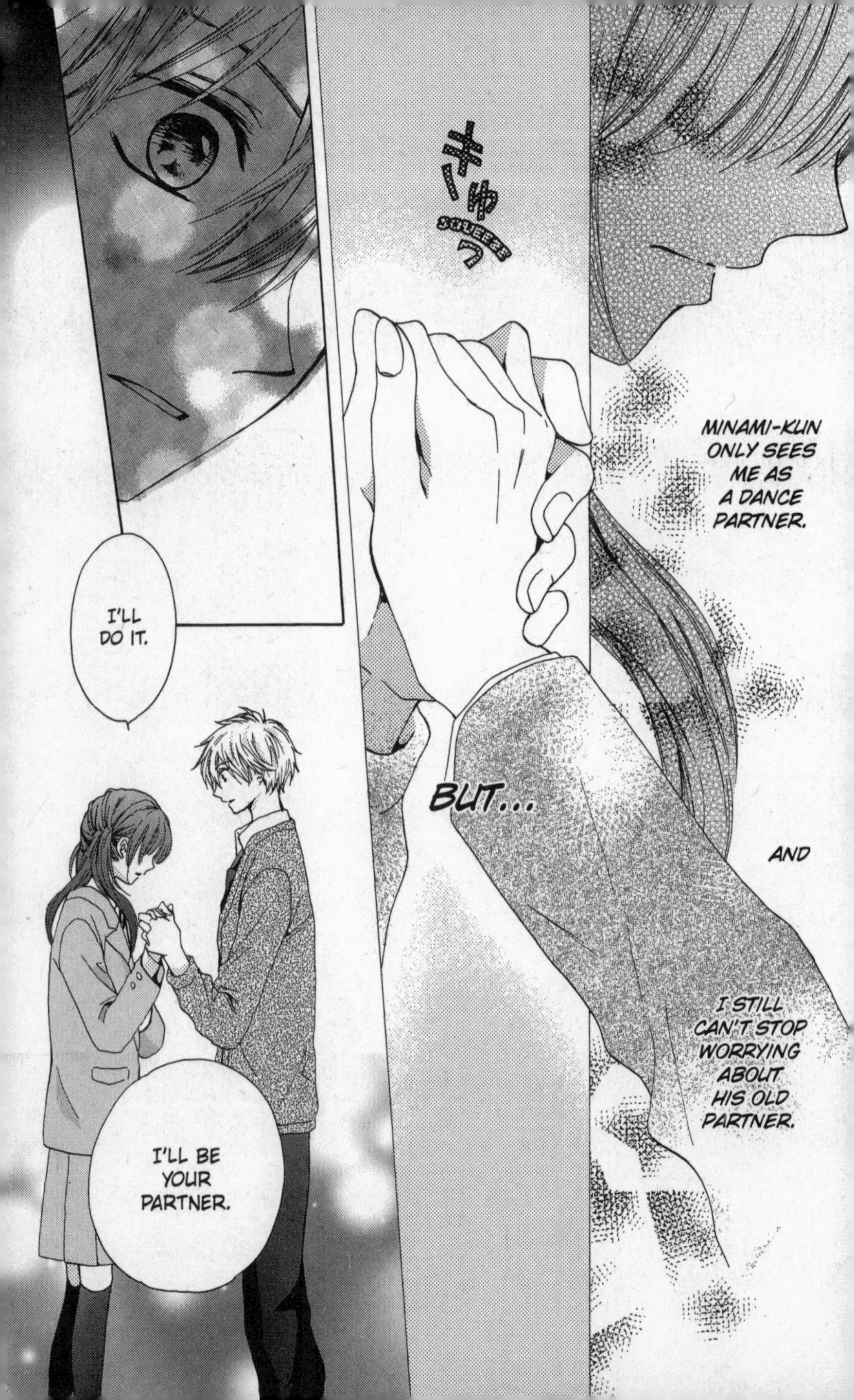
MINAMI-KUN ONLY SEES ME AS A DANCE PARTNER.
AND
I STILL CAN'T STOP WORRYING ABOUT HIS OLD PARTNER.
きゅっ
SQUEEZE
BUT...
I'LL DO IT.
I'LL BE YOUR PARTNER.

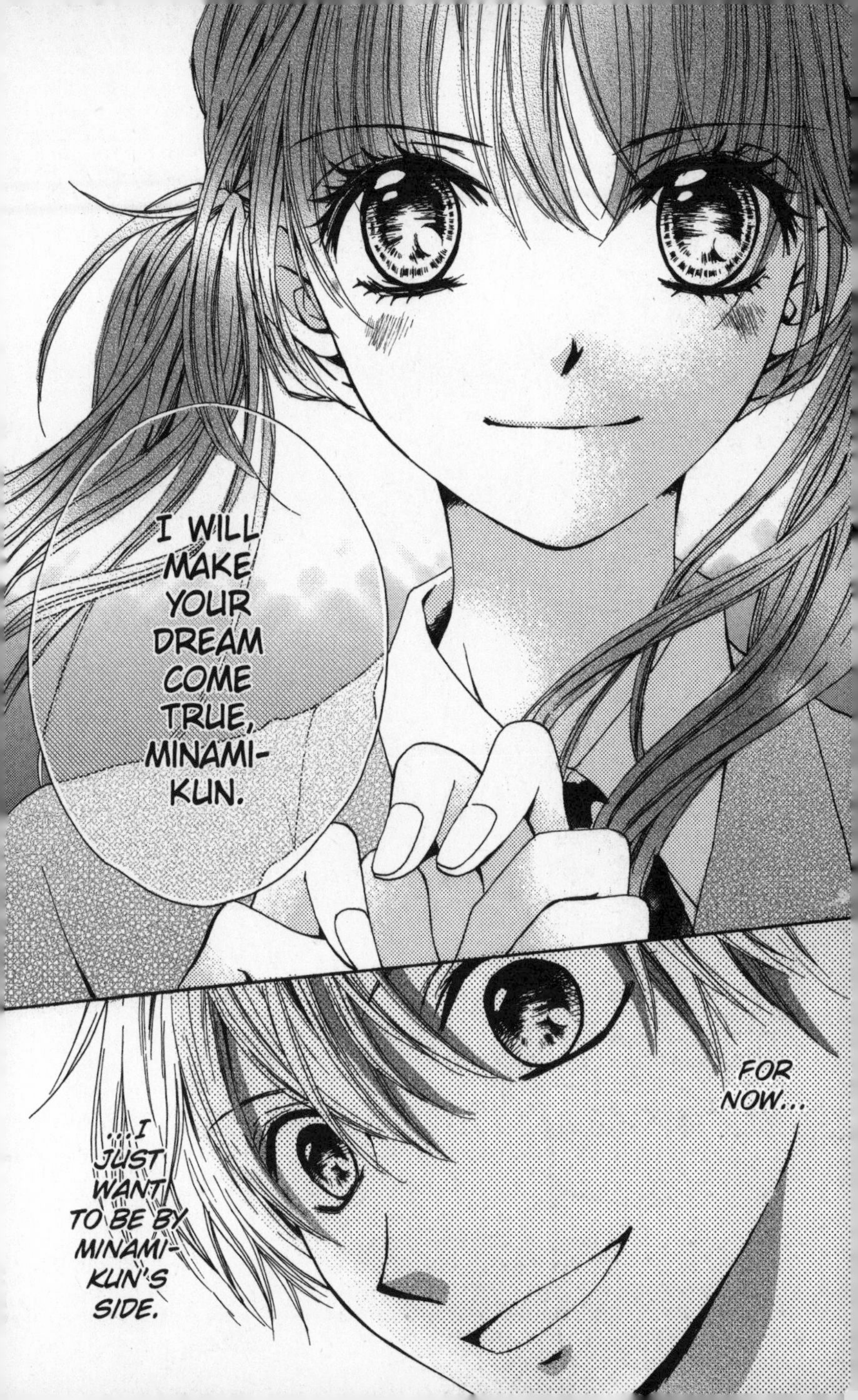
I WILL MAKE YOUR DREAM COME TRUE, MINAMI-KUN.
FOR NOW...
...I JUST WANT TO BE BY MINAMI-KUN'S SIDE.

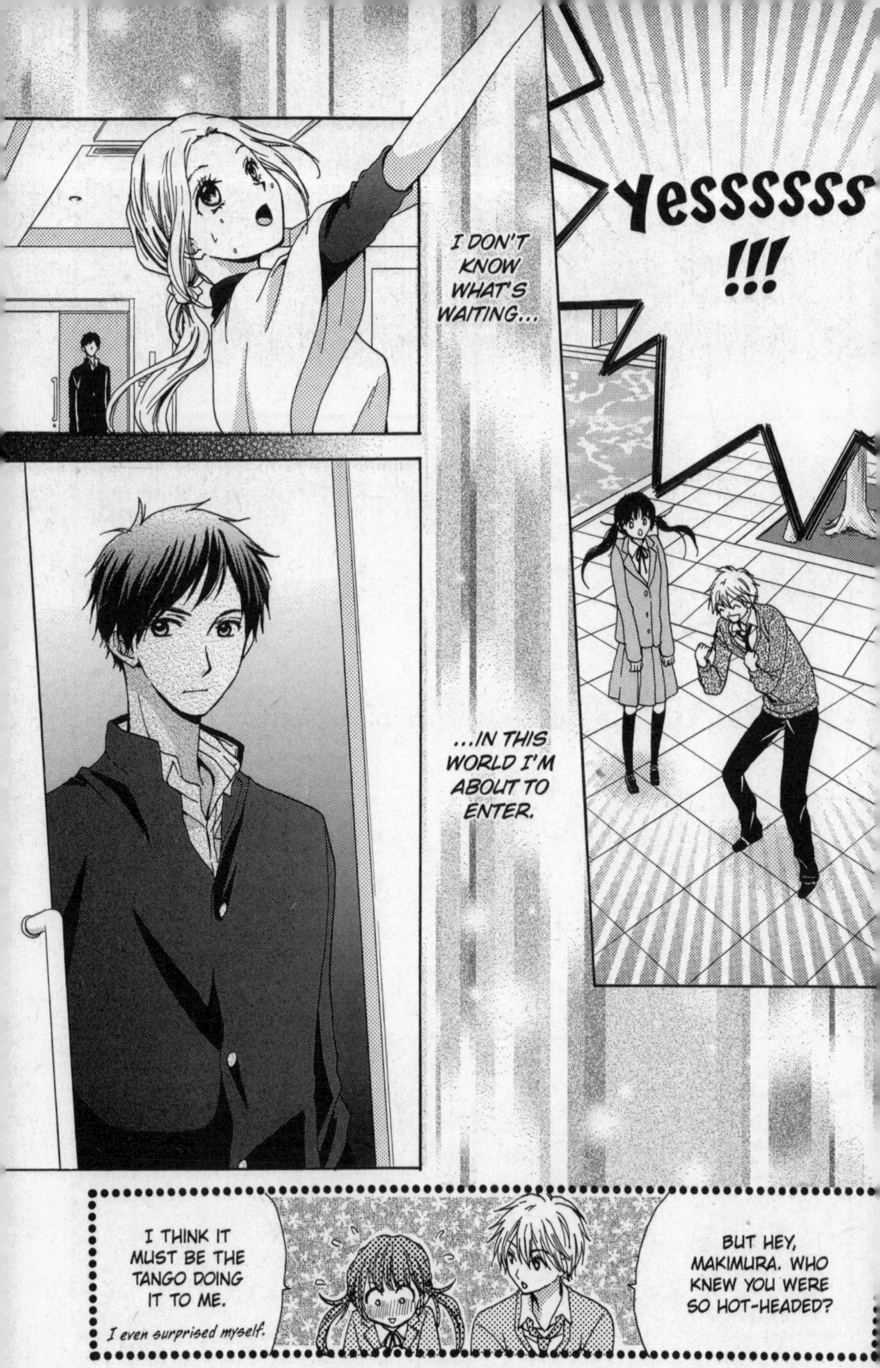
Yessssss !!!
I DON'T KNOW WHAT'S WAITING...
...IN THIS WORLD I'M ABOUT TO ENTER.
BUT HEY, MAKIMURA. WHO KNEW YOU WERE SO HOT-HEADED?
I THINK IT MUST BE THE TANGO DOING IT TO ME.
I even surprised myself.

LET'S READ A FOUR-PANEL COMIC

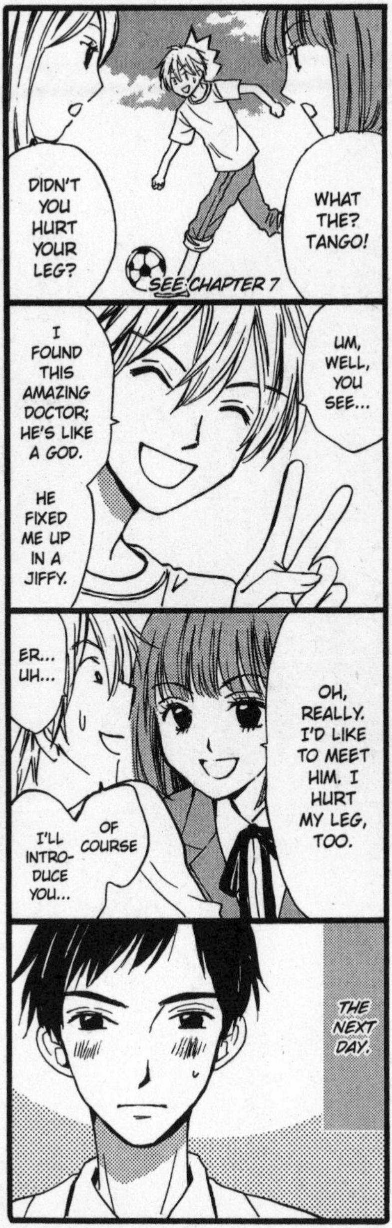
WHAT THE? TANGO!
DIDN'T YOU HURT YOUR LEG?
SEE CHAPTER 7
UM, WELL, YOU SEE...
I FOUND THIS AMAZING DOCTOR; HE'S LIKE A GOD.
HE FIXED ME UP IN A JIFFY.
OH, REALLY. I'D LIKE TO MEET HIM. I HURT MY LEG, TOO.
ER... UH...
OF COURSE
I'LL INTRO-DUCE YOU...
THE NEXT DAY.

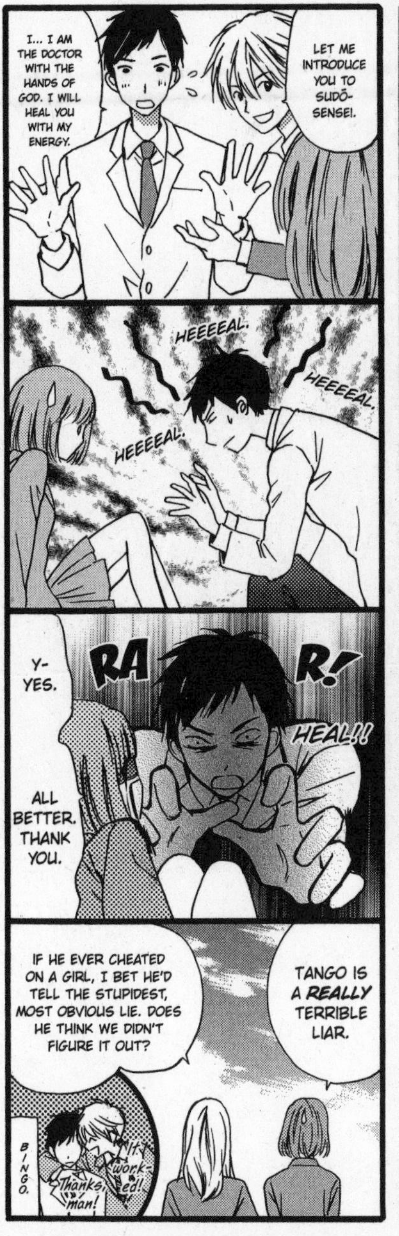
LET ME INTRODUCE YOU TO SUDŌ-SENSEI.
I... I AM THE DOCTOR WITH THE HANDS OF GOD. I WILL HEAL YOU WITH MY ENERGY.
HEEEEAL.
HEEEEAL.
HEEEEAL.
RA R!
HEAL!!
Y-YES.
ALL BETTER. THANK YOU.
TANGO IS A REALLY TERRIBLE LIAR.
IF HE EVER CHEATED ON A GIRL, I BET HE'D TELL THE STUPIDEST, MOST OBVIOUS LIE. DOES HE THINK WE DIDN'T FIGURE IT OUT?
It worked!
Thanks, man!
BINGO.

Chapter 8: Our Waltz

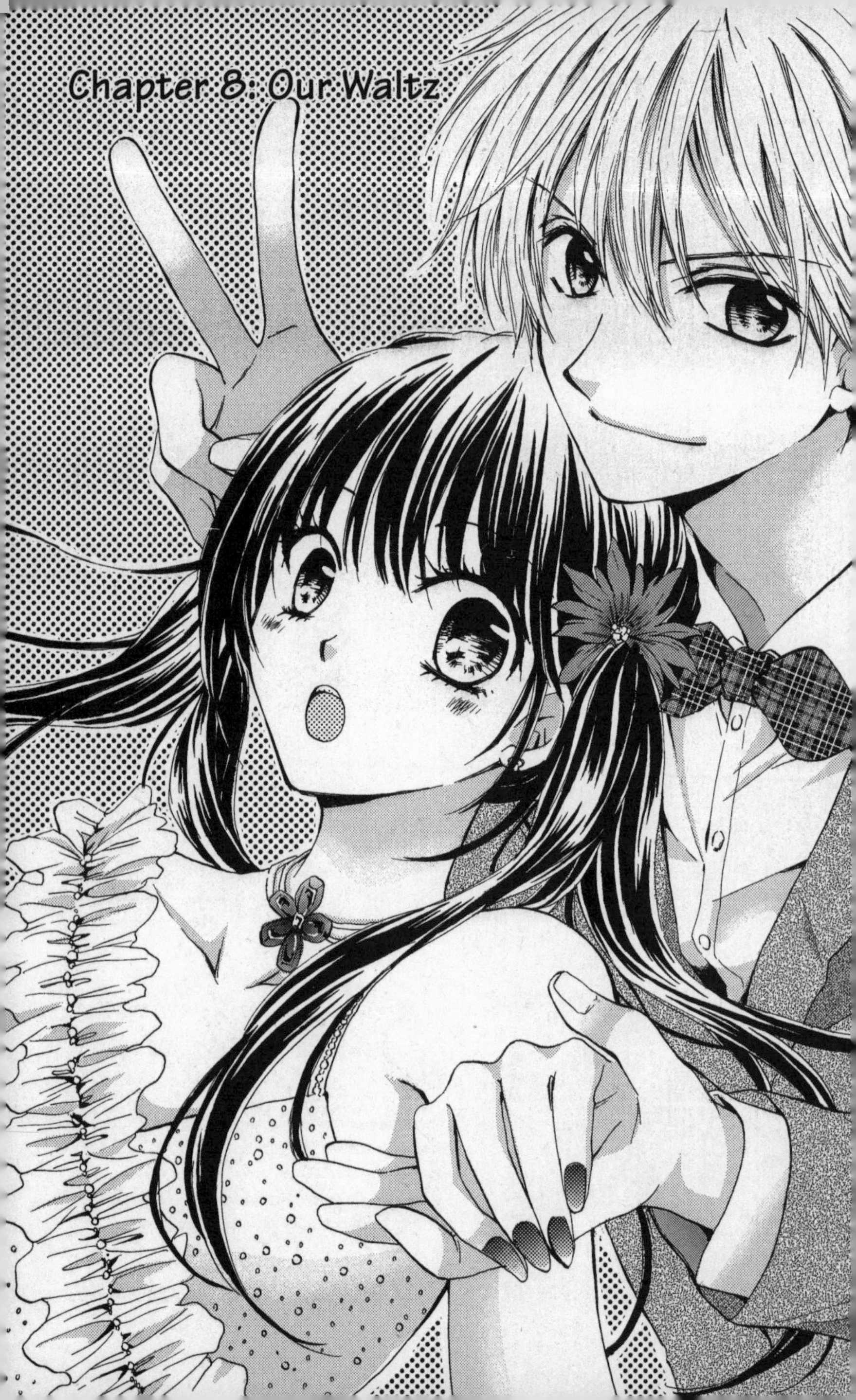

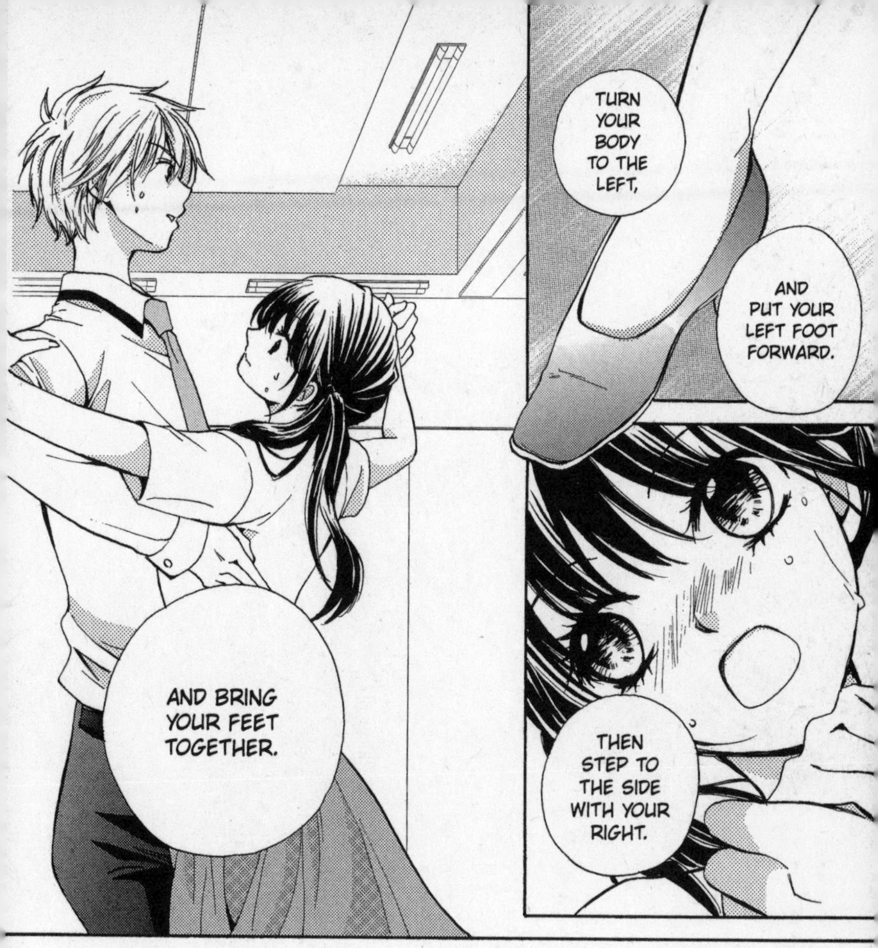
TURN YOUR BODY TO THE LEFT,
AND PUT YOUR LEFT FOOT FORWARD.
THEN STEP TO THE SIDE WITH YOUR RIGHT.
AND BRING YOUR FEET TOGETHER.

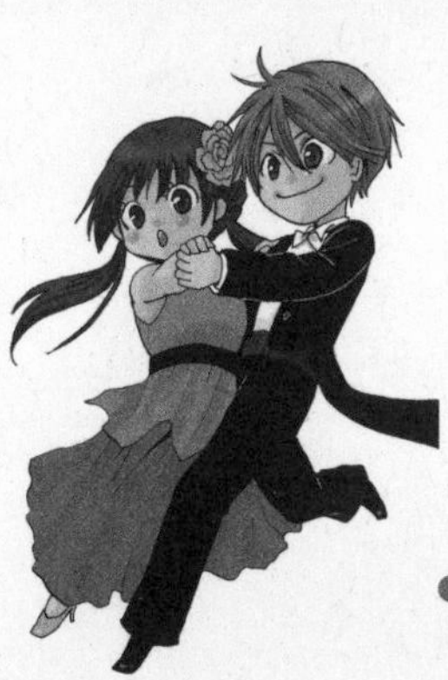

The Quickstep

The fastest-paced of the standard dances. There's plenty of bounding steps and speedy footwork as the dancers fly like the wind across the dance floor. Of the standard dances, it is usually the last one danced in a competition.

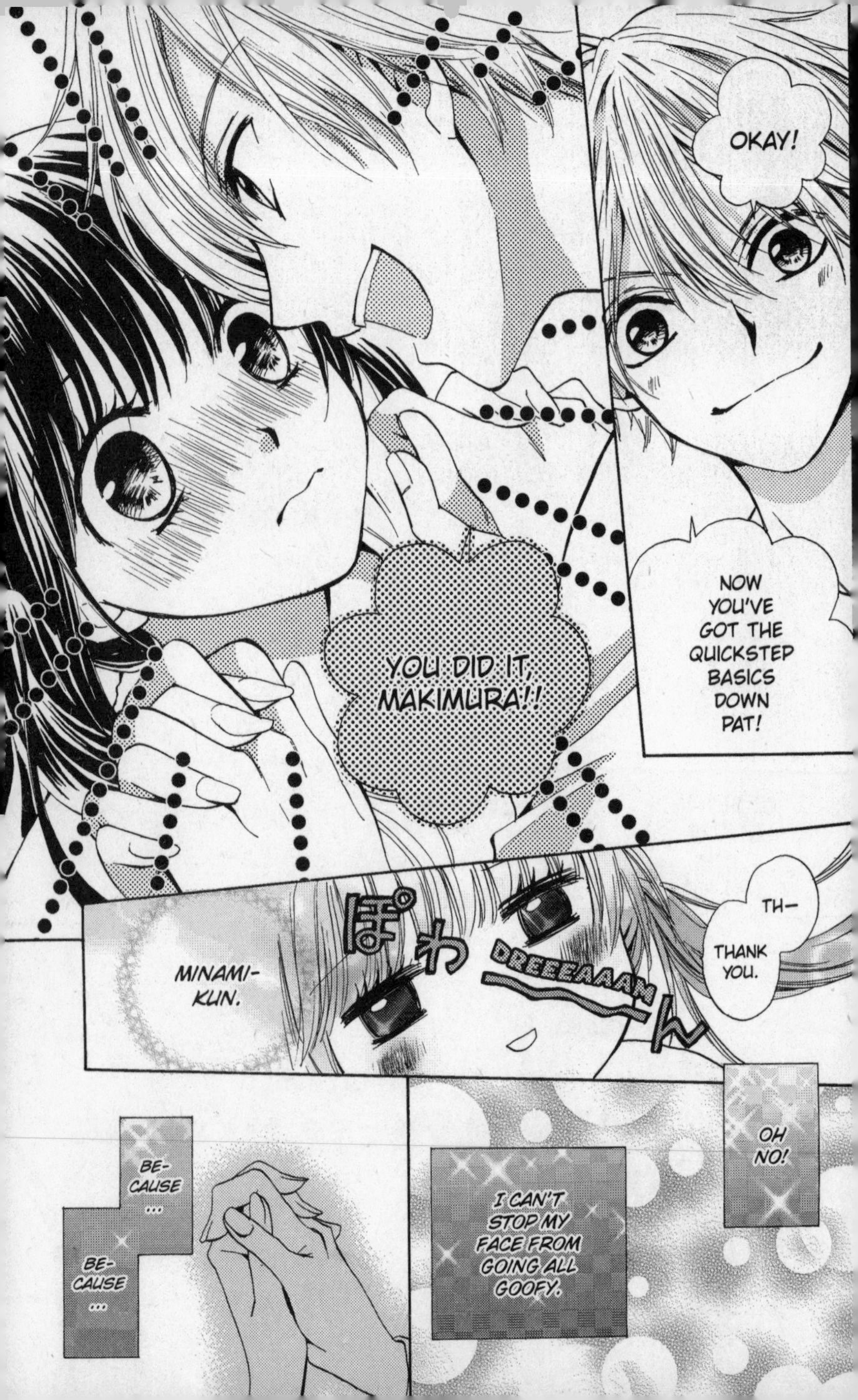
OKAY!
NOW YOU'VE GOT THE QUICKSTEP BASICS DOWN PAT!
YOU DID IT, MAKIMURA!!
TH- THANK YOU.
ぽわ
DREEEAAAAM
ん
MINAMI-KUN.
OH NO!
I CAN'T STOP MY FACE FROM GOING ALL GOOFY.
BE-CAUSE ...
BE-CAUSE ...

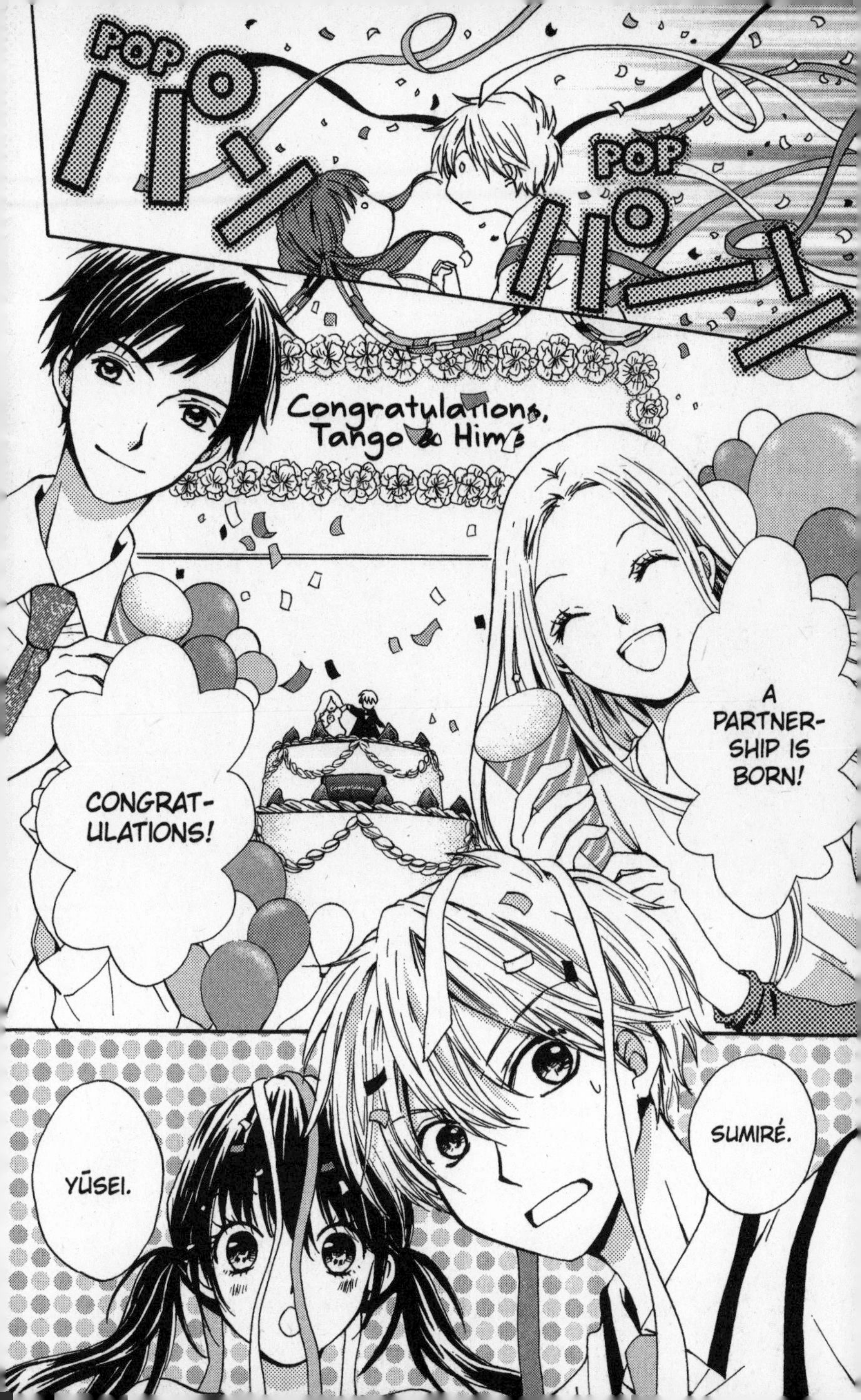
POP
POP
Congratulations, Tango & Hime
A PARTNERSHIP IS BORN!
CONGRATULATIONS!
SUMIRÉ.
YŪSEI.

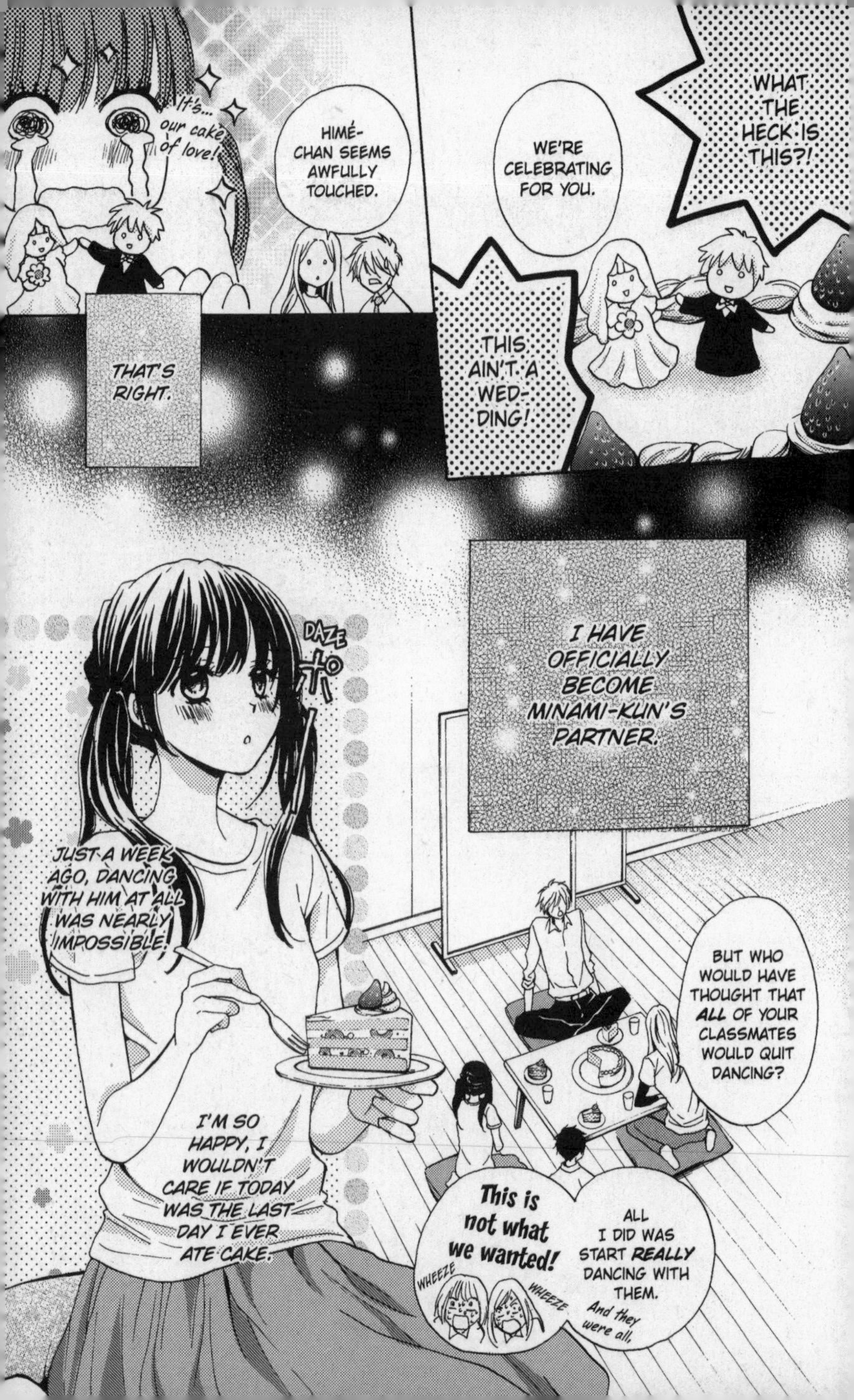
WHAT THE HECK IS THIS?!
WE'RE CELEBRATING FOR YOU.
THIS AIN'T A WEDDING!
HIMÉ-CHAN SEEMS AWFULLY TOUCHED.
It's... our cake of love!
THAT'S RIGHT.
I HAVE OFFICIALLY BECOME MINAMI-KUN'S PARTNER.
DAZE
JUST A WEEK AGO, DANCING WITH HIM AT ALL WAS NEARLY IMPOSSIBLE!
BUT WHO WOULD HAVE THOUGHT THAT ALL OF YOUR CLASSMATES WOULD QUIT DANCING?
ALL I DID WAS START REALLY DANCING WITH THEM.
And they were all,
This is not what we wanted!
WHEEZE
WHEEZE
I'M SO HAPPY, I WOULDN'T CARE IF TODAY WAS THE LAST DAY I EVER ATE CAKE.

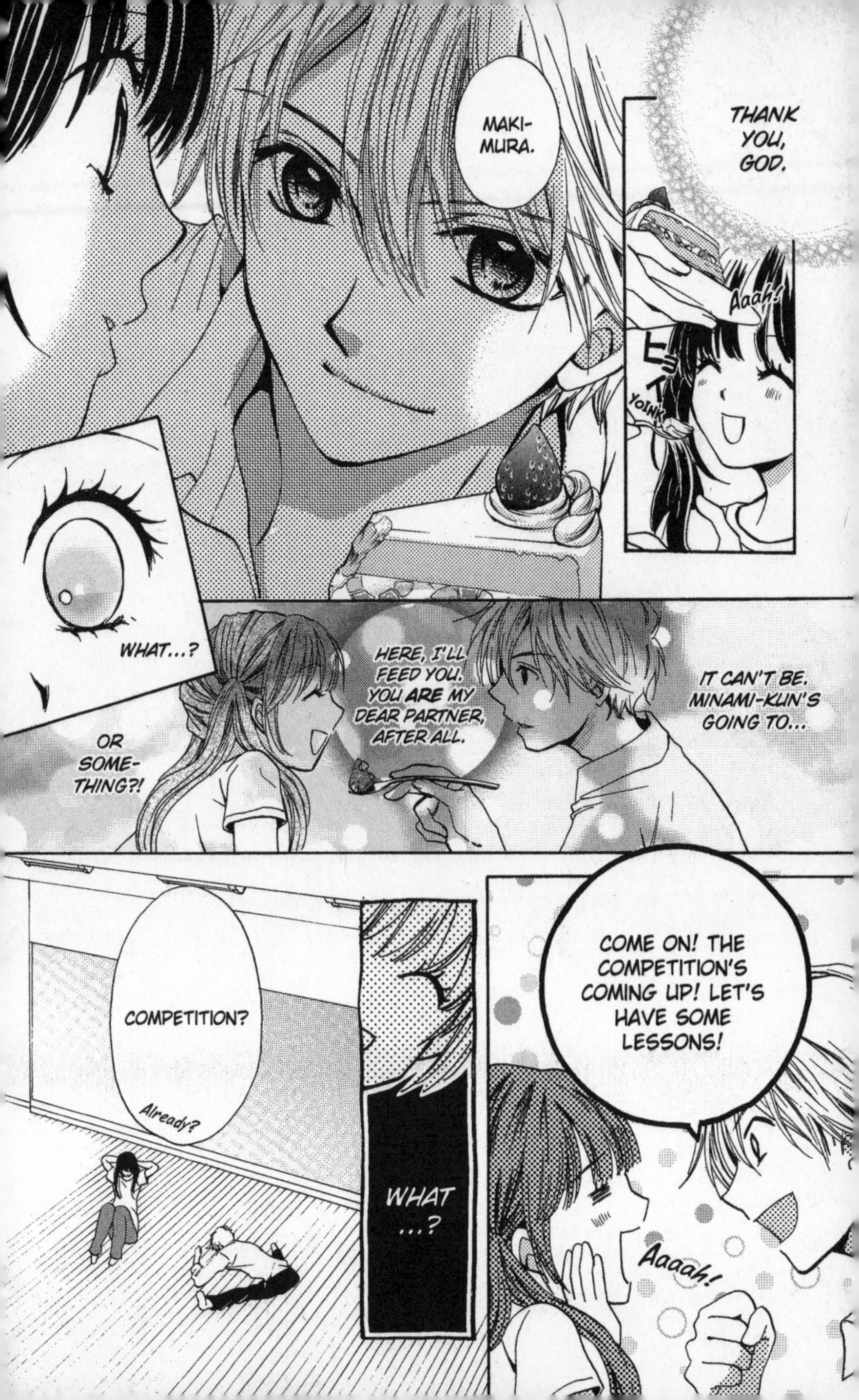
THANK YOU, GOD.
Aaah!
YOINK
MAKI-MURA.
WHAT...?
IT CAN'T BE. MINAMI-KUN'S GOING TO...
HERE, I'LL FEED YOU. YOU **ARE** MY DEAR PARTNER, AFTER ALL.
OR SOME-THING?!
COME ON! THE COMPETITION'S COMING UP! LET'S HAVE SOME LESSONS!
Aaaah!
WHAT ...?
COMPETITION?
Already?

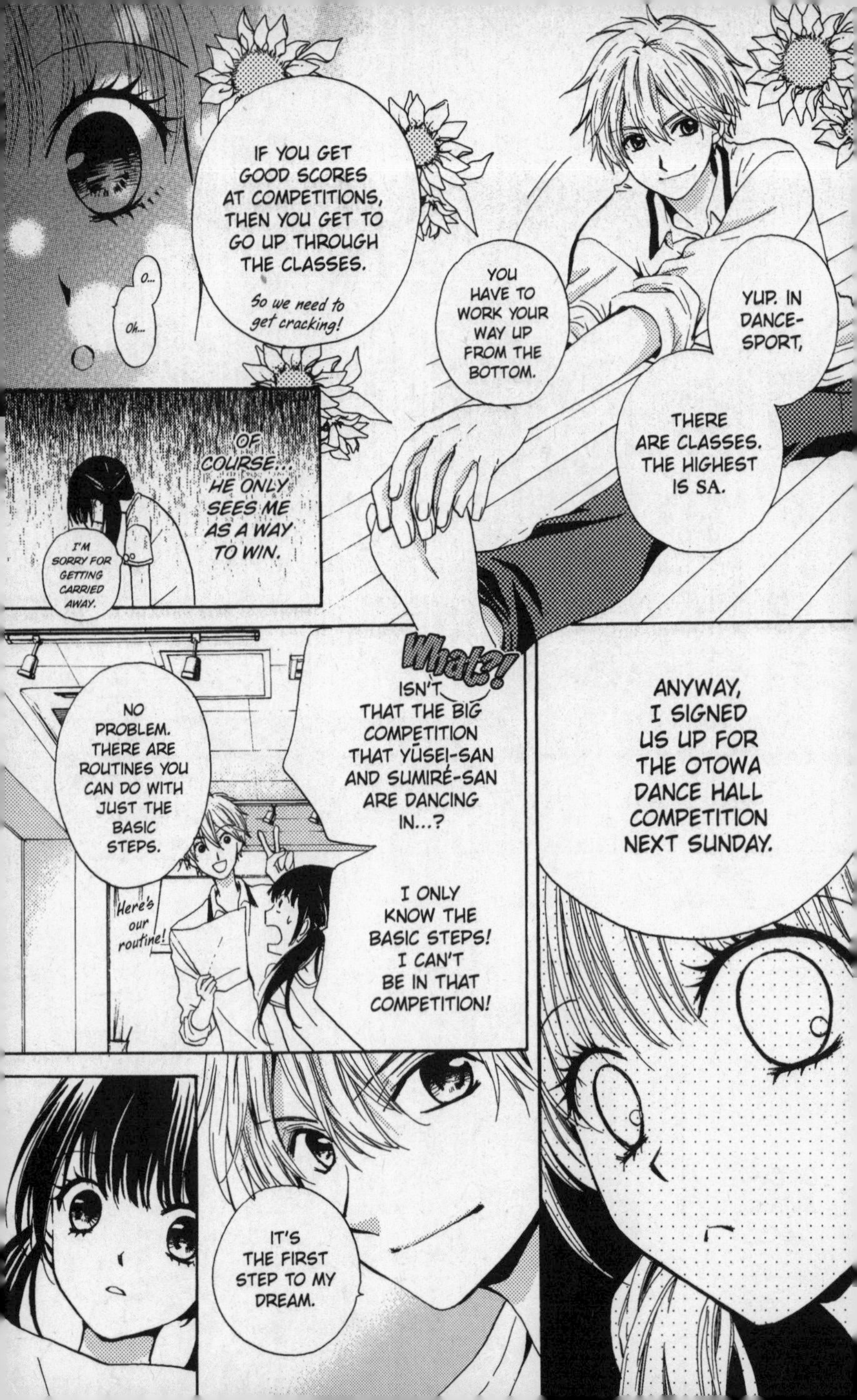
YUP. IN DANCE-SPORT,
THERE ARE CLASSES. THE HIGHEST IS SA.
YOU HAVE TO WORK YOUR WAY UP FROM THE BOTTOM.
IF YOU GET GOOD SCORES AT COMPETITIONS, THEN YOU GET TO GO UP THROUGH THE CLASSES.
So we need to get cracking!
O... Oh...
OF COURSE... HE ONLY SEES ME AS A WAY TO WIN.
I'M SORRY FOR GETTING CARRIED AWAY.
ANYWAY, I SIGNED US UP FOR THE OTOWA DANCE HALL COMPETITION NEXT SUNDAY.
What?!
ISN'T THAT THE BIG COMPETITION THAT YŪSEI-SAN AND SUMIRÉ-SAN ARE DANCING IN...?
I ONLY KNOW THE BASIC STEPS! I CAN'T BE IN THAT COMPETITION!
NO PROBLEM. THERE ARE ROUTINES YOU CAN DO WITH JUST THE BASIC STEPS.
Here's our routine!
IT'S THE FIRST STEP TO MY DREAM.

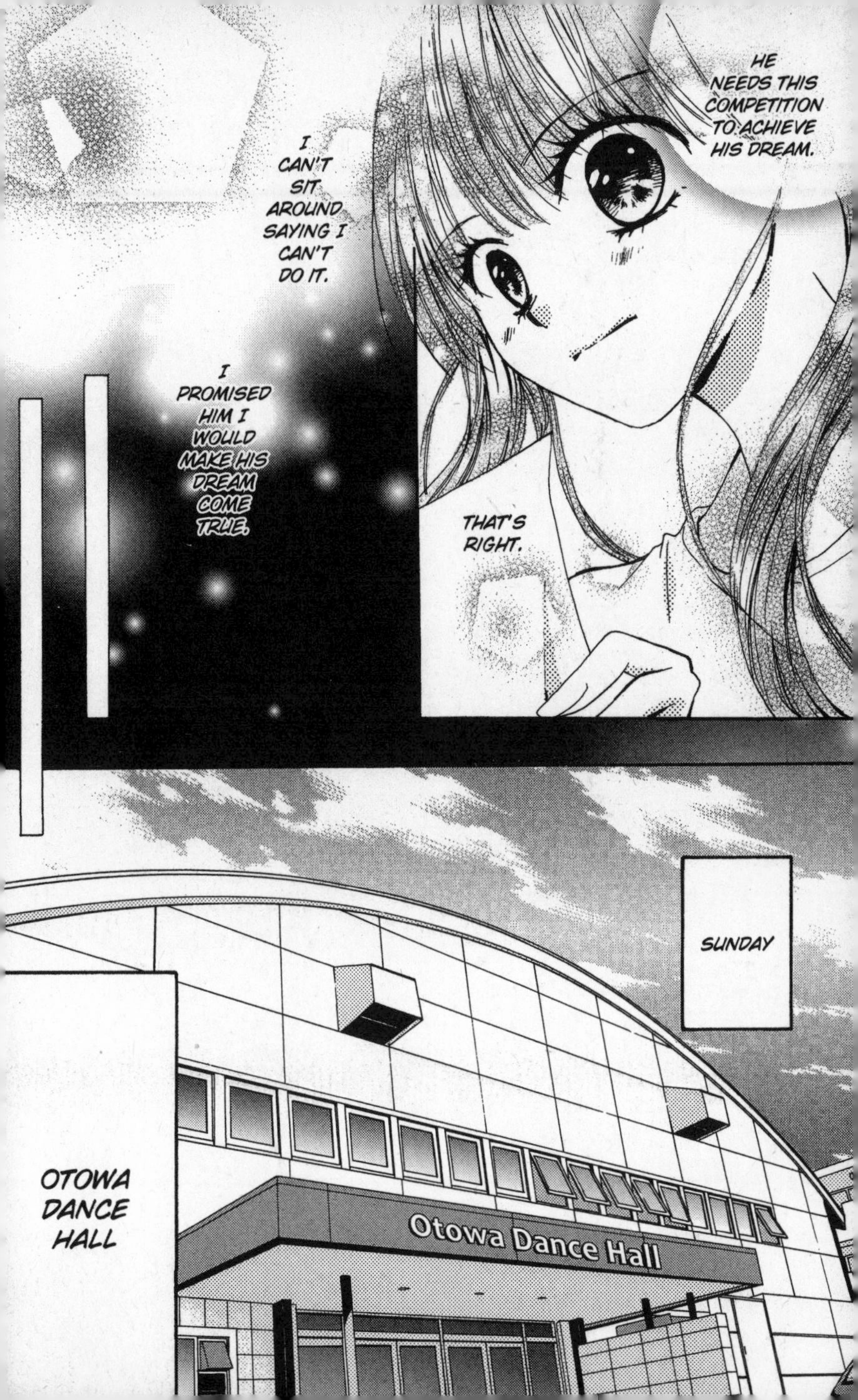
HE NEEDS THIS COMPETITION TO ACHIEVE HIS DREAM.
I CAN'T SIT AROUND SAYING I CAN'T DO IT.
THAT'S RIGHT.
I PROMISED HIM I WOULD MAKE HIS DREAM COME TRUE.
SUNDAY
OTOWA DANCE HALL
Otowa Dance Hall

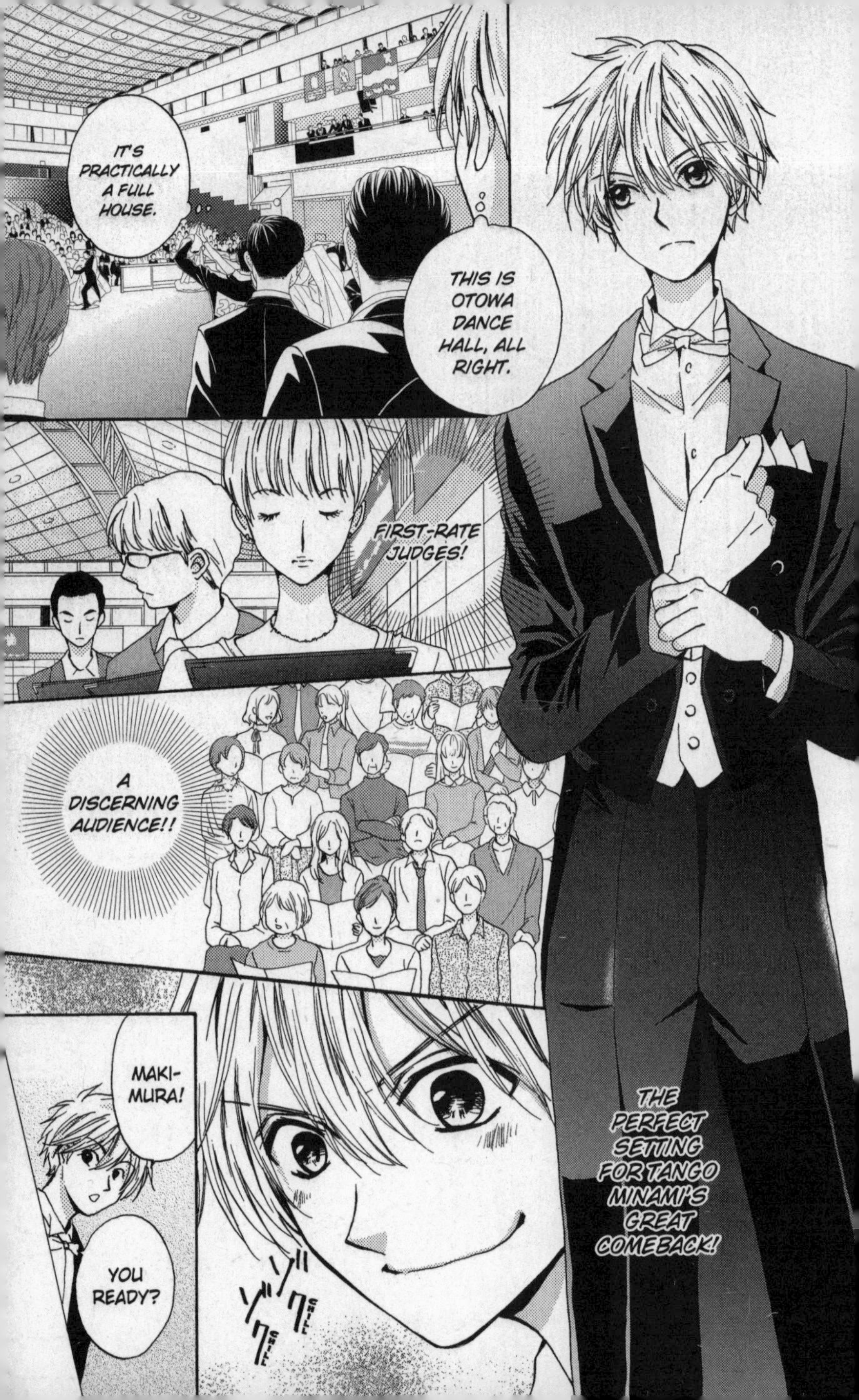
THIS IS OTOWA DANCE HALL, ALL RIGHT.
THE PERFECT SETTING FOR TANGO MINAMI'S GREAT COMEBACK!
IT'S PRACTICALLY A FULL HOUSE.
FIRST-RATE JUDGES!
A DISCERNING AUDIENCE!!
MAKI-MURA!
YOU READY?
ゾク ゾク
CHILL CHILL

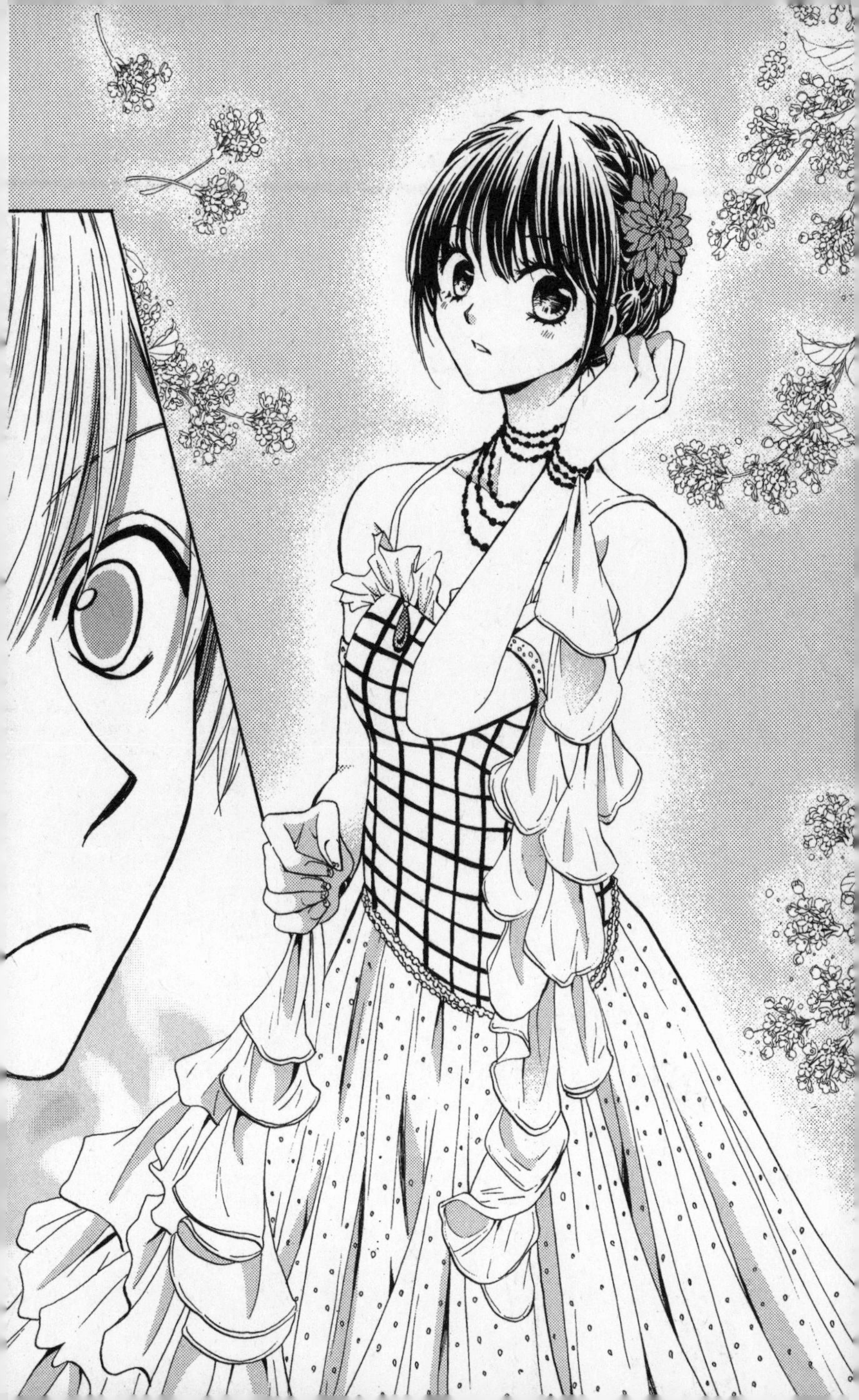

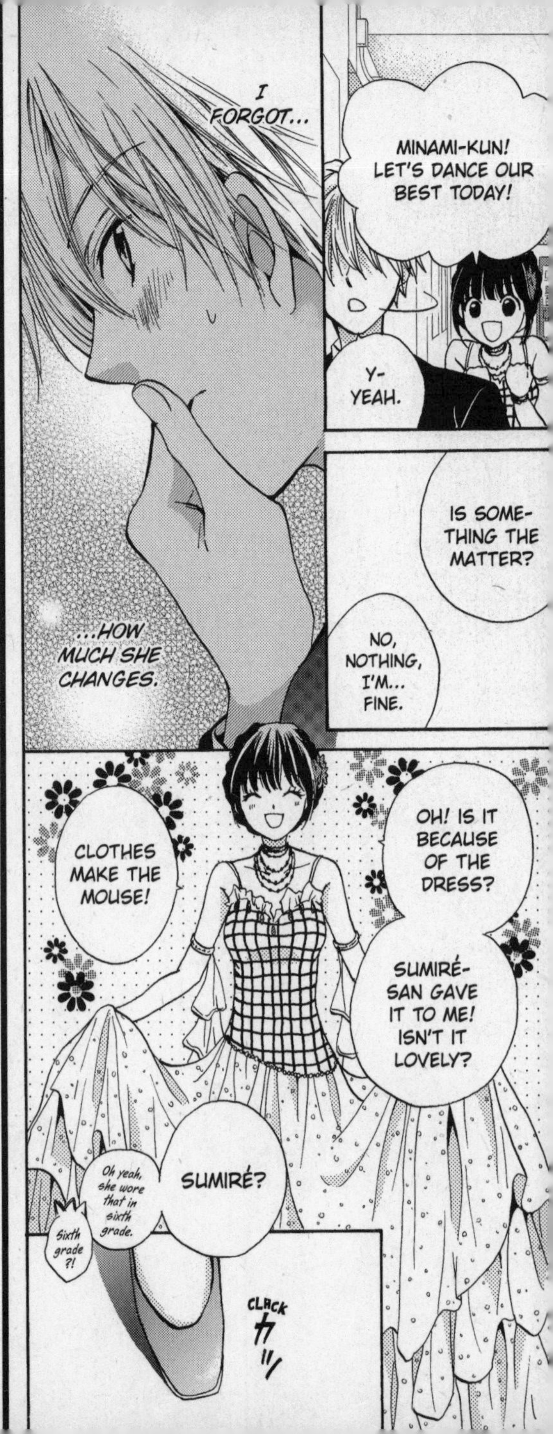
MINAMI-KUN! LET'S DANCE OUR BEST TODAY!
Y-YEAH.
IS SOME-THING THE MATTER?
NO, NOTHING, I'M... FINE.
I FORGOT...
...HOW MUCH SHE CHANGES.
OH! IS IT BECAUSE OF THE DRESS?
SUMIRÉ-SAN GAVE IT TO ME! ISN'T IT LOVELY?
CLOTHES MAKE THE MOUSE!
SUMIRÉ?
Oh yeah, she wore that in sixth grade.
Sixth grade ?!
CLACK

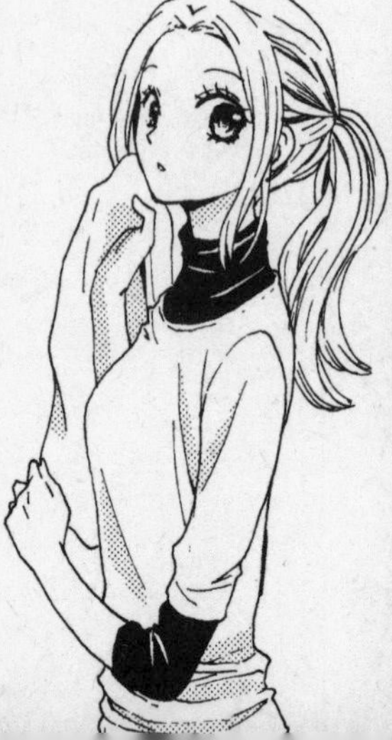

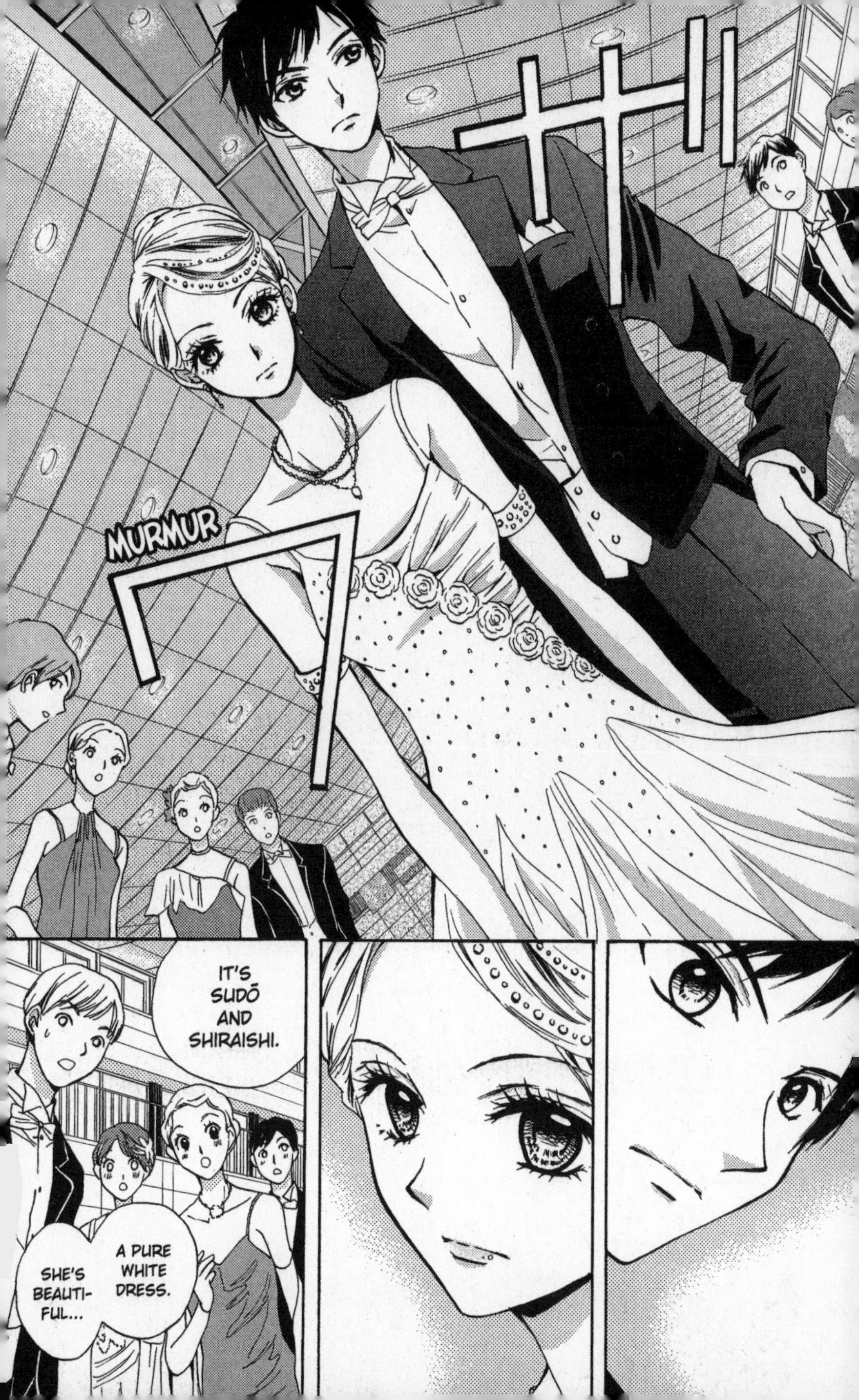
MURMUR
IT'S SUDŌ AND SHIRAISHI.
A PURE WHITE DRESS.
SHE'S BEAUTI-FUL...

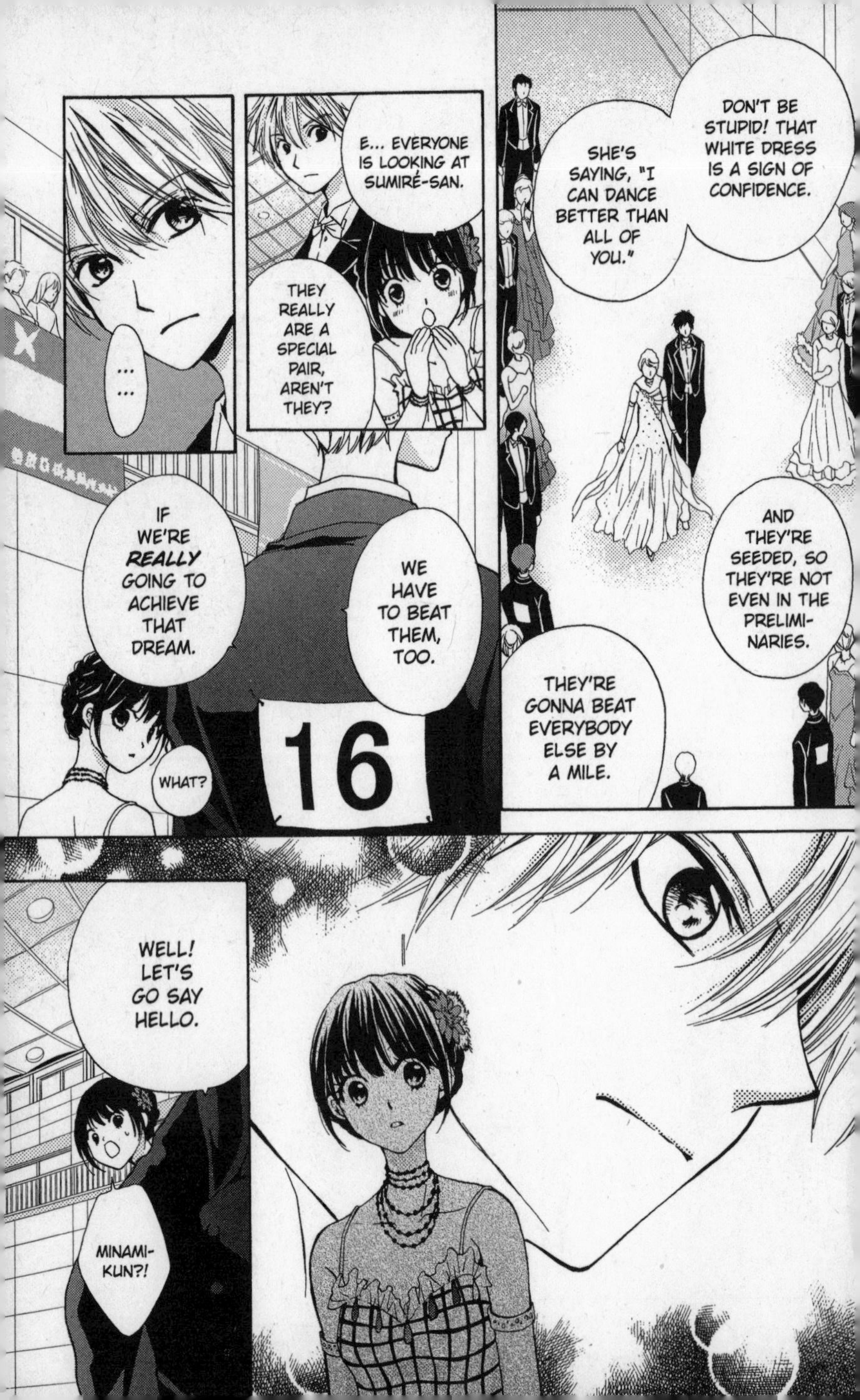

DON'T BE STUPID! THAT WHITE DRESS IS A SIGN OF CONFIDENCE.
SHE'S SAYING, "I CAN DANCE BETTER THAN ALL OF YOU."
AND THEY'RE SEEDED, SO THEY'RE NOT EVEN IN THE PRELIMINARIES.
THEY'RE GONNA BEAT EVERYBODY ELSE BY A MILE.
E... EVERYONE IS LOOKING AT SUMIRÉ-SAN.
THEY REALLY ARE A SPECIAL PAIR, AREN'T THEY?
......
WE HAVE TO BEAT THEM, TOO.
IF WE'RE *REALLY* GOING TO ACHIEVE THAT DREAM.
WHAT?
16
WELL! LET'S GO SAY HELLO.
MINAMI-KUN?!

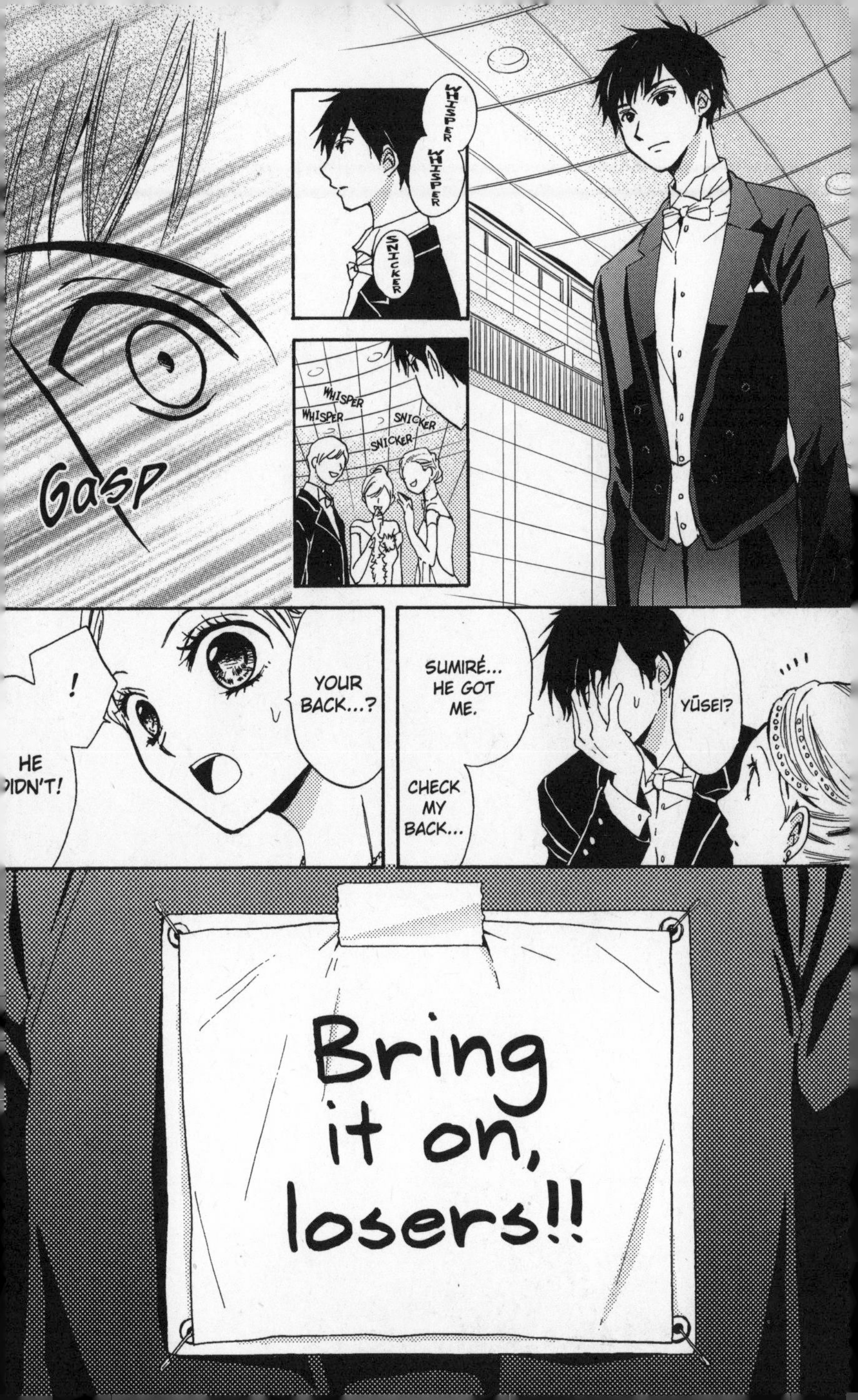
WHISPER WHISPER
SNICKER
WHISPER WHISPER
SNICKER SNICKER
Gasp
YŪSEI?
SUMIRÉ... HE GOT ME.
CHECK MY BACK...
YOUR BACK...?
!
HE DIDN'T!
Bring it on, losers!!

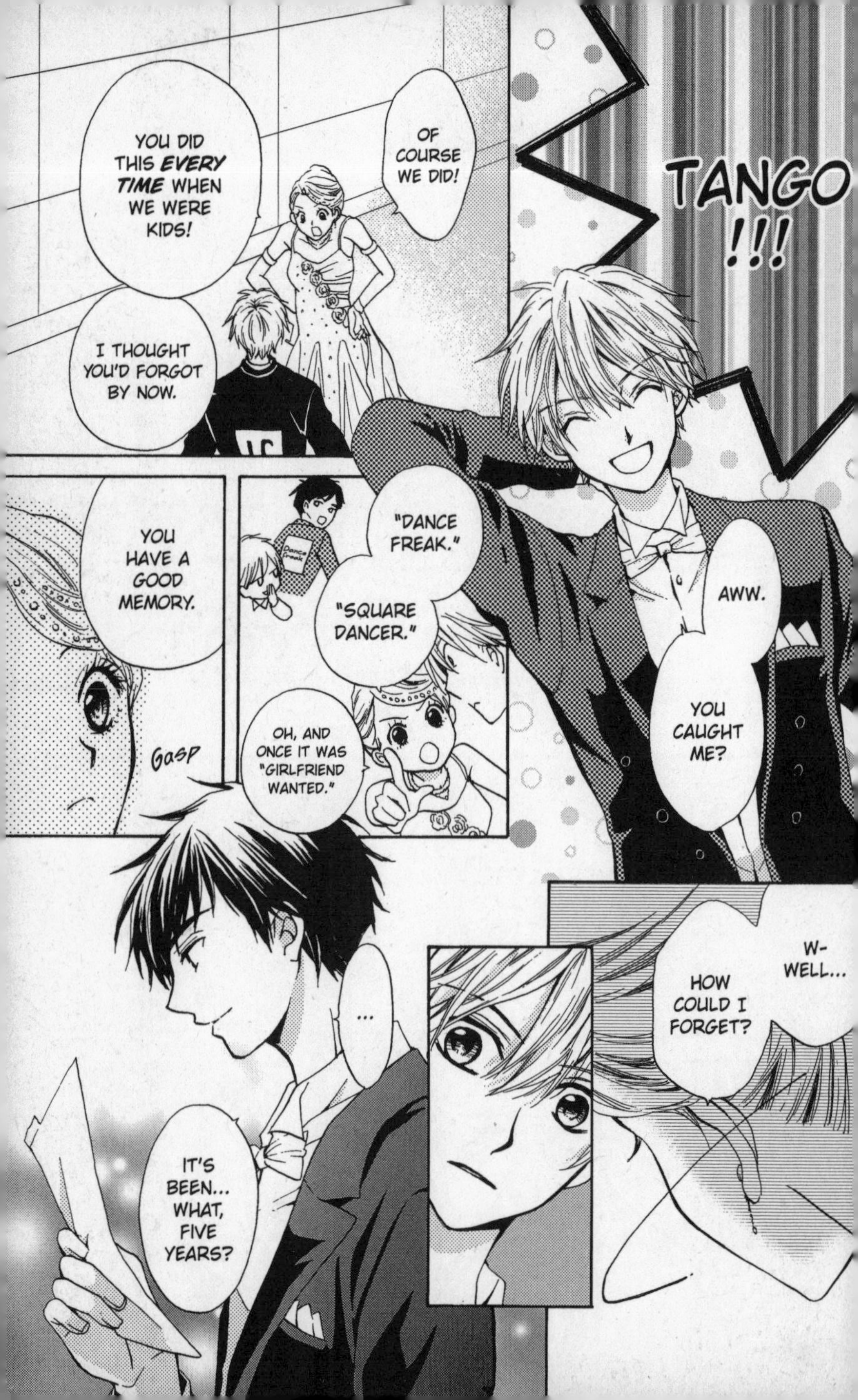
TANGO !!!
AWW.
YOU CAUGHT ME?
OF COURSE WE DID!
YOU DID THIS EVERY TIME WHEN WE WERE KIDS!
I THOUGHT YOU'D FORGOT BY NOW.
"DANCE FREAK."
"SQUARE DANCER."
OH, AND ONCE IT WAS "GIRLFRIEND WANTED."
YOU HAVE A GOOD MEMORY.
Gasp
W-WELL...
HOW COULD I FORGET?
...
IT'S BEEN... WHAT, FIVE YEARS?

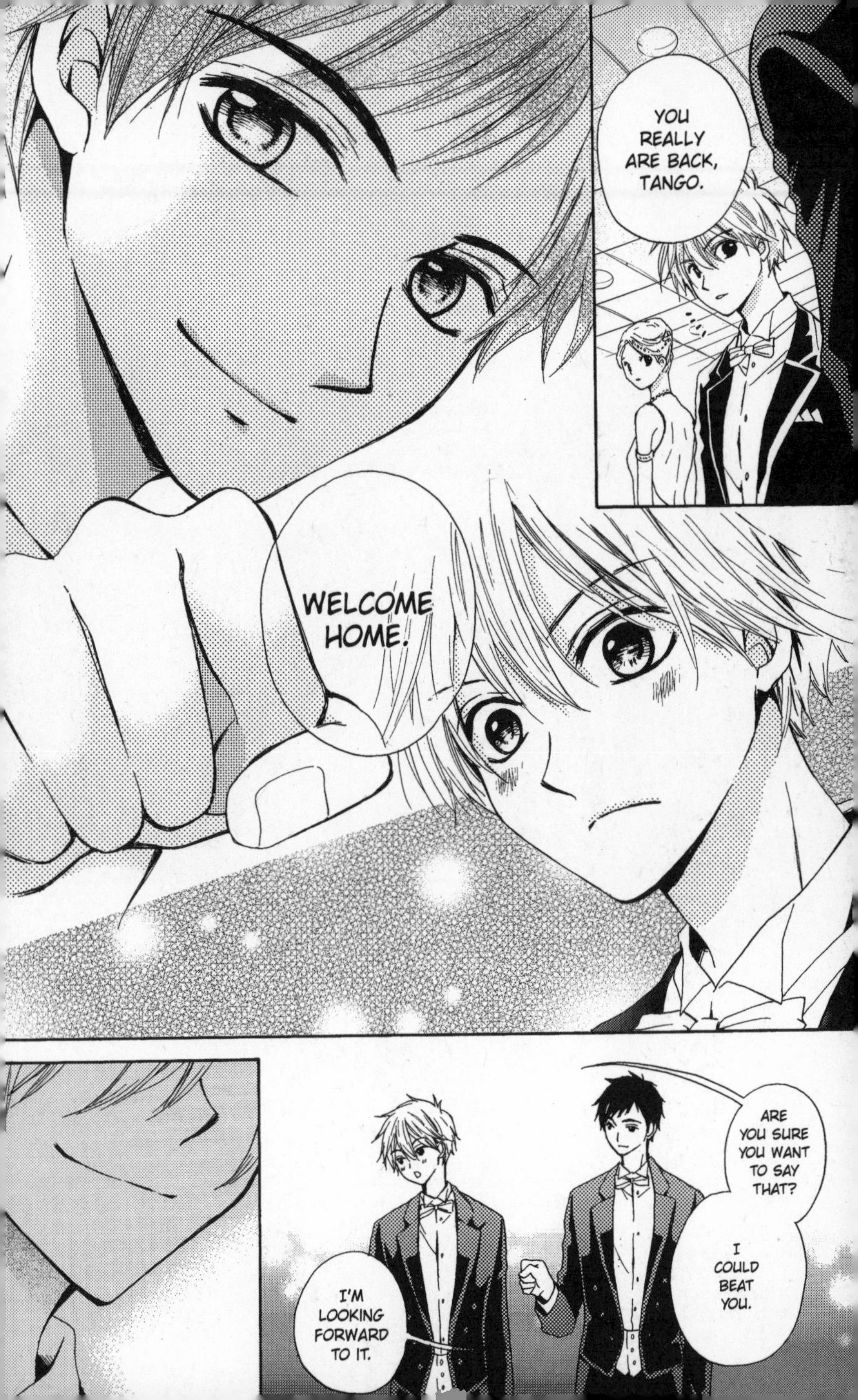
YOU REALLY ARE BACK, TANGO.
WELCOME HOME.
ARE YOU SURE YOU WANT TO SAY THAT?
I COULD BEAT YOU.
I'M LOOKING FORWARD TO IT.

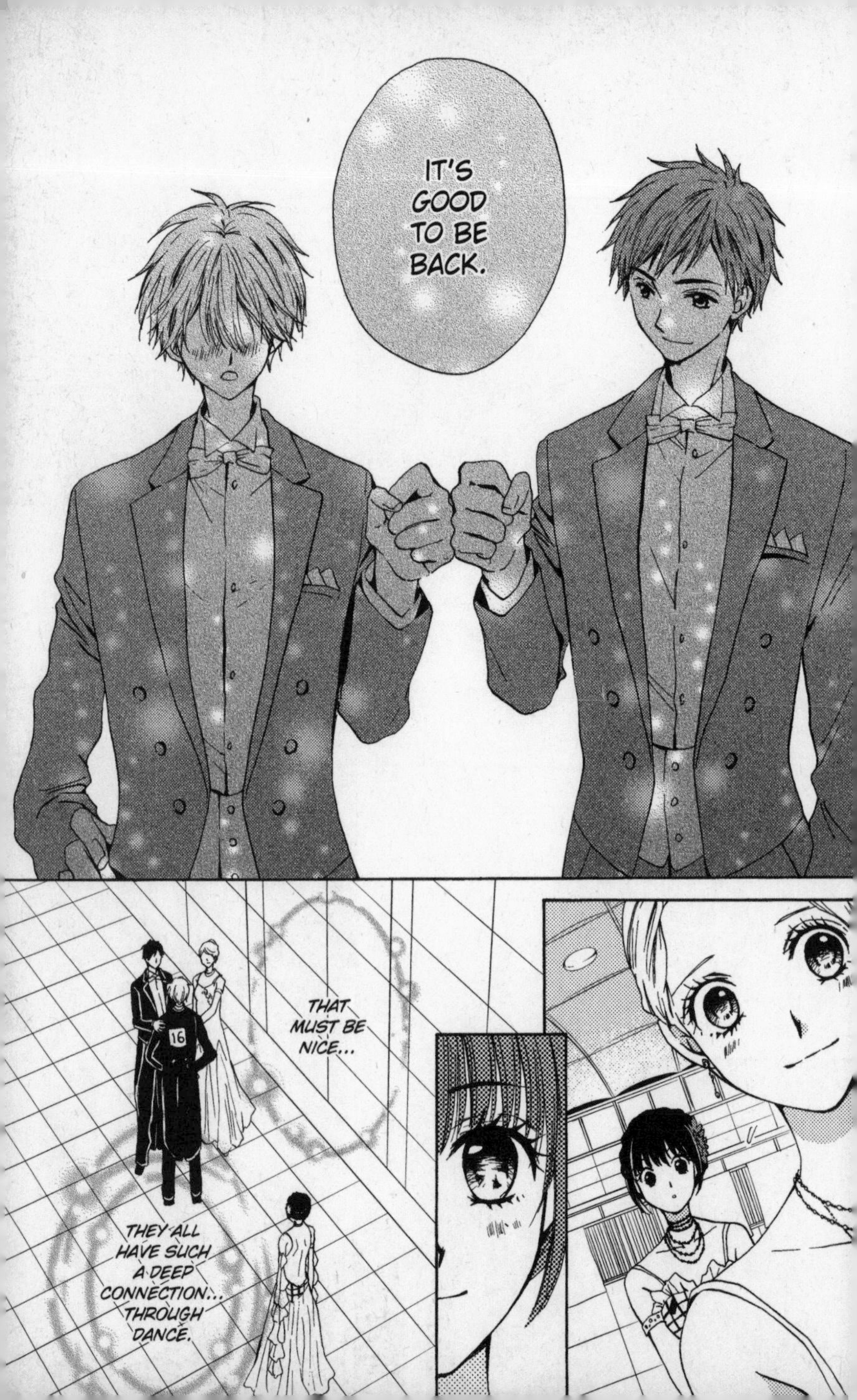
IT'S GOOD TO BE BACK.
THAT MUST BE NICE...
THEY ALL HAVE SUCH A DEEP CONNECTION... THROUGH DANCE.

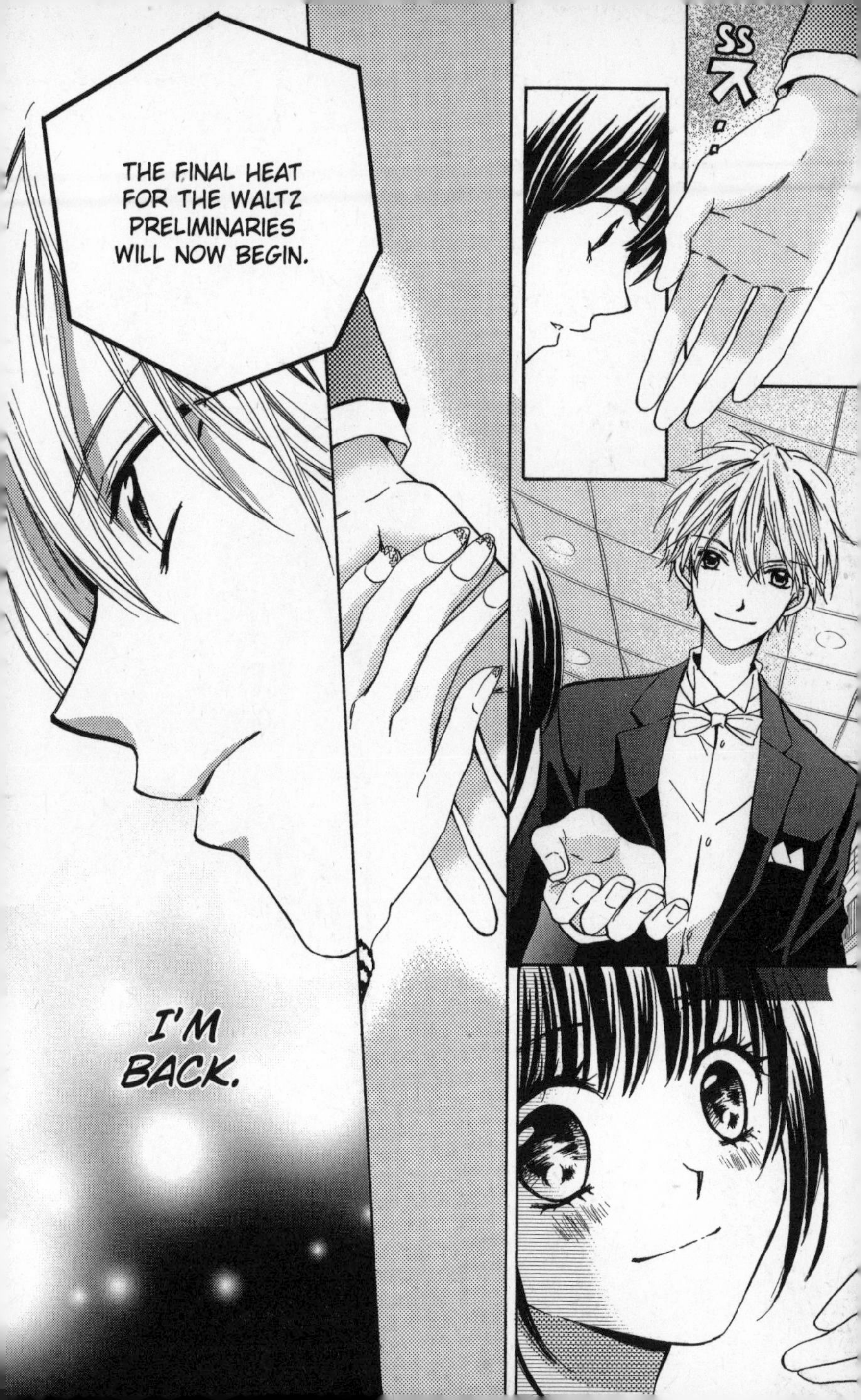
SS
ス
THE FINAL HEAT FOR THE WALTZ PRELIMINARIES WILL NOW BEGIN.
I'M BACK.

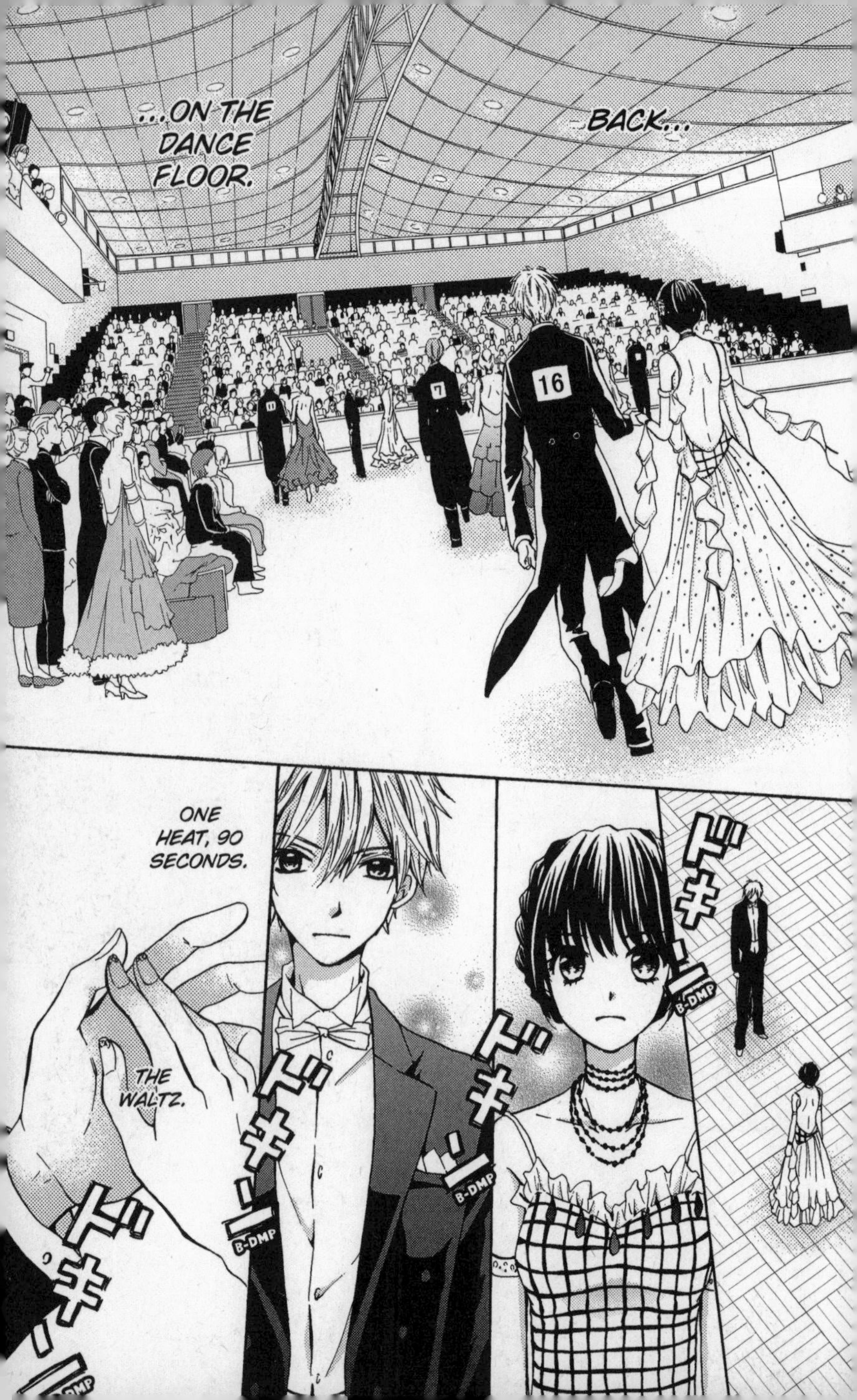
BACK...
...ON THE DANCE FLOOR.
B-DMP
B-DMP
ONE HEAT, 90 SECONDS.
B-DMP
THE WALTZ.
DMP

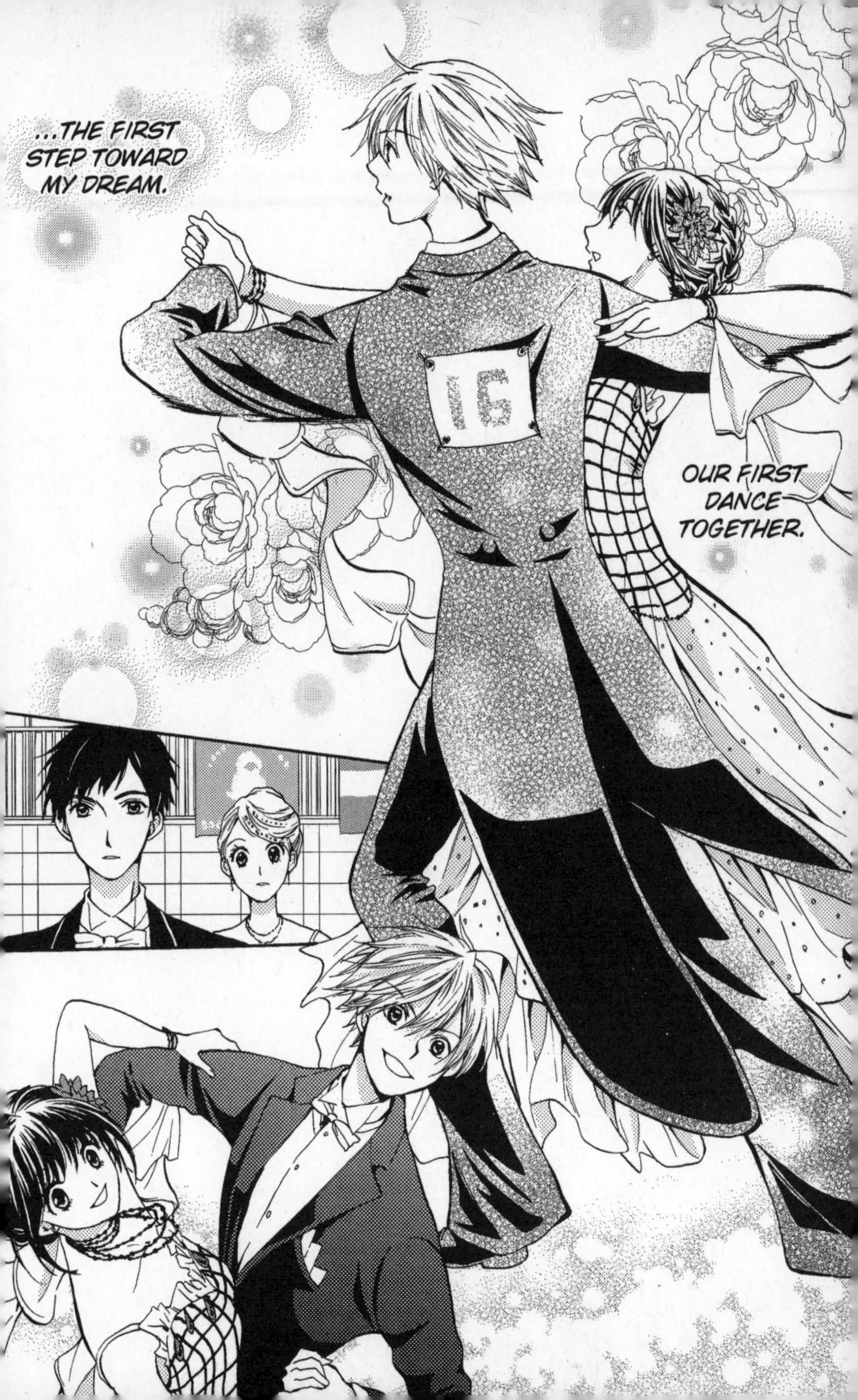
OUR FIRST DANCE TOGETHER.
...THE FIRST STEP TOWARD MY DREAM.

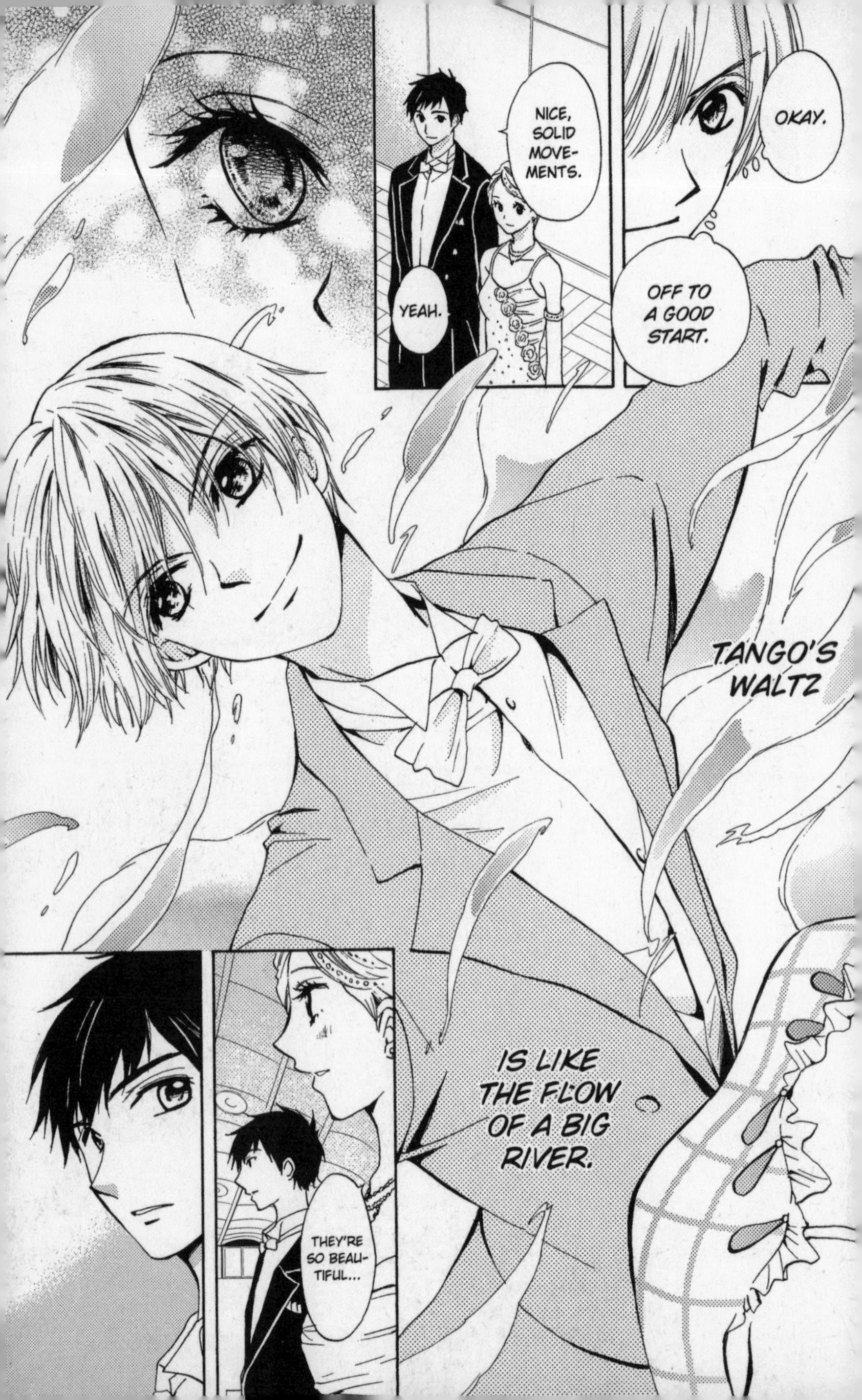
OKAY.
OFF TO A GOOD START.
NICE, SOLID MOVE-MENTS.
YEAH.
TANGO'S WALTZ
IS LIKE THE FLOW OF A BIG RIVER.
THEY'RE SO BEAU-TIFUL...

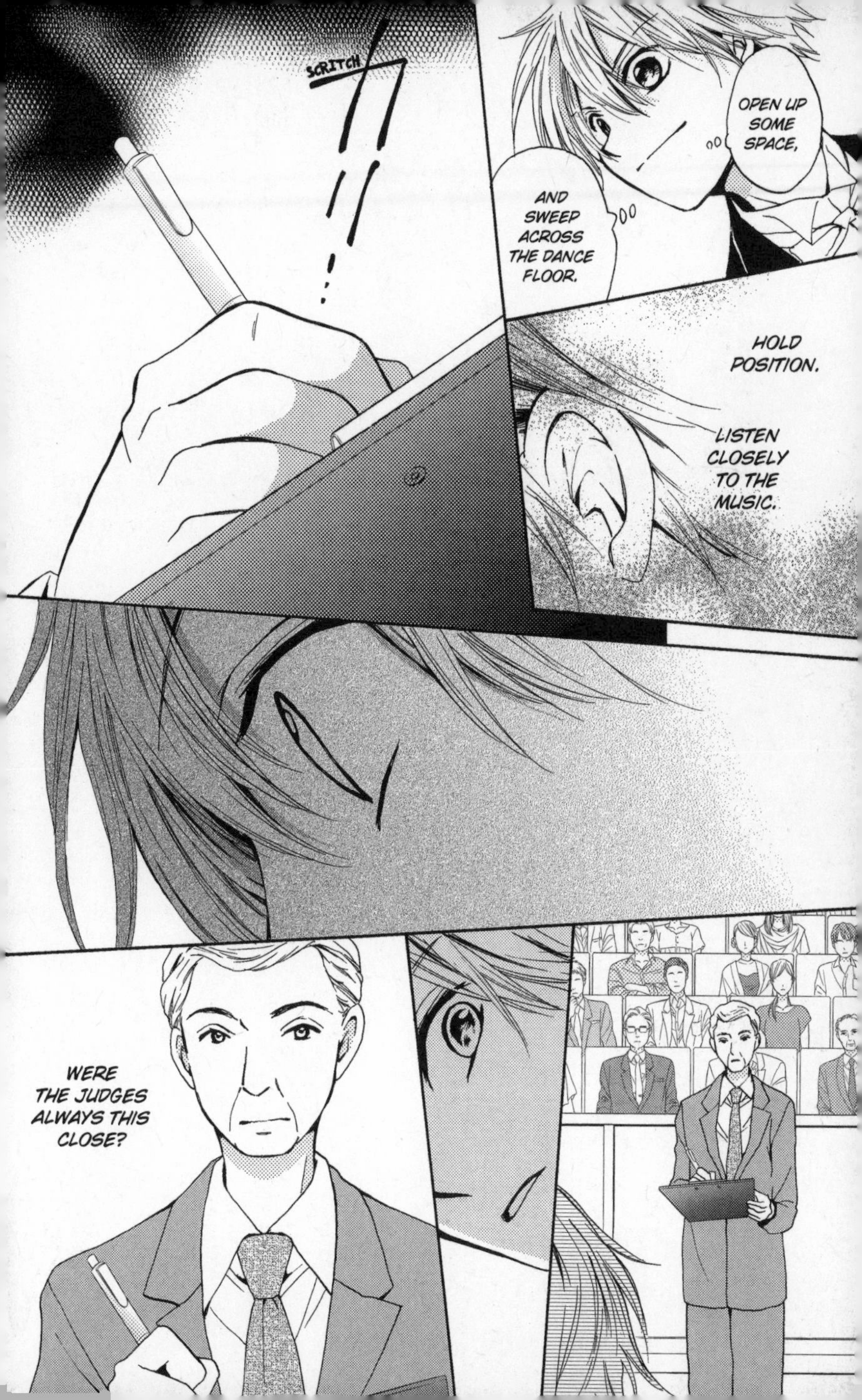
OPEN UP SOME SPACE,
AND SWEEP ACROSS THE DANCE FLOOR.
HOLD POSITION.
LISTEN CLOSELY TO THE MUSIC.
SCRITCH
WERE THE JUDGES ALWAYS THIS CLOSE?

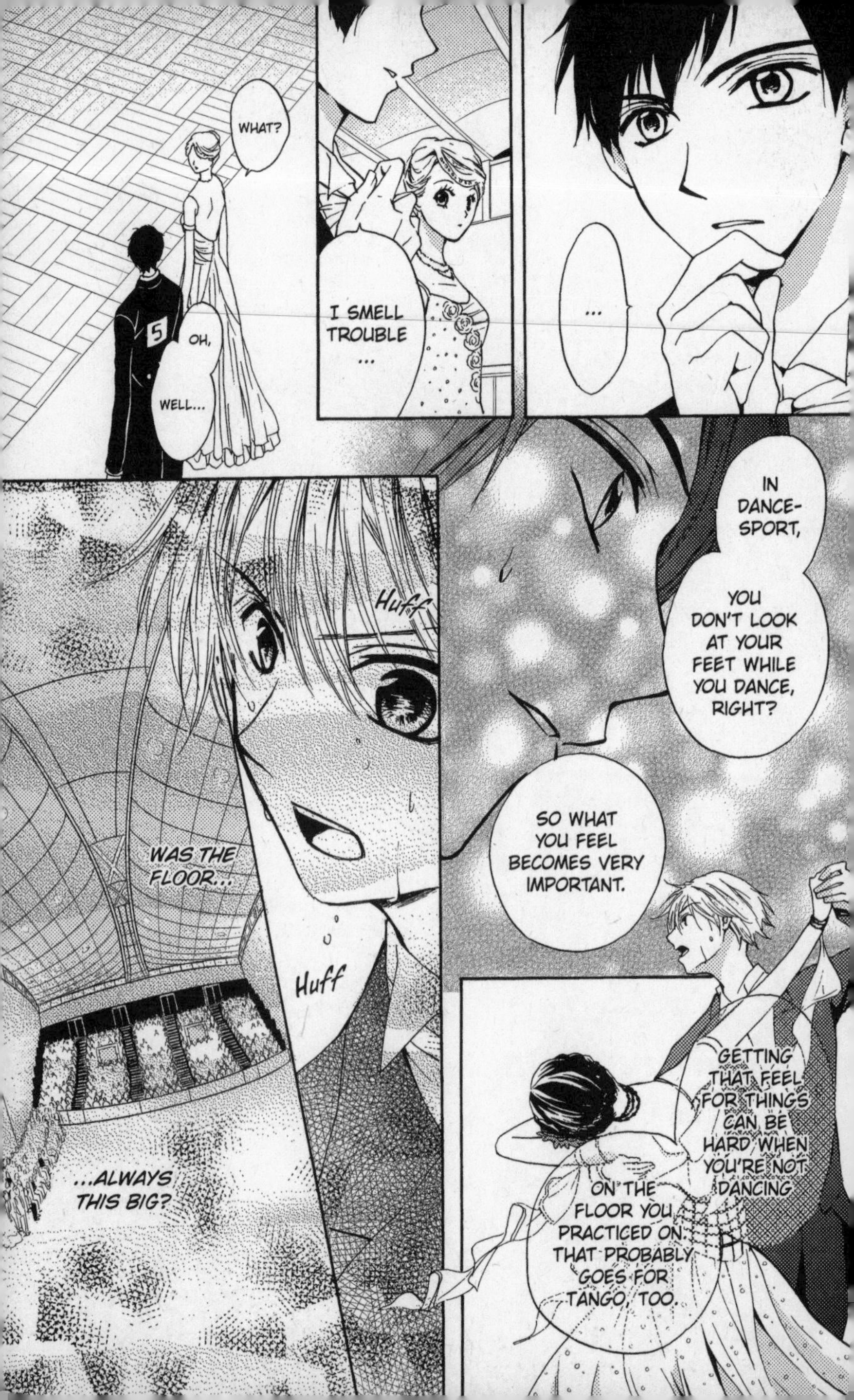
...
I SMELL TROUBLE ...
WHAT?
OH, WELL...
IN DANCE-SPORT,
YOU DON'T LOOK AT YOUR FEET WHILE YOU DANCE, RIGHT?
SO WHAT YOU FEEL BECOMES VERY IMPORTANT.
GETTING THAT FEEL FOR THINGS CAN BE HARD WHEN YOU'RE NOT DANCING
ON THE FLOOR YOU PRACTICED ON. THAT PROBABLY GOES FOR TANGO, TOO.
Huff
Huff
WAS THE FLOOR...
...ALWAYS THIS BIG?

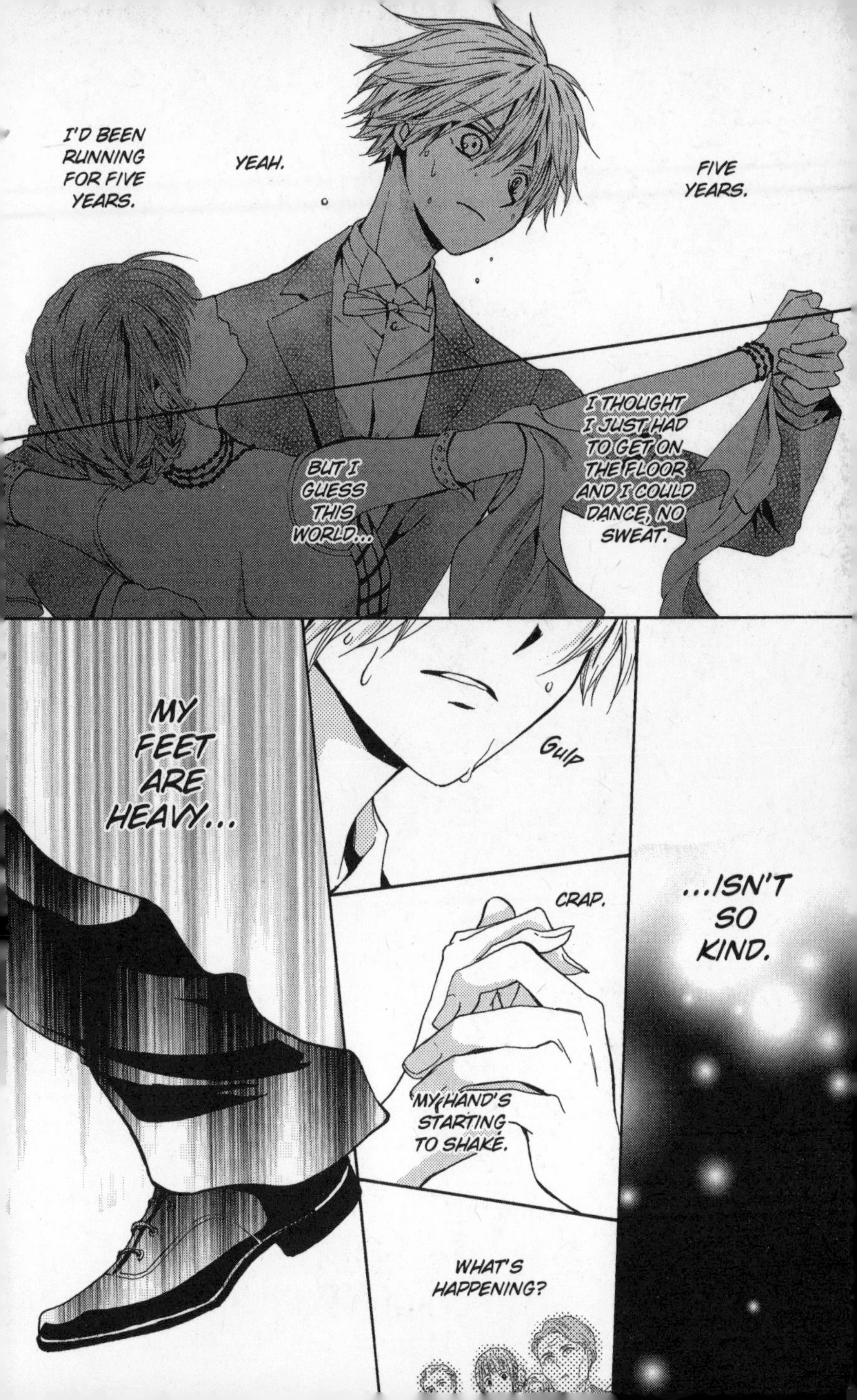
FIVE YEARS.
YEAH.
I'D BEEN RUNNING FOR FIVE YEARS.
I THOUGHT I JUST HAD TO GET ON THE FLOOR AND I COULD DANCE, NO SWEAT.
BUT I GUESS THIS WORLD...
...ISN'T SO KIND.
Gulp
CRAP.
MY HAND'S STARTING TO SHAKE.
WHAT'S HAPPENING?
MY FEET ARE HEAVY...

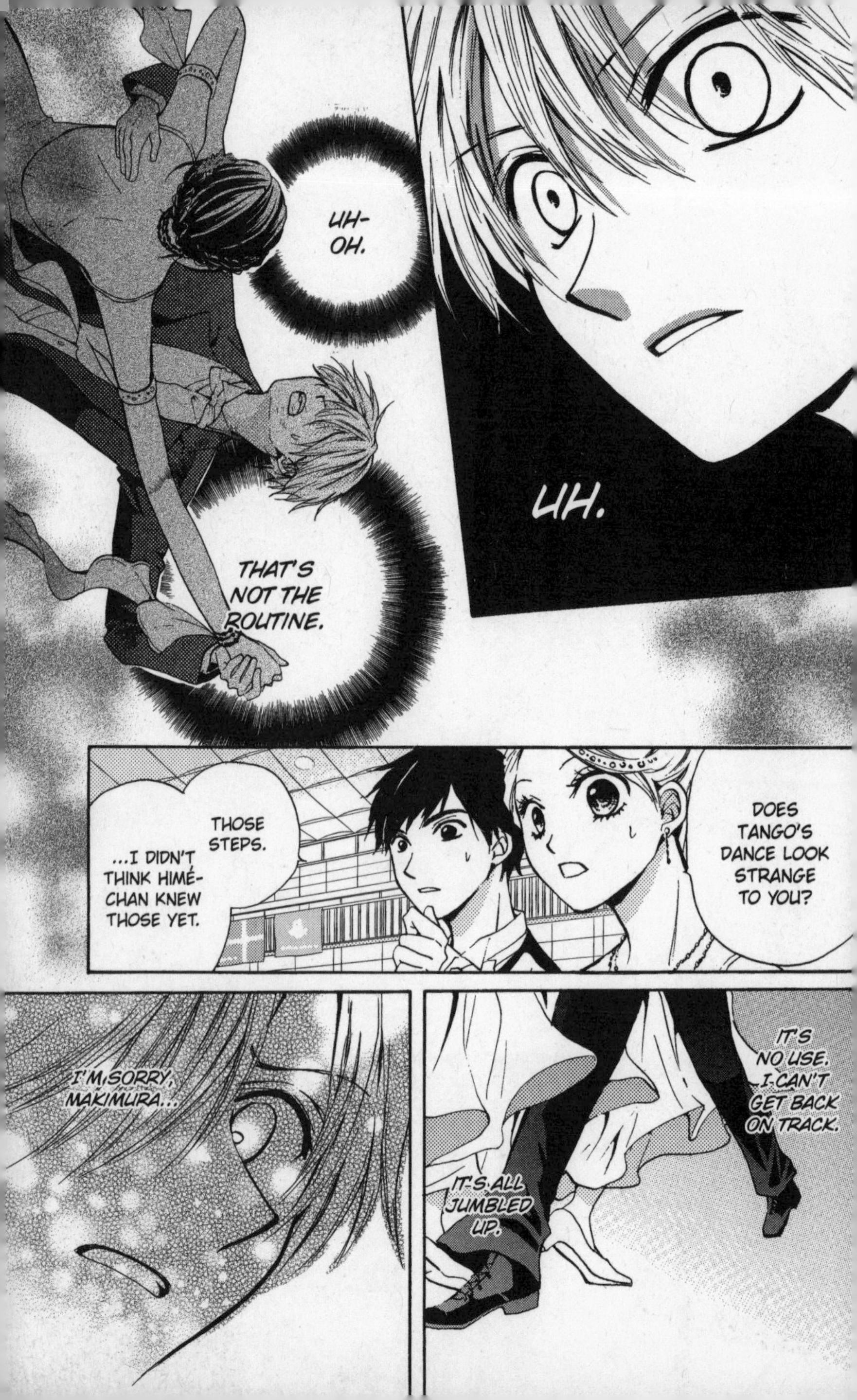
UH.
UH-OH.
THAT'S NOT THE ROUTINE.
DOES TANGO'S DANCE LOOK STRANGE TO YOU?
THOSE STEPS.
...I DIDN'T THINK HIME-CHAN KNEW THOSE YET.
IT'S NO USE. I CAN'T GET BACK ON TRACK.
IT'S ALL JUMBLED UP.
I'M SORRY, MAKIMURA...

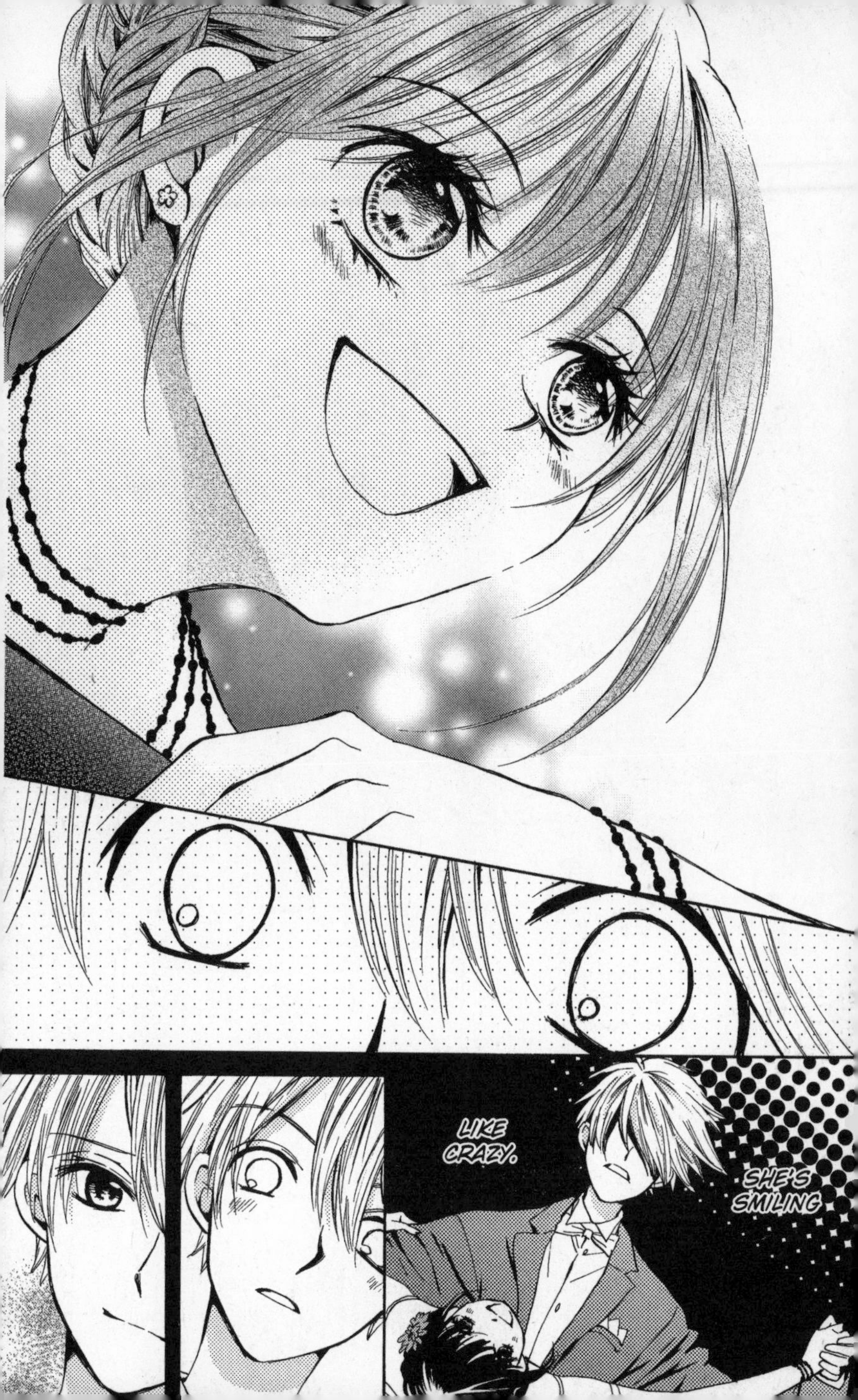
SHE'S SMILING
LIKE CRAZY.

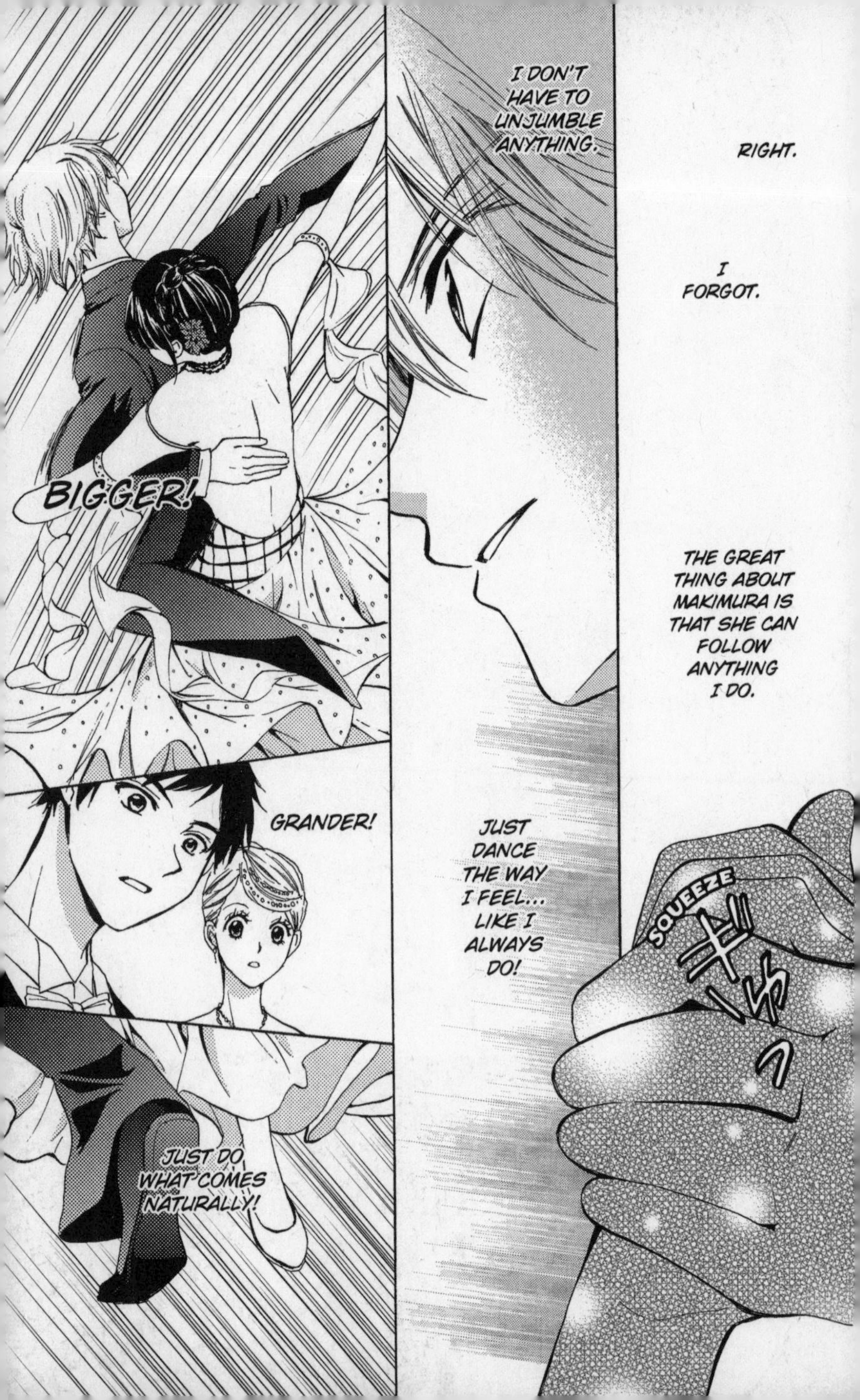
RIGHT.
I FORGOT.
THE GREAT THING ABOUT MAKIMURA IS THAT SHE CAN FOLLOW ANYTHING I DO.
SQUEEZE
I DON'T HAVE TO UNJUMBLE ANYTHING.
JUST DANCE THE WAY I FEEL... LIKE I ALWAYS DO!
BIGGER!
GRANDER!
JUST DO WHAT COMES NATURALLY!

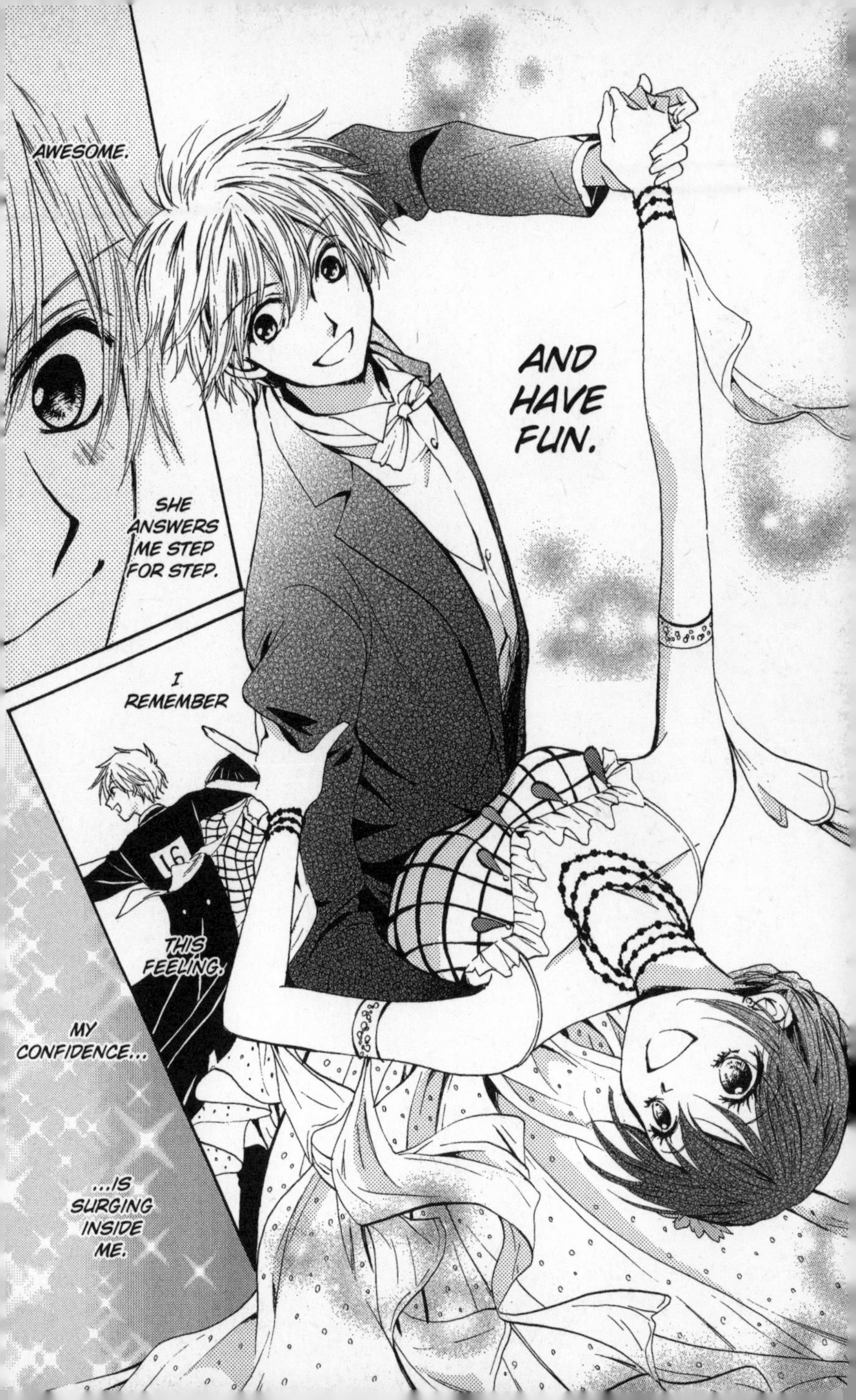
AND HAVE FUN.
AWESOME.
SHE ANSWERS ME STEP FOR STEP.
I REMEMBER
THIS FEELING.
MY CONFIDENCE...
...IS SURGING INSIDE ME.

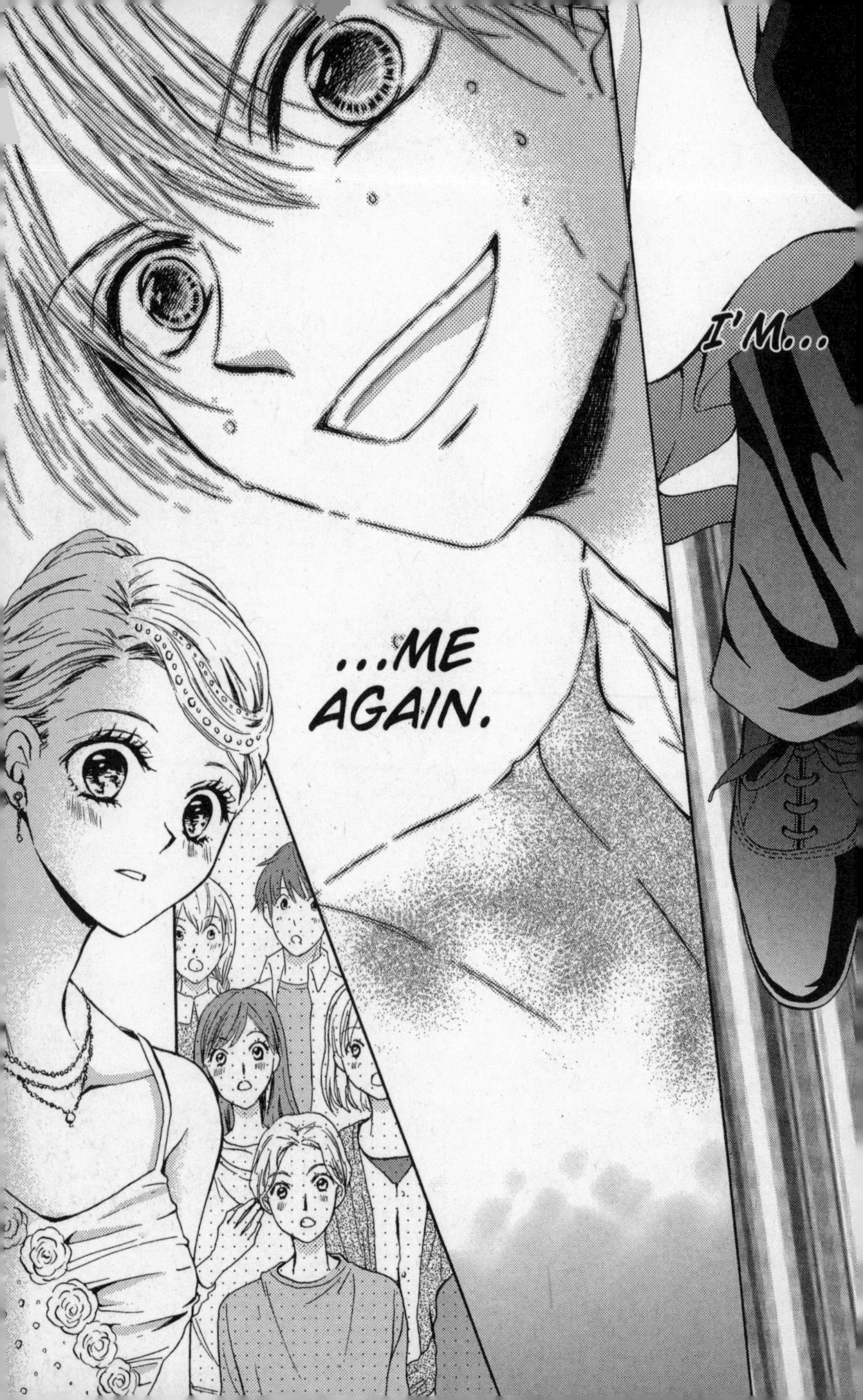
I'M...
...ME AGAIN.

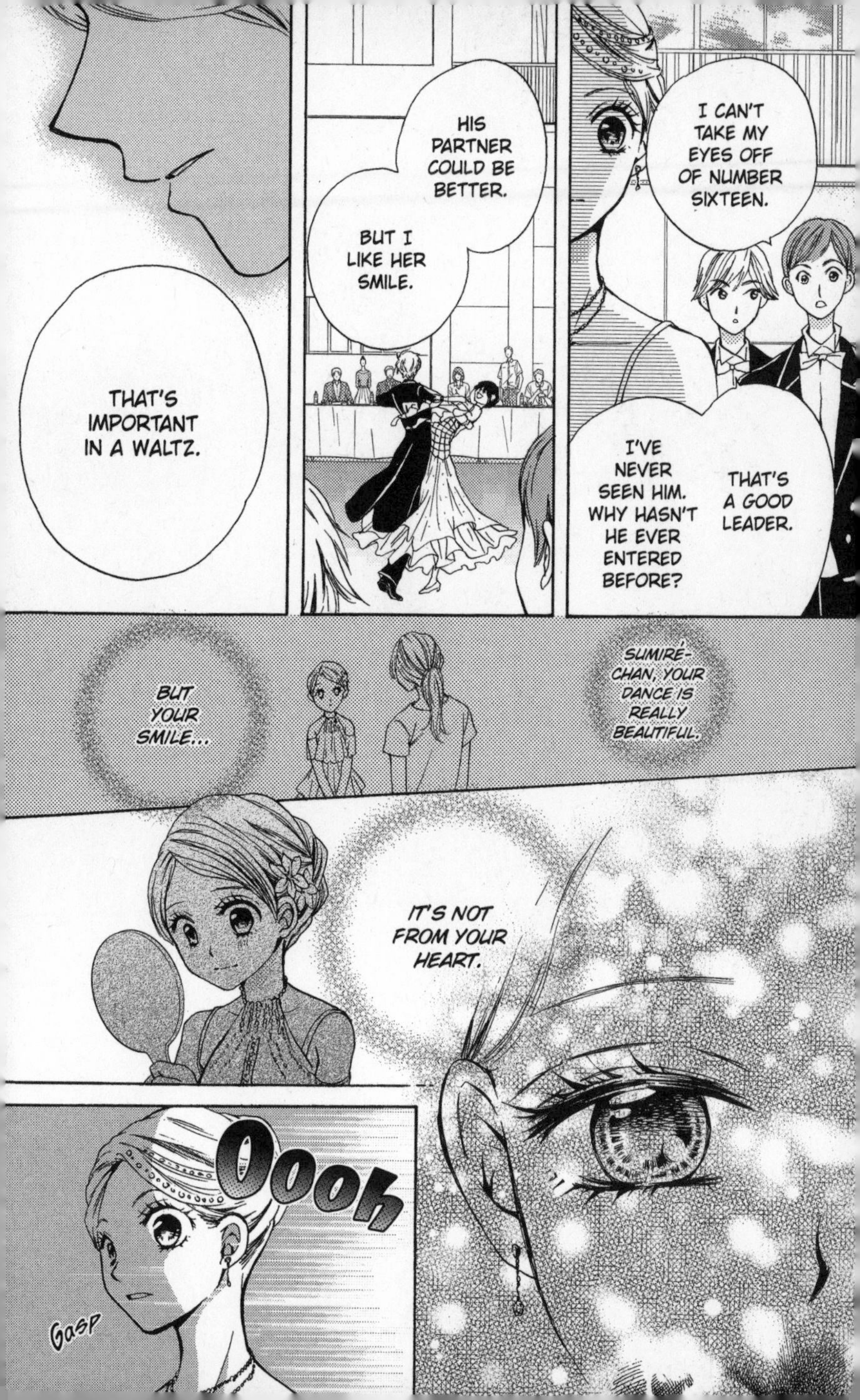
I CAN'T TAKE MY EYES OFF OF NUMBER SIXTEEN.
THAT'S A GOOD LEADER.
I'VE NEVER SEEN HIM. WHY HASN'T HE EVER ENTERED BEFORE?
HIS PARTNER COULD BE BETTER.
BUT I LIKE HER SMILE.
THAT'S IMPORTANT IN A WALTZ.
SUMIRÉ-CHAN, YOUR DANCE IS REALLY BEAUTIFUL.
BUT YOUR SMILE...
IT'S NOT FROM YOUR HEART.
Oooh
Gasp

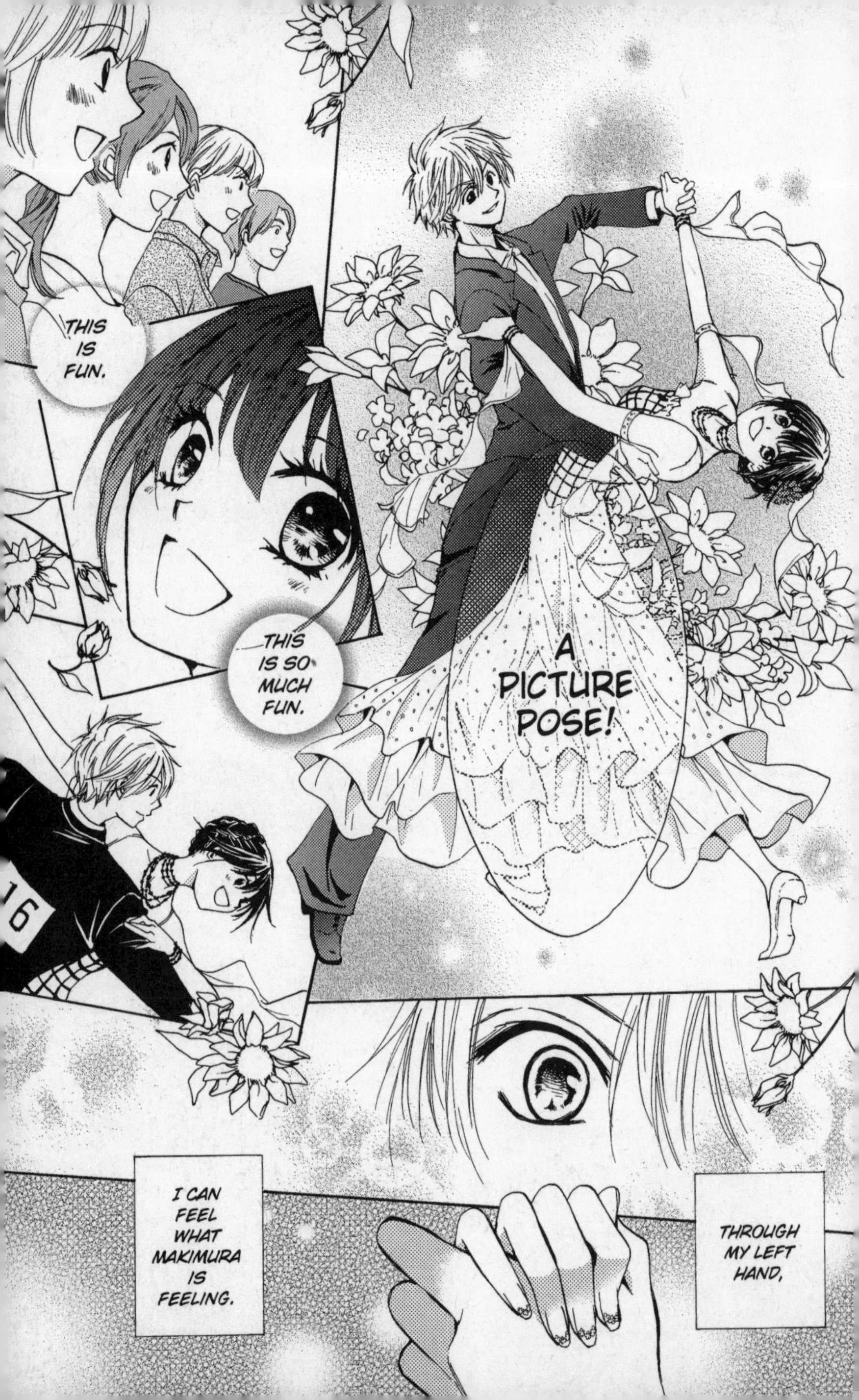
A PICTURE POSE!
THIS IS FUN.
THIS IS SO MUCH FUN.
16
THROUGH MY LEFT HAND,
I CAN FEEL WHAT MAKIMURA IS FEELING.

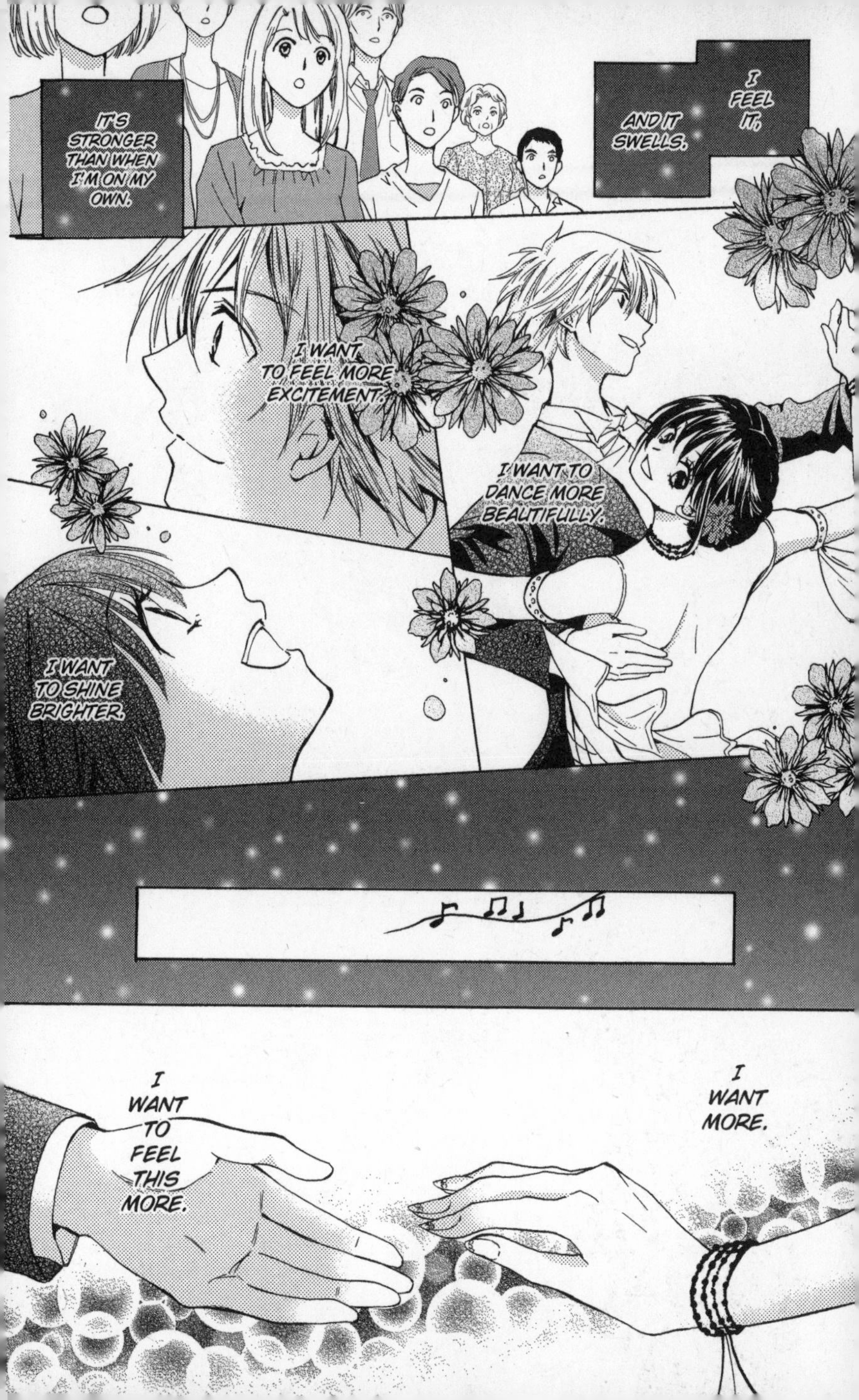
I FEEL IT, AND IT SWELLS.
IT'S STRONGER THAN WHEN I'M ON MY OWN.
I WANT TO DANCE MORE BEAUTIFULLY.
I WANT TO FEEL MORE EXCITEMENT.
I WANT TO SHINE BRIGHTER.
I WANT MORE.
I WANT TO FEEL THIS MORE.

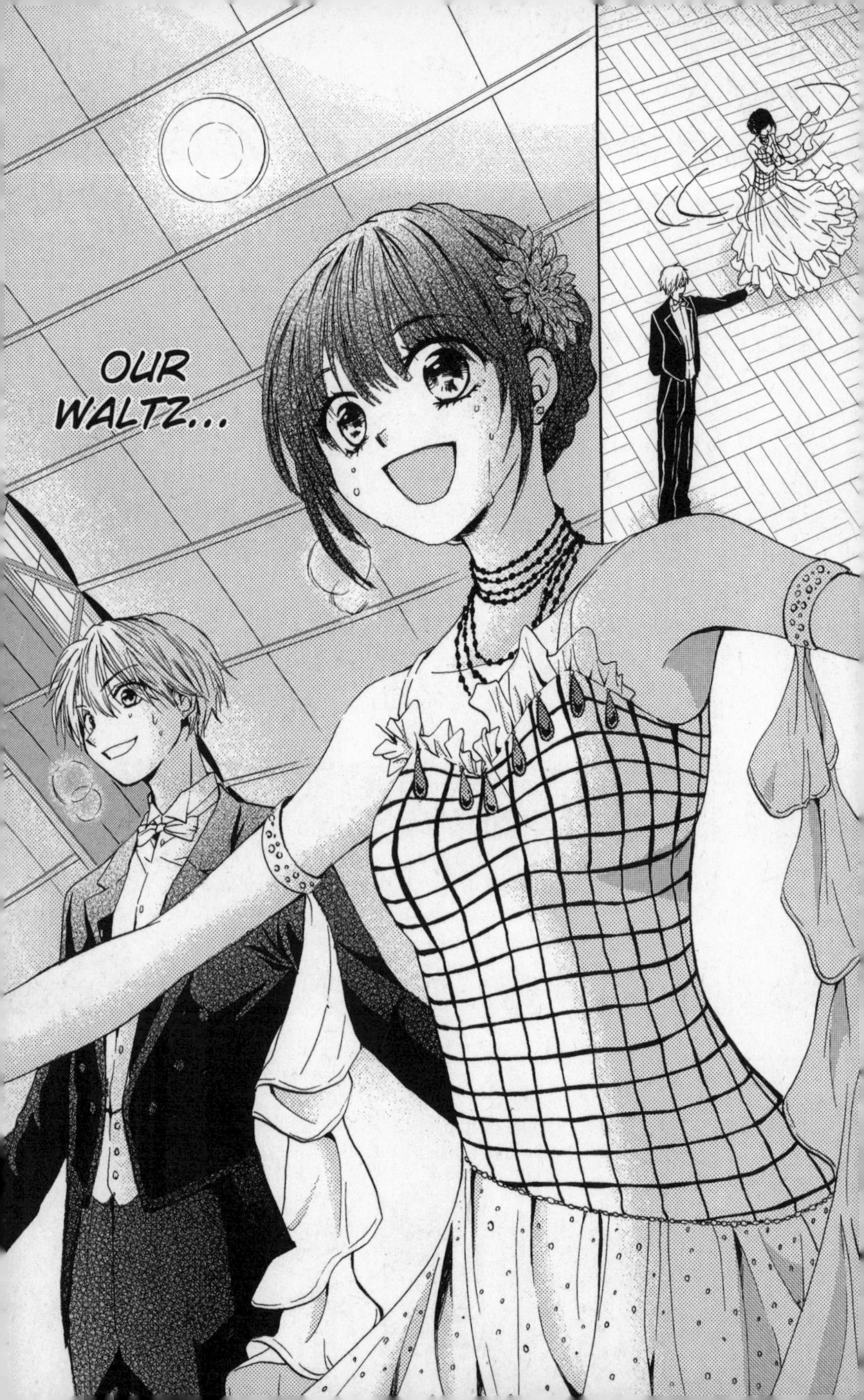
OUR WALTZ...

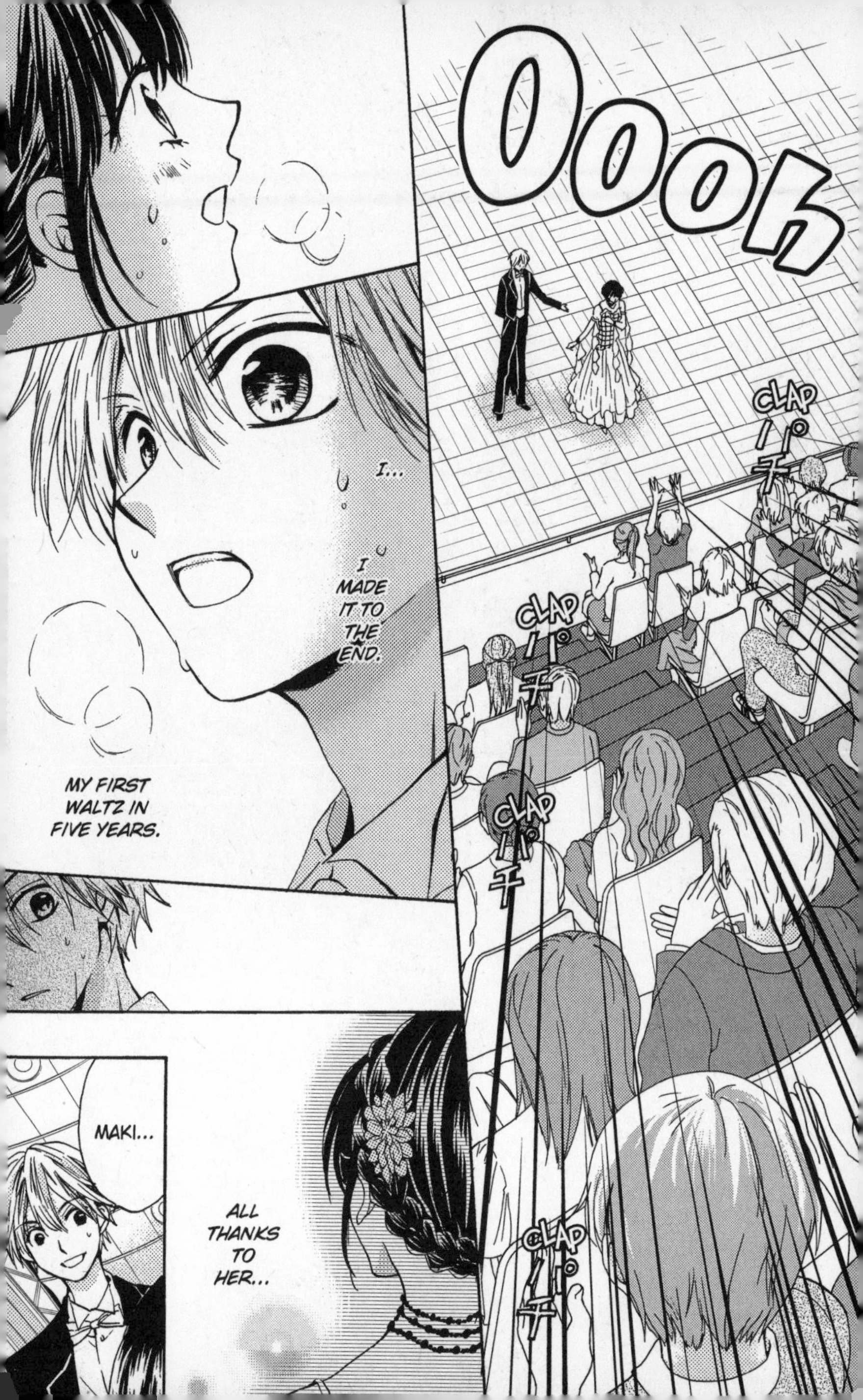
Ooooh
CLAP
パチ
CLAP
パチ
CLAP
パチ
CLAP
パチ
I...
I MADE IT TO THE END.
MY FIRST WALTZ IN FIVE YEARS.
MAKI...
ALL THANKS TO HER...

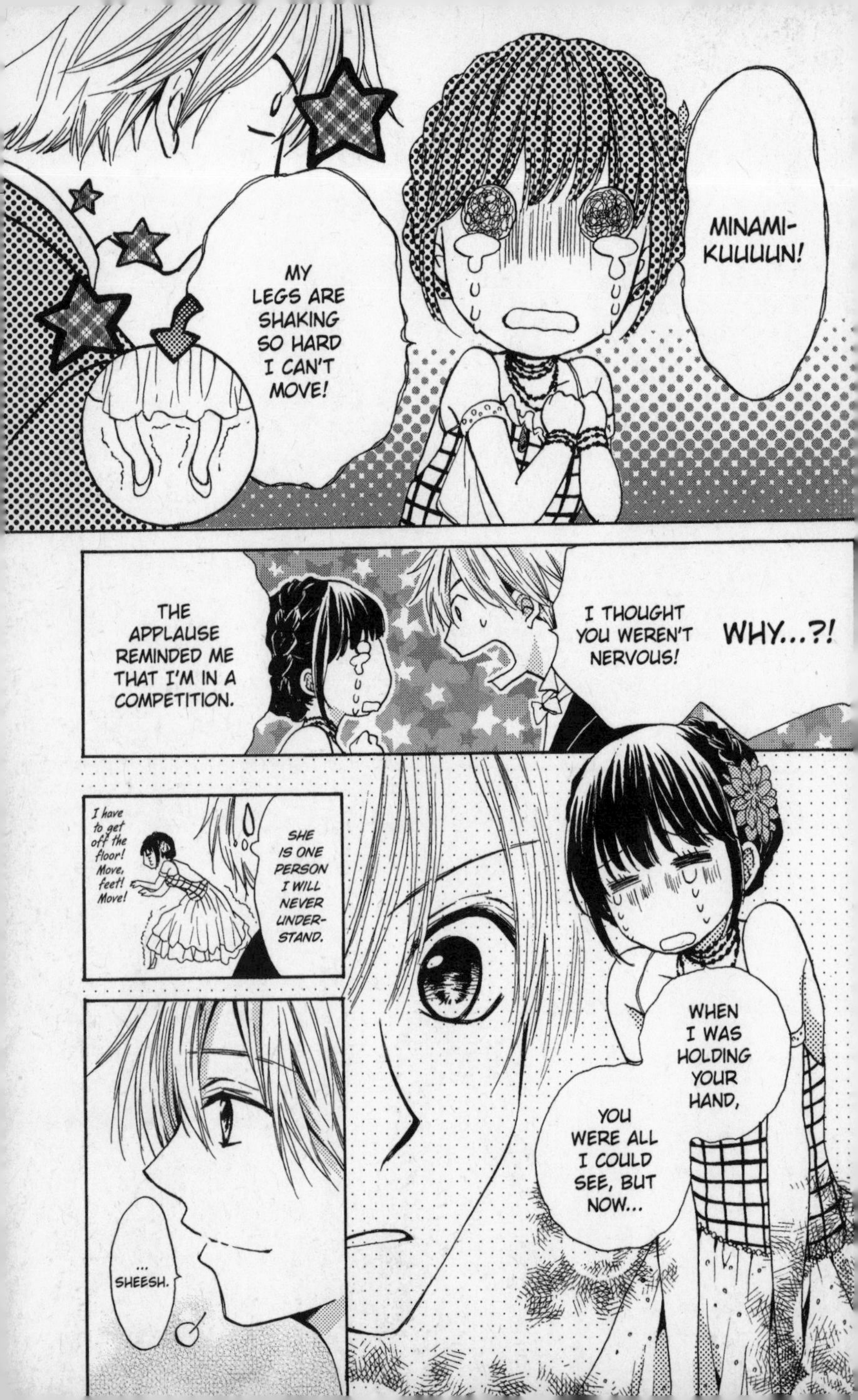
MINAMI-KUUUUN!
MY LEGS ARE SHAKING SO HARD I CAN'T MOVE!
WHY...?!
I THOUGHT YOU WEREN'T NERVOUS!
THE APPLAUSE REMINDED ME THAT I'M IN A COMPETITION.
WHEN I WAS HOLDING YOUR HAND,
YOU WERE ALL I COULD SEE, BUT NOW...
SHE IS ONE PERSON I WILL NEVER UNDERSTAND.
I have to get off the floor! Move, feet! Move!
...SHEESH.

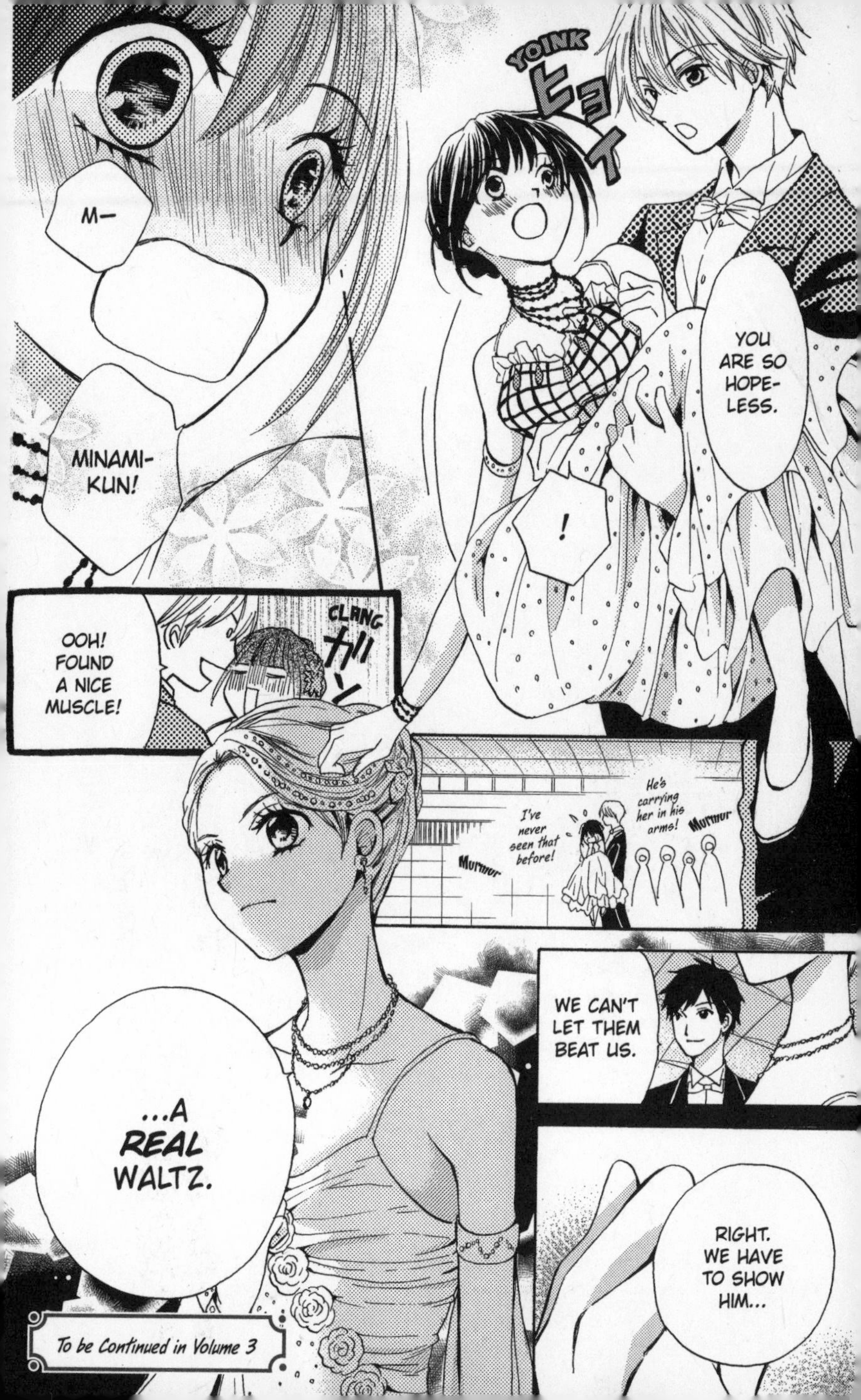
YOINK
ヒョイ
YOU ARE SO HOPE-LESS.
!
M—
MINAMI-KUN!
He's carrying her in his arms!
Murmur
I've never seen that before!
Murmur
OOH! FOUND A NICE MUSCLE!
CLANG
ガン
WE CAN'T LET THEM BEAT US.
RIGHT. WE HAVE TO SHOW HIM...
...A *REAL* WALTZ.
To be Continued in Volume 3

Special Thanks!!

Nakamura-sama
Miyaji-sama
Hirano-sama
Nakayama-sama
Ueno-sama

M's Dance Academy
Wakashiro-sensei
Tatsumi-sensei
My editor-sama
Everyone in the Editorial Department
Kawatani Design-sama
And all of my readers.

Thank you very much.

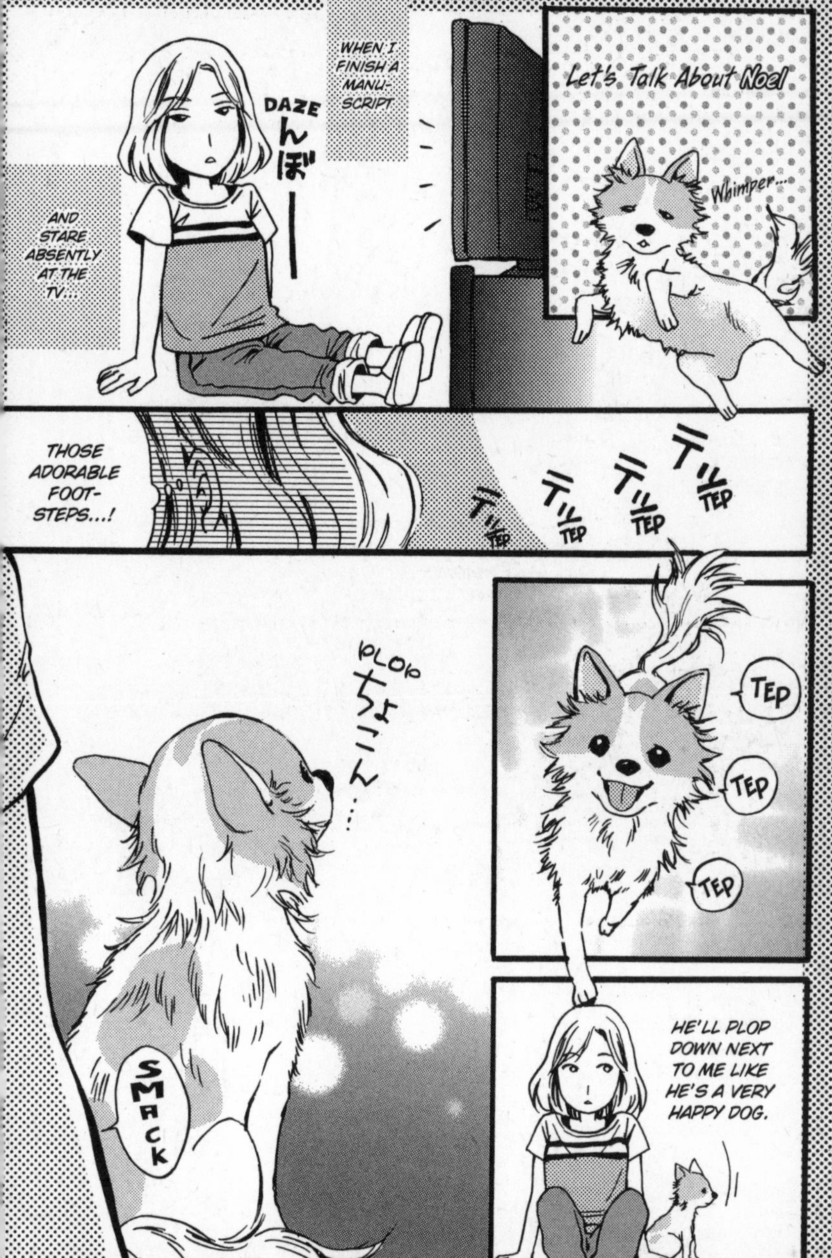
Let's Talk About Noel
Whimper...
WHEN I FINISH A MANUSCRIPT
DAZE んぼー
AND STARE ABSENTLY AT THE TV...
テッ TEP
テッ TEP
テッ TEP
テッ TEP
THOSE ADORABLE FOOT-STEPS...!
TEP
TEP
TEP
HE'LL PLOP DOWN NEXT TO ME LIKE HE'S A VERY HAPPY DOG.
PLOP ちょこん...
SMACK

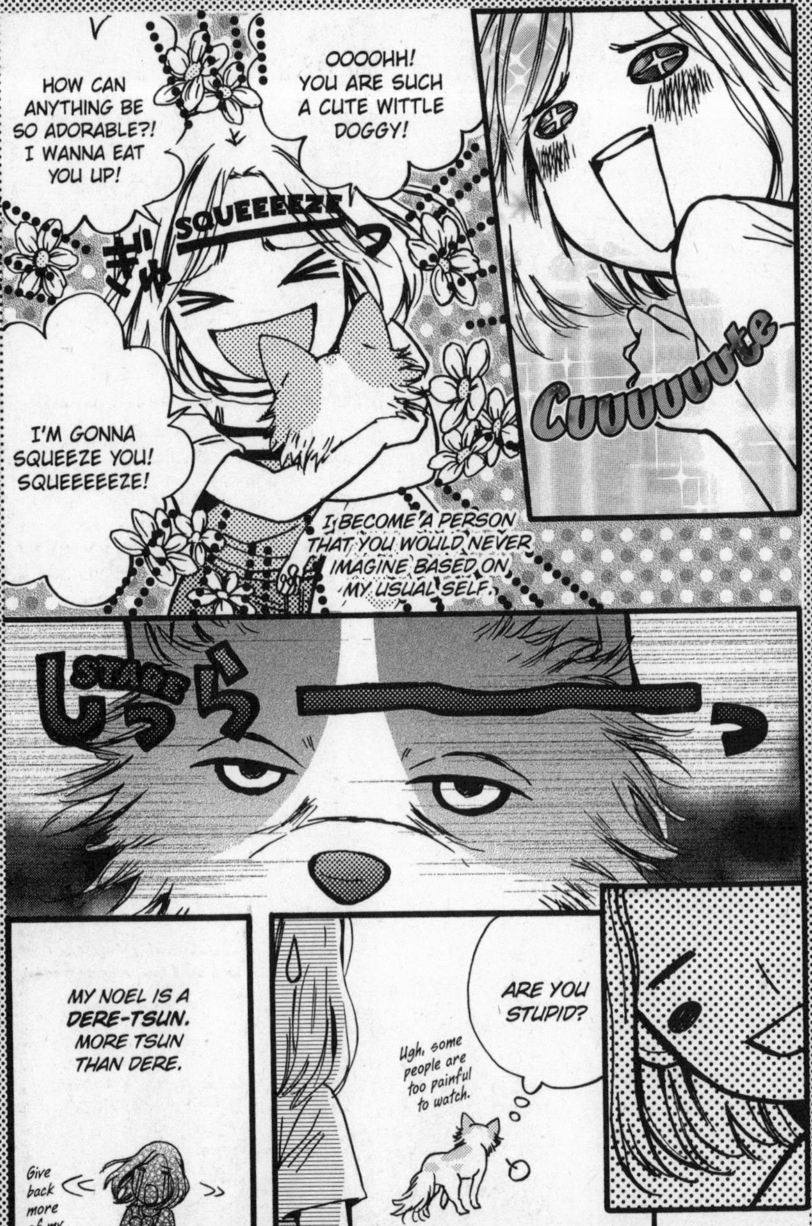
Cuuuuute
OOOOHH! YOU ARE SUCH A CUTE WITTLE DOGGY!
HOW CAN ANYTHING BE SO ADORABLE?! I WANNA EAT YOU UP!
SQUEEEEEZE
I'M GONNA SQUEEZE YOU! SQUEEEEEZE!
I BECOME A PERSON THAT YOU WOULD NEVER IMAGINE BASED ON MY USUAL SELF.
STARE
ARE YOU STUPID?
Ugh, some people are too painful to watch.
MY NOEL IS A DERE-TSUN. MORE TSUN THAN DERE.
Give back more of my love!

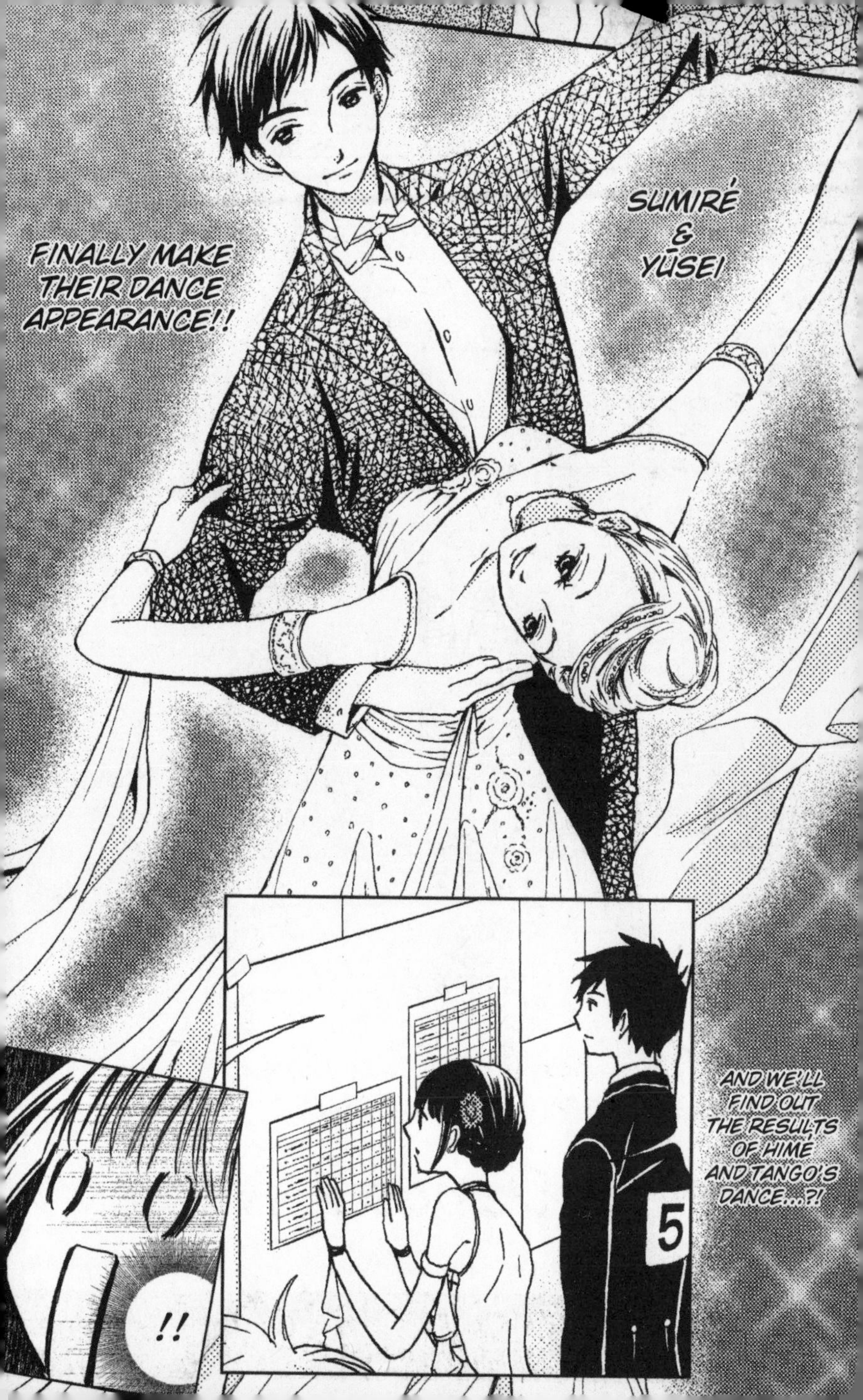
SUMIRÉ & YŪSEI
FINALLY MAKE THEIR DANCE APPEARANCE!!
AND WE'LL FIND OUT THE RESULTS OF HIME AND TANGO'S DANCE...?!
5
!!

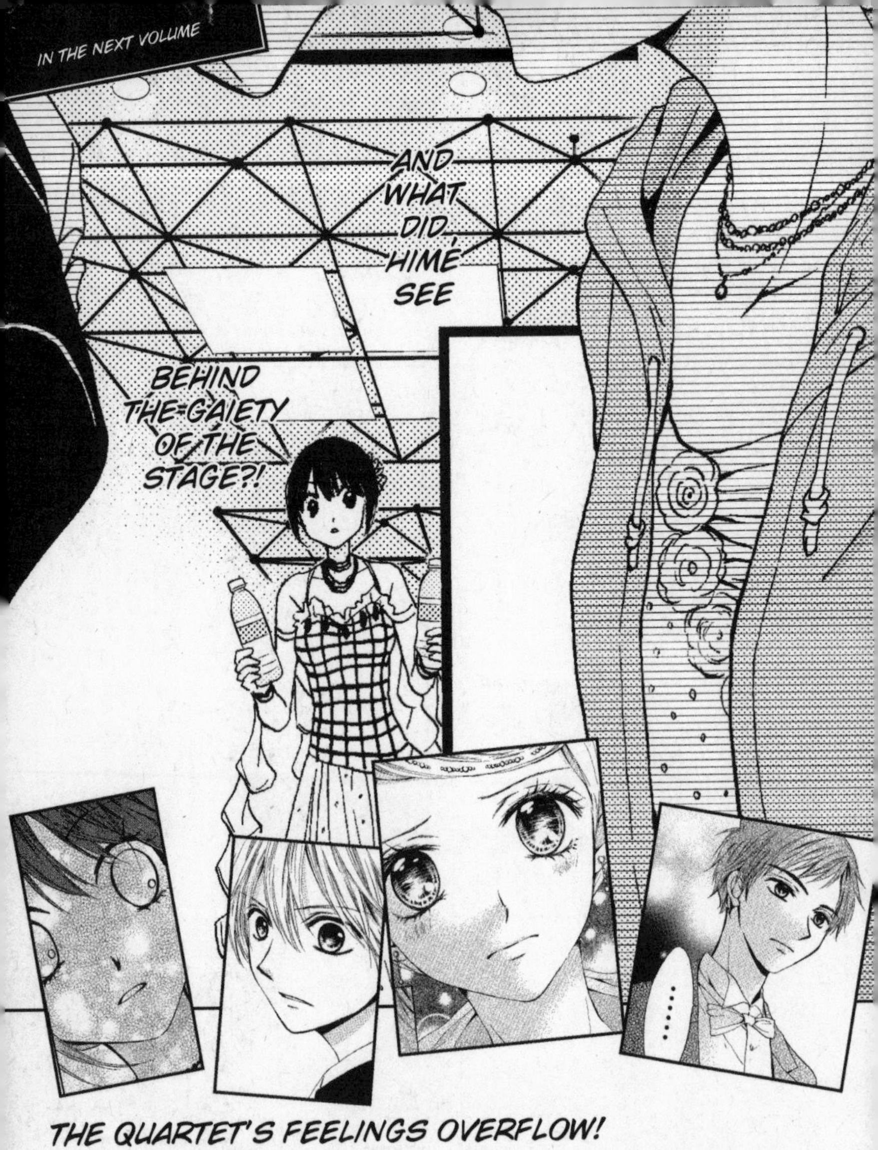
IN THE NEXT VOLUME
AND WHAT DID HIME SEE
BEHIND THE GAIETY OF THE STAGE?!

THE QUARTET'S FEELINGS OVERFLOW!

Let's Dance a Waltz

VOLUME 3, ON SALE SOON!!

♪
If I want to be Minami-kun's partner, I have to lose weight.
I'll go on that enzyme diet I've heard about.
I just juice some apples and carrots together.
GULP
This is something I can keep up with. I'll lose tons of weight! ♥
GULP
Yummy!
Oh, but it might taste even better if I added honey!
We have bananas! Those will taste good, too! And oranges!
Speaking of oranges, Mr. Chocolate is not going to stay quiet about this.
I'll add some fresh cream and cook the whole thing together.
WOW!
This tastes great on pancakes!
Hey. What happened to your diet?
You're a genius, Himé!
It's too delicious!

Translation Notes

Japanese is a tricky language for most Westerners, and translation is often more art than science. For your edification and reading pleasure, here are notes on some of the places where we could have gone in a different direction with our translation of the work, or where a Japanese cultural reference is used.

Dancesport classes, page 123
Tango tells Himé that the highest class in dancesport is SA, but this is not true in all countries. In Europe, the classes go from A down to E, E being the lowest. In Japan, the lowest class is D.

Square dancer, page 131
First, the translators would like to apologize for this very sad attempt at poking fun at Yūsei. Tango's real taunt was "Komanechi," which is a Japanese one-shot gag popularized by the comedian Beat Takeshi. The word is the Japanese pronunciation of Comăneci, the name of a famous gymnast. The gag involved striking a "gymnastics" pose and saying the name. Tango's reference to the gag may have been his way of saying that Yūsei's dancing is a joke. Or maybe he just liked the gag.

Carrying her in his arms, page 152
While this move is romantic in and of itself, it might have an extra special meaning for our princess Himé because the Japanese term for it translates roughly to "carry like a princess."

Dere-tsun, page 155
For readers unfamiliar with Japanese anime and manga tropes, dere-tsun is a variant of tsun-dere, from *tsun-tsun* (meaning prickly) and *dere-dere* (meaning lovestruck). A tsun-dere is a character whose first reaction to his or her love interest is prickly and mean, but because they care deep down, sometimes those ooey-gooey emotions will show through. Noel appears to be a bit of a reverse of this trope—he starts out being sweet and sappy, but quickly switches to being quite stand-offish.

e 2 is a work of fiction. Names, characters, places, and incidents are the products of the author's imagination or are used fictitiously. Any resemblance to actual events, locales, or persons, living or dead, is entirely coincidental.

A Kodansha Comics Trade Paperback Original.

Published in the United States by Kodansha Comics, an imprint of Kodansha USA Publishing, LLC, New York.

Publication rights for this English edition arranged through Kodansha Ltd., Tokyo.

First published in Japan in 2013 by Kodansha Ltd., Tokyo, as *Waltz no Ojikan*, volume 2.

ISBN 978-1-63236-047-2

Printed in the United States of America.

www.kodanshacomics.com

9 8 7 6 5 4 3 2 1

Translator: Alethea Nibley & Athena Nibley
Lettering: Jennifer Skarupa